THE WORLD ALMANAC®

BOOK OF
CROSSWORDS

WORLD ALMANAC BOOKS

World Almanac books may be purchased in bulk at special discounts for sales promotion, corporate gifts, fund-raising, or educational purposes. Special editions can also be created to specifications. For details, contact the Special Sales Department, 307 West 36th Street, 11th Floor, New York, NY 10018 or info@skyhorsepublishing.com.

Published by World Almanac, an imprint of Skyhorse Publishing, Inc., 307 West 36th Street, 11th Floor, New York, NY 10018.

The World Almanac® is a registered trademark of Skyhorse Publishing, Inc. All rights reserved.

www.skyhorsepublishing.com

10 9 8 7 6 5 4 3 2 1

Puzzles and text by Diego Jourdan Pereira
Interior design by Chris Schultz
Cover by David Ter-Avanesyan
Cover image by Shutterstock

Library of Congress Cataloging-in-Publication Data is available on file.

ISBN: 978-1-5107-7029-4

Printed in China

PUZZLES

1

ACROSS

1. Stylish excellence
6. ___-Cola
10. Flowering plants often compared to lilies
14. Zippy the Pinhead's twin brother
15. A very dark black
16. ___ Roach (band)
17. A step before stabling
19. Place of complete bliss and peace
20. ___ *Sunshine of the Spotless Mind*
21. Swerving
23. Bo Derek in 1979, e.g.
24. Prosperous: 3 wds.
25. Locke's ___ *Concerning Human Understanding*
28. *Mad ___*
29. Commotion
30. ___ *v. Wade*
31. ___ *Story* (1995)
32. Henry Threadgill, Fred Hopkins, and Steve McCall, collectively
33. Potentially attractive charge
40. Mowed grass fodder
41. DC's "Bat Hound" superhero
42. One of a European range
43. Fluffy mass
45. Yasmina Reza's 1994 play
46. Known as a *chadaree* in Afghanistan
48. Pacifist
50. An amusing person
51. Nectars in Hindu mythology
52. ___ duo
56. Rigid circular necklace
57. Enlighten
59. ___ *Lies*
60. Meat from a calf
61. Shape a material like stone or wood
62. High-pitched barks
63. Sports award
64. "___ Bells" by AC/DC

DOWN

1. Murder mystery board game
2. Fluff
3. Semicircular church recess
4. "This is ___!"
5. Author Sheldon
6. 2006 Stephen King novel
7. ___-Wan Kenobi
8. Concave's opposite
9. Michael or Gabriel, e.g.
10. Hole or opening (photography)
11. Sends a wireless message
12. Turns upside down
13. Spanish clothing company
18. Martial arts ranking system
22. Small and delicate
24. A point on a route of travel
25. Before
26. Martian day
27. "I ___ dead people"
28. Bovine noise
31. Attempt
32. Ice ___
34. Chocolate-coated ice-cream treats (UK)
35. Musical term also known as a rest
36. A subdivision of a play, opera, or ballet
37. Dark and thick liquid
38. Kind of people
39. Bean counter: Abbr.
43. The plural of femur
44. Beating
45. Passageways
46. Cast out
47. Usage
48. *Miracle Worker* actress ___ Duke
49. Showing lack of guile
50. Workout location
52. Appropriately
53. Darth ___
54. It will: Contr.
55. Mushroom also known as porcini
58. ___ pool

ACROSS

1. Seasoned rice dish
6. Irish police officer
11. *Game of Thrones*, to fans
14. Spanish for "friend"
15. Led by Hannibal Smith
16. Uncooked
17. ___ of Longinus
18. Make an exact copy
20. Possessive pronoun
22. Otalgia
23. Blocks
28. Examination
29. French vineyard classification
30. Fishing implement
31. Carrington portrait "___ of the Dawn Horse"
33. Decompose
34. Vexed
36. Roof overhang
40. So soon
42. Catherine Tramell's weapon of choice: 2 wds.
44. Astronaut and politician John ___
45. Extremely dangerous
47. ___ and the Family Stone
48. Carrot ___
50. *Atlas Shrugged* author
51. Spinal ___
52. Streamlined 1920s design
55. Constituency
58. A Christian hermit
60. Be in debt
61. Cruel disposition
64. Become hardened
68. Indigenous people who gave a southwest state its name
69. High IQ society
70. ___ tag
71. George Burns and Morgan Freeman played Him
72. Short, high-pitched, electronic sound
73. Domesticated South American camelid

DOWN

1. Ballet step
2. Small, mischievous devil or fairy
3. TV's ___ *to Me*
4. Once more
5. Loud, then soft
6. Freshwater fish species
7. Consumed
8. Force away
9. Gambian currency
10. 2018 Iranian film
11. Princess Kelly
12. Solemn promises
13. Say with a character limit
19. Doze
21. Long metal blade weapon
23. D&D marine troll
24. Internet bully
25. Unusual and startling
26. Durable synthetic resin
27. Marvel giant Stan ___
32. Incompetent: 3 wds.
35. Paul A. M. ___
37. Successor to XP
38. Enthusiastic display
39. Pioneering videoconferencing app
41. Place in a grave
43. ___ Fine Foods
46. Wrath
49. Tube-nosed seabird
52. Identify and remove computer errors
53. Greek muse of poetry
54. Wrapped in waxcloth (Middle Ages)
56. Director Sergio ___
57. Related to the kidneys
59. Metrical unit used in poetry
62. Employ
63. Vascular plant fluid
65. One of NATO's founding members: Abbr.
66. "Losing My Religion" band
67. A major division of geological time

3

ACROSS

1. Farm tool component
10. *The Untouchables* actor Robert ___
15. Impulsive
16. Synthetic DuPont yarn
17. Achieving a goal
18. *Watchmen* writer Alan ___
19. A rose's defender
20. ___-hee!
21. Right a wrong
22. It has needles instead of leaves
24. Full of rage
26. Pigpen
29. Small lump
31. Each one is made for gliding over snow
32. "___ ___, there's a place you can go," 2 wds.
35. Acerbically
40. The longest river in Africa
41. Two of a kind
43. A.k.a. viola da gamba
44. Rolled into a ball
47. Dusko Popov's MI5 codename
50. Spanish for "sea"
52. Large flightless Australian bird
53. *A Nightmare on ___ Street*
54. Relating to vessels which carry blood
59. ___ Research Center
61. Base-eight numbering system
62. Wild animal shelter
64. Iraqi city
68. Juvenile insect
69. Medium for sculpture
71. Attribute
72. Produced as a consequence of something
73. Move sideways
74. Arya Stark's first victim

DOWN

1. Excellent, slangily
2. Averse (UK)
3. Spiderman villain Dr. Octopus's first name
4. Mooring locale
5. Fishing with a large, vertical net
6. ___ Solo
7. Horizontal entrance to an underground mine
8. Take action on a subscription, e.g.
9. Lawn trimming tools
10. Affecting the body
11. Early photographer Henry ___
12. Remote in manner
13. Snail species ___ aspersum
14. "___ before Zod!"
23. Distilled sugarcane liquor
25. Abbr. preceding a nickname
26. Short for synchronization
27. Labor strenuously
28. Word with "tide" or "log"
30. Singer ___ Bunny
33. Old's opposite
34. Word with "hazel" or "pea"
36. Batman villain Poison ___
37. "Roll the ___" (Bukowski poem)
38. Hang loosely
39. The primordial matter of the universe
42. Valuable mineral deposit
45. Strive to match
46. Delta stock symbol
48. A mischievous child
49. All white, in billiards
51. Wireless detection systems
54. Units named after Italian physicist Alessandro
55. Mite
56. String music publication, with "The"
57. Make a petty objection
58. Lease again
60. Throw away
63. They put man on the Moon: Abbr.
65. Wound with a knife
66. ___ *911* comedy series
67. A RISD student, likely
70. Wolverine's favorite slang

4

ACROSS

1. Proverb
6. Includes credit, medical, and student loan types
10. A person with pretensions
14. R&B group ___ Me Badd
15. Acquire by one's efforts
16. ___-___ list
17. *Superman* actor Christopher ___
18. Troublesome child
19. Solemnly affirm
20. Gaelic language
21. There are three in a half-inning
22. Vicious growl
23. Domineering
26. Eye bruises
29. Perform in an exaggerated way, 3 wds.
33. Congressional Medal of ___
34. Italian composer Niccolò ___
35. Gelatinous substance made from algae
36. 1950's subculture
38. A horse's pace
39. Most gangling
41. The human body's largest artery
42. Patella
43. A campaign act
45. Acute nerve pain
47. A riding horse
50. Fencing sword
51. Indigenous people of the Amazon
55. Blacken
56. Expression of incredulity
57. ___ mortis
58. ___ Major
59. "Ain't" synonym
60. Loud cry
61. 1971 made-for-TV Spielberg film
62. Units of wood
63. "Bloomin'___" (appetizer)

DOWN

1. Land unit
2. Not a slacker
3. Brewskis
4. William Howard Taft in the Philippines, e.g.
5. Earlier than
6. Corrects
7. L. Ron Hubbard's *Battlefield* ___
8. High-ranking officer (slang)
9. 1976 AC/DC song
10. Enthusiastic audience response
11. George Taylor's companion in *Planet of the Apes*
12. Distinctive smell
13. NFL's Super ___
21. Belonging to us
22. *Brave New World*'s happiness-producing drug
24. Poetic "over"
25. Crones
26. Great white or hammerhead
27. Wrestler Hulk ___
28. Fatuous
30. Demi-crown
31. Inches, e.g.
32. Round flatbreads
34. American politician ___ Buchanan
36. Male admirer, once
37. Pressure-brewed coffee
40. Frosted
41. Folk singer ___ DiFranco
43. Indentations
44. Edith Wharton's The ___ of Innocence
46. Copying
47. 1991 Gulf War missile
48. Word on a fast-food sign
49. Effortlessness
52. Tangerine-grapefruit hybrid
53. Marco ___
54. Marvel's ___ Man
56. Trouble
57. Seventeenth letter of the Greek alphabet

5

ACROSS

1. The Who's "___ O'Riley"
5. Earth has an elliptical one
10. Prayer conclusion
14. Excited
15. River in France
16. Ready to eat
17. Daughter of Gaia and Uranus
18. "___ thou bind the sweet influences of Pleiades, or loose the bands of Orion?" (Job 38:31, KJV)
19. Elm or oak
20. Related to marriage
22. Flourished
24. Not any
25. Brand of casual sandals
26. Improper use
29. Most scaly
34. Outdoor shelters
35. Time taken by a sequence of events, 2 wds.
36. Death notice
37. Destined
38. Country bordered to the west by Iraq and Turkey
39. Showing signs of age
41. Simultaneous discharge of artillery
42. Quickest
43. Merchant or trader
44. Salvador Dalí's wife
45. Servant or helper
47. Frosted vessel
50. A set of baby clothes
54. Site of the Taj Mahal
55. Renovate a ship
57. ___ 51
58. A raja's wife
59. One related on the mother's side
60. French streets
61. *I Dream of Jeannie* star Barbara ___
62. Remains
63. Pup ___

DOWN

1. Yeast
2. Ottoman honorific
3. War ended with Peace of Vereeniging
4. Counter to natural inclination, 3 wds.
5. Dead language of southern Italy
6. Homemaker? 3 wds.
7. Osama ___ Laden
8. Cordwainer Smith's *The ___ of Mankind*
9. Attached
10. Surgically installed blood pump
11. Multi-warhead ballistic acronym
12. Dueling sword
13. Not a mere want
21. "Head, Shoulders, Knees, and ___"
23. They call flags on plays: Abbr.
26. Particles
27. Anime series *Cowboy ___*
28. Bring together
30. Quotes
31. ___ bird
32. Solomon Northup's *12 Years a ___*
33. Luciano Pavarotti, e.g.
37. Deficiencies
40. Dutch cheese
41. Sterilize
46. Buddies (UK)
47. ___ knuckle fighting
48. Mild exclamation of surprise
49. Sea eagle
51. False's opposite
52. Tween, in a few years
53. A compass point
56. U.S. aviation authority: Abbr.

ACROSS

1. Deep red garnet mineral
7. Parasitic nematode worm
15. ___ and fishes
16. Unique person, 2 wds.
17. Passionate
18. Avida Dollars and Genuine Class, e.g.
19. Research subject
21. Japanese currency
22. Video game musician Takeshi ___
23. High
25. Attempt or effort
28. A narrow strip of wood
30. Thomas Alva ___
32. Travel quickly
33. Dines at home
35. Break away
37. Plural of cilium
39. *The ___ of Adaline* film
41. Wheeled trash bin
42. Eyespots
44. Dress
46. Baseball ___
47. Butt against
49. *Carmina Burana* composer
52. ___ and aahs
54. Meat or fish seasoner
56. Duran Duran's second studio album
57. ___ Father
59. Fully and completely
61. Gums, technically
64. Render capable
65. Operating a plane in flight
66. Army supplier, once
67. Make or become smaller
68. Accelerates

DOWN

1. ___ cadence or mode
2. Southwestern Nigerian language
3. Two-way wireless sound transmission
4. Kitchen appliance used for baking or roasting
5. Plural of a male organ
6. *Back to the Future*'s Lyon ___
7. Educational institution for teachers, once
8. Scopes
9. *Rosemary's Baby* author ___ Levin
10. Cautious
11. Largest lagomorphs
12. Russia's first czar
13. Game where two players take turns in taking objects from several piles
14. *Free Your Mind… and Your ___ Will Follow* album by Funkadelic
20. Plural of podium
24. Early OS: Abbr.
26. White House Chief of Staff, e.g.
27. ___ Hall Putsch
29. Pellets of frozen rain
31. UK alternative to net, sometimes
34. 1938 poetry book by Gabriela Mistral
36. ___ salmon
37. ___ Chanel
38. UN air transport agency: Abbr.
40. Spanish teen drama on Netflix
43. Must-haves for air travel
45. Quality of being united
48. Tokyo, Yokohama, Osaka: ___ major cities
50. Sated
51. Entrance halls
53. Sweetener
55. Hoisted
58. Religious ceremony
60. Amount of charge or payment
61. ___ about: aimlessly on-the-go
62. Former Apple designer Jonathan ___
63. By way of

ACROSS

1. The capital of Norway
5. ___, Roebuck and Co.
10. Long-range nuclear weapon delivery device: Abbr.
14. Barge
15. Tashkent resident
16. Famous projectile targeted at President George W. Bush
17. Fleshy seed cover
18. TV sitcom *The ___ Bunch*
19. Fulminate
20. French cocktail of crème de cassis and white wine
21. Pursuit
22. Comedian Silverman
23. Single-celled animals
25. Deliberately stay away from
27. Sultanate of the Arabian Peninsula
29. The study of bird's eggs
32. St. Louis landmark
35. Impurity used to alter conductivity
38. Cow's vocalization
39. British TV series *Top ___*
40. Objects of worship
41. Nation south of Ecuador
42. Unit of corn
43. In place (Latin), 2 wds.
44. George Washingtons
45. Batman artist Dick ___
47. Highly spiced stew
49. Counterbalance
52. Parts of some theater sets
56. Preamble
58. Effusive
60. Large bird of legend
61. Small shelter for domestic animals
62. India's capital territory
63. Track made by treading
64. Conscious minds
65. Semi-legendary Greek fabulist
66. Individual article
67. Second-year undergraduate: Abbr.
68. Attracts
69. Currency of multiple countries

DOWN

1. 2021 Australian Open women's singles champ
2. Singular of 52-across
3. Longest river in France
4. Solitary, nocturnal bird of prey
5. Section dividers, as in a magazine article
6. American poet ___ Pound
7. Mortify
8. Advises: Archaic
9. *Vanilla ___* film
10. Neighbor of Egypt, Jordan, and Syria
11. Cleaning ladies: Archaic
12. ___ fide
13. An upper
21. Small digital recorder: Abbr.
22. Photographed
24. Danish physicist Niels ___
26. Some foreign diplomatic posts
28. Assents
30. American politician Al ___
31. Y'all
32. Lifetimes
33. You ___ what you sow
34. Comedian Scott Thompson's stage name, 2 wds.
36. Hawaiian dish made from the fermented root of the taro
37. Spanish for both "tall" and "stop"
41. Impoverished
43. Intel
46. Anew
48. Frosty
50. Chief or ruler: var.
51. Second-largest city in Oklahoma
53. Infuriated
54. Particles
55. Yiddish word for a stupid or obnoxious person
56. Glazes
57. Not ready, 2 wds.
59. Spectacle
62. Pop
63. *Great Expectations* narrator

ACROSS

1. Thriller author Daniel ___
6. Warships, collectively
11. Female sheep
14. Romanced
15. Direct the attention of someone to
16. Assist
17. Bristled
18. More than enough
19. Music combining jazz and Caribbean elements
20. Wind instrument
22. Yiddish word for Gentiles
24. Rascal
26. The projecting arm of a crane
27. Lurid horror franchise originating in 2004
30. Road congestions, 2 wds.
35. From Ivan the Terrible to Nicholas II
37. Novak Djokovic, e.g.
38. Give off
39. Rend
40. Beneficiary
41. Pepsi-___
42. Notion
43. ___ of Green Gables
44. Dangerous feat
45. Allowable
48. Latin for "thing"
49. Blockchain currency: Abbr.
50. In a highly spirited manner
52. The third gift of the Magi
55. Cut off
59. Affirmative answer
60. Exocrine duct sacs
64. Digression
65. Bother persistently
66. Punctuation mark preceding a list
67. Stone with a crystal-lined cavity
68. "Take on Me" band
69. As a companion
70. Bar

DOWN

1. Nasal ___
2. Johnny Carson was born there
3. Chandler novel *The ___ Goodbye*
4. Quayle, Gore, Pence, et al.
5. Junkies
6. Members of a certain fraternal organization
7. Superman villain ___ Luthor
8. A newt's terrestrial stage
9. Poetic always
10. Very sad
11. ___ *Rider* (1969 film)
12. A website that's collaboratively edited and managed
13. Dutch cheese
21. Golf standard
23. Express opposition
25. Former German penny
26. Insulting remark
27. A certificate of recognized value
28. A linear anion
29. Hesitate
31. Some cocaine use
32. Michael Haneke's 2012 film
33. *Winnie the Pooh* author A.A. ___
34. Some data: Abbr.
36. Citrus ___(kitchen tool)
40. Super speedy offspring of *The Incredibles*
44. Fabric edge woven to prevent raveling
46. College town known for gorges
47. False assertion
51. Plural of "yes"
52. Asian starling
53. Informal for "yes"
54. Melodic mode in Indian music
56. Disturbance of the peace
57. Taro
58. Genesis's "In Too ___"
61. Blake or Potter, in TV's *MASH*: Abbr.
62. UN working standards agency: Abbr.
63. Opposite of "oui"

ACROSS

1. Sketch
5. TMZ subject
10. Hairstyle of tight curls in a rounded shape
14. Apiece
15. Idealized image of someone
16. Burrowing marine mollusk
17. Disappointing outcome
19. ___ d'Ivoire
20. Concealed
21. A favorite fall pie
22. Spanish for "more"
23. Rest in Peace: Abbr.
24. Russian pancake
28. Kidnappers
34. Equate
35. Fictional country setting for *The Prisoner of Zenda*
36. Affirm solemnly
37. Sea nymph
38. TV host ___ Maher
39. Lacking meaning
41. Flowering succulents
42. Writers of creative nonfiction, maybe
43. Latin for "table"
44. Group of whales
45. A 5-centime piece
47. Dwarf planet
50. Stick used to support a painter's brush hand
56. "Ding Dong! ___ Calling!"
57. Prefabricated dwelling
58. Microprocessor type using highly optimized instructions: Abbr.
59. Web browser originally developed in Norway
60. Took unauthorized time off: Abbr.
61. Kill
62. They may hold things up
63. Desire

DOWN

1. *Night of the Living* ___ film
2. Hindu queen
3. Fifth book of the New Testament
4. Supporter of a 19th-century American political party
5. Hairlike structures in a cell
6. Envoys
7. Unable to move without difficulty
8. Expression of surprise
9. Container
10. Satisfactory
11. Loosely clumped mass of fine particles
12. Spanish for "rat"
13. 1976 horror film *The* ___
18. Dried spice used frequently in Latin American and Asian cuisine
21. Member of a northern Scotland people during Late Antiquity
23. Destroy
24. Apathetic
25. 2006 German film *The* ___ *of Others*
26. Box set featuring material recorded by rock band KISS
27. Reuters, e.g.
29. Blowout
30. Garment sometimes paired with a suit
31. Satirical media company The ___
32. Bothers
33. Popular condiment
37. Eminem song "The Real ___ Shady"
40. A nestling hawk
41. ___-bouche
46. Spanish for "pots"
47. Autos
48. *Masters of the Universe* villainess ___-Lyn
49. Civil rights activist ___ Parks
50. Brood
51. Cain's brother
52. Melt
53. State known for caucuses
54. Encouraging word: Contr.
55. Salmon after spawning
57. Horde

ACROSS

1. Hard to change pattern
4. French abbots
9. The "I" in M.I.T.
13. Peruvian river in the eastern Andes
14. Operate an airplane
15. Make dim
16. Pointed tool
17. Branch of pediatrics concerned with newborns
19. Gift
21. An old French coin
22. Walmart and Apple, e.g.: Abbr.
23. Small earthenware pot
24. Roadside guide
26. Morals specialists
28. Vessel for beans or soup
29. Hanna-Barbera character ___ Ant
30. Abbr. preceding a pseudonym
31. Tributary of Germany's Fuhse river
33. "The biggest little city in the world"
34. Linoleums, in the UK: Abbr.
37. White and salty Greek goat cheese
39. *Scream* actor ___ Campbell
41. ___ *Hard* action film franchise
42. Foundation promoting STEM scholars
43. Protagonist of the *Matrix* film series
44. Grammatical cases expressing motion away from something
46. Ecclesiastically
49. Spud
50. "Everybody Hurts" band
51. Before, poetically
52. Dampen
53. Uncontrolled expansion of cities, 2 wds.
56. Retirement account: Abbr.
57. Hammurabi's code was engraved in one
58. Person receiving a check
59. Family vehicle
60. *The Flash* star ___ Miller
61. Artistic style that uses lines or patterns to make illusions: Abbr.
62. Miami time zone

DOWN

1. Emerge
2. In the oral tradition
3. Most people don't memorize this anymore, 2 wds.
4. Related to transient cessation of respiration
5. Event occurring every two years
6. Pat dry
7. Proterozoic or Archean
8. Stability
9. Unwell
10. Ben Shapiro, e.g.
11. Tapiocas
12. Secret rendezvous
15. Eject
18. Togo's IOC code
20. Read something quickly, 2 wds.
24. Readiness for duty
25. Layered desserts
27. Glide on water or snow
32. Miscellanies
35. Upton Sinclair's 1926 novel
36. Naval supremacy, 2 wds.
38. Having the same vowel sound
40. Epoch that began about fifty-six million years ago
44. Syrian city
45. A.k.a. the "throne"
46. American cartoonist Howard ___
47. Car rental service
48. Measures of time: Abbr.
52. *Bridesmaids* actress ___ Rudolph
54. "In the manner of," 2 wds.
55. Hip hop

ACROSS

1. Light throw
5. Small, bony fish
10. Printed characters
14. Marvel Comics' anthology ___ *Illustrated*
15. Winter weather phenomenon ___ vortex
16. Successor
17. Formerly known as Facebook
18. Tree native to the Philippines, known for its resin
19. Anne Frank's father
20. Foundation of many consumer electronics, 2 wds.
23. Smoothed, as a piece of wood
24. Chinese unit of value
25. Novelist Louis L'___
27. Mind over ___
32. It's usually covered by hair
35. *West Side Story* song
37. Military science fiction video game franchise
38. They preceded email
39. Freedom from constraint
40. January 20 speech
42. Vexed
43. In opposition to
44. Fly effortlessly
46. CT or PET
48. Emmy Award-winning writer Michael ___
52. Amenity or luxury
57. Harvest
58. Pose or simulate, 2 wds.
59. Prong
60. Hearing organs
61. Japanese cartoon style
62. Otherwise
63. Northwestern river in Ireland
64. Worked as fast as possible
65. Done working: Abbr.

DOWN

1. Short-term workers: Abbr.
2. Puccini's *Madama Butterfly*, e.g.
3. Occupy an area for a protest
4. John Singer Sargent's *Portrait of Madame X*, e.g.
5. Swimsuit brand
6. Fungus
7. ___ wave or spectrum
8. Female demon who haunted Keats
9. Ancient galleys with three banks of oars
10. "___ shall not kill"
11. Abominable snowman
12. *Troy* actor Brad ___
13. Desire
21. Measure of heat or cold: Abbr.
22. *Inspector Gadget* villain Dr. ___
26. One who employs a service
28. From then on
29. Furniture wood
30. Gaelic language
31. A type of tall grass
32. Prison-made weapon
33. Walking stick
34. Banned plant growth regulator
36. Daniel Defoe's 1722 novel ___ *Flanders*
38. Brawny
41. Strong wind
42. Ditto
45. Pressed
47. "The Man in the ___" speech passage by Theodore Roosevelt
49. Sheer fabric
50. German Dadaist Max ___
51. Patrick Macnee in 1960s TV show *The Avengers*
52. One of Canada's largest First Nations
53. Backside
54. Merit
55. Chapel part
56. 2006 Jay-Z album *Kingdom ___*

12

ACROSS

1. Latin for "souls"
7. NY Giants Super Bowl XLIV center David ___
11. "Easy as 1-2-3!"
14. Second-most populous city in Switzerland
15. Diarist Frank
16. Supportive garment
17. Died away
18. Lively dance
20. "The Safety Dance" band ___ Without Hats
21. Historical region in the Czech Republic
22. Adidas and Nike product
27. Basic unit of all organisms
28. External abdominal pouches
29. *Evil Dead* franchise protagonist ___ Williams
31. Eggs
32. ___ -to-riches
33. Formal agreements
37. Felix the ___
38. Induct
41. Leftover morsel
42. Understood
44. Major waterway of central Europe
45. Call of pigeons and doves
46. Edge of a cloth folded and sewn
48. BBC and PBS series *Antiques* ___
50. ___ and sound
53. Properties
55. Cradle song
57. Family
58. *Zantedeschia aethiopica*
60. Kerala Kasavu ___ (plural)
63. 2002 film *Catch Me If You* ___
64. Biggest bones in human hips
65. Canadian capital
66. Small barrel
67. Swarming with
68. Methodism founder John ___

DOWN

1. ___ Kahn
2. Omaha state: Abbr.
3. Male lover
4. Metric length measures
5. A form of translucent quartz
6. Lou Reed's "___ Song"
7. ___ mitzvah
8. ___ Mundi (museum in the Vatican)
9. Director Ed Wood's favorite wool
10. Singe
11. "As ___, so below"
12. Grill
13. Artificial waterway
19. Russian country house
22. Garment to wear while painting
23. Actress in *The Man in the Gray Flannel Suit* Marisa ___
24. Width of the human hand
25. Hair pieces
26. ___ Orthodox Church
30. Winter Olympic activity, 2 wds.
34. Insect from which red dye is derived
35. A group of soldiers or scouts
36. Packs
39. Succulent plant
40. Ski lift
43. Overcome
47. Kinetic sculpture
49. Garibaldi's forces wore red ones
50. Messaging app
51. Sensations that precede the onset of some seizures
52. Thrown away
54. American chef Dufresne
56. Dismounted
59. Sweet potato
60. Plant seeds
61. Dolly, for one
62. Express in words

ACROSS

1. Disney's *Lady and the* ___
6. Fast-moving card game
10. Enrich, in a way
14. *Almost Famous* actress ___ Phillips
15. Alcoholic
16. Affirm
17. Wrangles
18. "Not to mention…"
19. "Wine in España
20. Chipper
21. Vulgar term for feces
22. Leisurely walk
23. Glass vessel for *Carassius auratus*: 2 wds.
26. The Great White North
29. Dessert option, for short
30. *Compadres*
31. Puts in stitches
32. Canadian rock band The Guess ___
35. Go-carts
36. One who moves diagonally
38. Not merely "a"
39. Boost
42. Horsey
43. Put down
44. Made a sudden move
45. Not from Ikea
49. Karaoke selections
50. Neuter
51. Don Juan, e.g.
55. HBO series starring Thomas Jane
56. Quick talk
57. Swampy
58. Chill
59. Came's opposite
60. Set ___
61. Blender sound
62. Cafeteria carrier
63. *The Maltese Falcon* actress Mary ___

DOWN

1. Cookbook abbr.
2. Opportune
3. Open
4. Homebuyer's note
5. Boil stuff
6. Grassy surface
7. Seasoned rice dishes (var.)
8. Fire up
9. "___ bad!"
10. Oblation bowl
11. Dispatch boat
12. Extend
13. Salivate
21. Enduring works
22. Mr. Universe's focus
24. Argon, e.g.
25. Salt pork
26. Links rental
27. Asian nurse
28. "Good going!"
32. John Quincy Adams, e.g.
33. Better
34. Kind of column
37. Hot weather wear
40. Less stale
41. Eardrums
43. Jimi Hendrix's "Dolly ___"
45. Exclamation of disbelief
46. Fairway boundary
47. Boredom
48. Crackers
52. "Don't bet ___ ___!": 2 wds.
53. Annul
54. Appraiser
56. One hundred pounds
57. U.S. flight agency

ACROSS

1. Rhyme-matching word game
7. Emotionally hardened
15. Put down again
16. Provides commentary
17. Lacking pathways
18. Revolving anglers' lures
19. Infuses
20. English for "unagi"
21. *Glee* actress ___ Michele
22. Ankle bones
23. John Water's 1990 film ___-*Baby*
24. ___ *Toons* animated show
25. Ginger ___ soft drink
26. Spiteful
29. Britney Spears song "___ of Me"
30. Lysergic acid diethylamide: Abbr.
31. Wheeled vehicle
32. Fought
33. Motley
36. Unite by interweaving
39. 2021 Nicolas Cage film
40. Noah's vessel
43. Put an end to
44. German philosopher Georg Wilhelm Friedrich ___
46. Mild expression of surprise
47. Cornel West's ___ *Matters*
48. Spanish for "sun"
49. Vestment
51. 1990s rapper Vanilla ___
52. Sick
53. Imbecile
54. Minimal meaningful language unit
57. Suggestive of a lyre
58. Infectious agent
59. Joins
60. Most proper
61. "Squeeze"

DOWN

1. Related to the Earth's outer layer
2. Available to lease (plural)
3. Tailored
4. Female horses
5. *Gandhi* or *Ali*, e.g.
6. ___ and ends
7. Pesticide, 2 wds.
8. Table linens
9. Laconically
10. Keats's "Ode on a Grecian ___"
11. Akira Kurosawa's 1985 film
12. French for "workshop"
13. *The Limey* actor ___ Stamp
14. Put to the test
24. Exhaust
27. Land unit
28. Brittany Murphy's *Clueless* character
29. "Love Is a Battlefield" singer ___ Benatar
32. Hourly payment
33. Found attached to a workbench
34. Original KISS lead guitarist ___ Frehley
35. Booking for a band
36. Economizes
37. Wool jacket
38. Latin for "lizard"
40. Score instruction meaning "restless"
41. Speaker
42. Most acute
44. Sherlock's surname
45. Voice box
48. Surround a fortified place
50. Boy Scouts' ___ badges
53. Lead
55. Twenty-first letter of the Greek alphabet
56. Open box attached to a long pole handle

15

ACROSS

1. "That's disgusting!"
5. "By yesterday!"
9. "Beat it!"
14. Shivering fit
15. Prefix with -phone
16. Hint
17. "Ali ___ and the 40 Thieves" folk tale
18. Punctuation mark
20. Tube from the bladder
22. Sick
23. Listen
24. Boosts
25. Dad's side
29. Lethargy
33. Almond liqueurs
35. Lying *Canterbury Tales* pilgrim
36. 1993 standoff site
37. *Phenomenology of Spirit* author
39. Drumming rudiment
40. Online publication
42. Italian composer Gaetano ___
44. Loathe
46. Author W. ___ Maugham
47. "Cut it out!"
49. Automatic
50. Catch
53. Foolishness
57. Dabblers
59. Small salmon
60. Occupied, as a lavatory, 2 wds.
61. Checked item
62. The America's Cup trophy, e.g.
63. Bakery output
64. Northern European language
65. All there

DOWN

1. Hindu Mr.
2. Biology lab supply
3. Bumpkin
4. Get rich at others' expense
5. Gluten-free grain
6. Apart
7. "Give it ___!" (2 wds.)
8. Ziti, e.g.
9. Harsh sound
10. Dictionary features
11. Absorbed
12. Advil target
13. Reward
19. Blockhead
21. "Catch!"
25. "Knocked" on the door, like Lassie
26. Astound
27. Implied
28. Corporate symbols
30. Animal hides
31. Egg-shaped
32. Send, as payment
34. Spanish for "girls"
38. Type of iron ore
41. Subjects of wills
43. Actress Catherine ___-Jones
45. Cause for a lawsuit
48. Christmas wish
50. Blue-pencil a work
51. "Feeling Good" singer ___ Simone
52. Aspersion
54. *Field of Dreams* setting
55. Accordingly
56. Auld lang syne
58. "___ any drop to drink": Coleridge

ACROSS

1. Latin dances
8. Complete loser (UK)
15. Mob action
16. Cow
17. Pilot
18. Sound qualities
19. Impede, with "down"
20. Staked
22. "C'___ la vie!"
23. "Great ___!"
26. Nipper
27. *People* or *The New Yorker*: Abbr.
29. Russian composer Sergei ___
34. *1984* working class
36. Ancient Roman coins
37. Become more profound
38. Rubbing
39. Corrode
41. Violin precursors
42. Archetypal sauropod, once
44. ___ *gestae*
45. Time div.
46. Leaf opening
50. Big Apple attraction
52. Bedouin
54. "Oui or ___?"
55. Musical passages
58. 1988 Melanie Griffith film ___ *Girl*
61. Extraction
62. Vertebrate
63. Entrance
64. Wishful dreamer

DOWN

1. Grouches
2. Devastation
3. Friend
4. Bean counter, for short
5. Pillbox, e.g.
6. Excited
7. Sistine Chapel figures
8. Tablet
9. Roman poet contemporary of Virgil and Horace
10. Shorten pants
11. Sun, e.g.
12. Camphorated tincture of opium
13. Female sheep
14. Medical advice, often
21. Doublemint or Hubba Bubba
24. Also called 3-tropanol
25. Gifts
27. A.k.a. a van
28. Metrical foot
30. "One-hundred," in Italian
31. Not older
32. Fivers
33. Fruit of a Ficus
34. Bartlett or Bosc
35. Responding in a quick and clever way
37. Samuel Pepys's young maid ___ Willet
40. Effortless learning styles?
41. Easy victory
43. Order between "ready" and "fire"
47. Part of "the works," usually
48. ___ Carlo
49. 2003 Jack Nicholson comedy ___ *Management*
50. Formerly French Sudan
51. ___ *Brockovich*
52. Strong ales
53. Capitol feature
56. "___ the fields we go"
57. Outdated abbreviation
59. Code for amino acids: Abbr.
60. White wine aperitif

ACROSS

1. "One More Time" singer Stewart
4. Fur pieces
10. Mud dauber, e.g.
14. Anger
15. Polished
16. ___ Minor
17. "*Comprende?*"
18. Rembrandt's birthplace
19. Lodgings, informally
20. Lacking nothing
22. Imagined
24. The Beatles' final studio album ___ *It Be*
25. Astronaut's employer: Abbr.
27. Down vote
28. *Billy Budd* director
32. Gossip
34. Beach bird
35. Dismissed lightly
40. Accord
42. 1969 Peace Prize grp.
43. Like ground around a tree
44. One way to be left
47. Wrestling hold
48. ___ gin fizz
49. Poem part
51. *Seinfeld* uncle
54. Ripped
56. Sheep or doe in its second year of life
57. Bit of progress
59. Drifting
64. "Lulu" composer
65. Made of stone
67. Neither
68. Arabic for "commander"
69. Barely make
70. James Clavell novel ___-*Pan*
71. Beam intensely
72. Water-based anti-aging solutions
73. Electrical unit

DOWN

1. Microprocessor type using highly optimized instructions: Abbr.
2. Ice cream topper, perhaps
3. Adjudge
4. Gloomy
5. "Rock-a-bye Baby" location
6. Final notice
7. Burdened
8. Charlotte-to-Raleigh dir.
9. Lampoons
10. 1973 Supreme Court decision name
11. ___ and Pacific Islander (U.S. census designation)
12. Fraternity letter
13. Hardly ruddy
21. Column bases
23. Gillette product
26. Can't abide
28. Its state motto is "Industry"
29. Eighteen-wheeler, for short
30. H.S. class
31. Official who can invalidate
33. The study of animals
36. Aged
37. Basketball goal
38. Carve in stone
39. Actor Dick Van ___
41. World War II conference site
45. Pasta
46. Element No. 39
50. Answers back
51. Actionable words
52. Blink-182's ___ *of the State*
53. Iris root
55. Banana oil, e.g.
58. Shrek, e.g.
60. Ten C-notes
61. "What's gotten ___ you?"
62. Wyle of *ER*
63. Bleak, as an outlook
66. Mamie's man

ACROSS

1. *Frasier* actress ___ Gilpin
5. Hindu nobleman
9. Sail supports
14. Impulse transmitter
15. ___ *probandi*
16. Beginning
17. Golden chains
19. Ribbon holder
20. File
21. Erupt
23. ___ Hoop
24. Atoll protector
26. Echoed
28. Superlative suffix
30. Control
32. Apprehend
33. Declaration of affirmation
34. Actress specializing in heartrending roles
39. Jagged, as a leaf's edge
41. Guy Fawkes Day month: Abbr.
42. Animal in a roundup
43. Enlisted personnel
46. Neon, e.g.
47. 1969 Peace Prize grp.
48. Bird ___
49. His "4" was retired
50. Cajole
54. Pluck
57. Injured
58. Food for sea urchins
60. Dispatch boat, for French and Portuguese navies
63. Bikini, e.g.
65. Celtic people dwelling in central Anatolia
67. Flycatcher
68. Clickable image
69. And others, for short
70. German for "serious"
71. Aug. follower
72. Ségolène Royal's nickname

DOWN

1. Drained of color
2. Final, e.g.
3. Cliff ___, of *Spider-Man* trilogy (2002-2007)
4. Accustom
5. Howard of *Happy Days*
6. Digestive tract opening
7. Starting point
8. Revenue-generating property
9. More, in Madrid
10. Kind of soup
11. Gush forth
12. Oar pin
13. "Rabbit food"
18. Salinger's *The Catcher in the* ___
22. Make (one's way)
25. In favor of
27. Bring up
28. Appraiser
29. "Buona ___" (Italian greeting)
31. Potter's tool
34. Dabbling ducks
35. "… there is no ___ angel but Love": Shakespeare
36. Bargain
37. "Cool!"
38. At one time, at one time
40. Variation of ninepins
44. Breakfast area
45. Big galoot
50. Contour
51. Exterior
52. Show displeasure
53. Auspices
55. Backstabber
56. Harvard, Yale, Brown, etc.
59. Alka-Seltzer sound
61. Catch
62. Christiania, now
64. Affranchise
66. Carpenter or fire insect

19

ACROSS

1. Bird not to be confused with a type of bread
6. Admits, with "up"
10. Lowlife
14. Broadcasting
15. Large watercraft
16. By way of, briefly
17. Completely motionless
19. Barbecue entree
20. *Rocky* ___ (debut feature of Mr. T)
21. Set of tools
22. Medicinal syrup
24. Dash lengths
25. Blue hue
26. Bantu people of Southern Africa
27. Asian appetizer
29. Catch a glimpse of
31. After expenses
32. Exam part, often
34. Those who surrender
36. Dwarf buffalo
38. ___ in comparison
39. Like some sentences
43. Settles
46. Egg cells
47. Vex, with "at"
48. Ancient city northwest of Carthage
50. Captain Ahab feature
52. Wax-coated cheese
55. "___, humbug!"
56. Primps
57. Chop (off)
58. "My man!"
59. "Empedocles on ___" poem by Matthew Arnold
60. Gossiper
64. Decomposes
65. Freudian topics
66. Clairvoyants
67. Clash
68. Stage musical by Jonathan Larson
69. Antiquated

DOWN

1. Carried by the pocket full, as in a nursery rhyme
2. Innermost organ membranes
3. *I Ching* readers, perhaps
4. ___-tac-toe game
5. Noah built one
6. Old Roman port
7. NY museum with an Edward Hopper collection
8. Bubkes
9. Main ingredient in a green soup
10. Scatter
11. Cheat
12. More debonair
13. Sweet grapes
18. A shade of blue
23. Fleawort
25. Colorless, almond-smelling toxic gas
28. "By yesterday!"
30. Bit of a draft
33. Child
35. Batman villain Harvey ___, a.k.a. Two-Face
37. Nurses' org.

39. Police officers
40. Surpass
41. Fuchsia red
42. Overemphasize
44. ___ 'n Bits dog food brand
45. Bogeymen
49. Traveling in a saddle
51. Minimal
53. Accomplish, as thou might
54. Appropriate
61. "Act your ___!"
62. Clairvoyance, e.g.
63. Grassland

ACROSS

1. "Silly Love ___" by Wings
6. Bender
9. Faint smell
14. Disguise
15. "I ___ you one"
16. Kidney-related
17. Accused's need
18. Egg-layer
19. English exam finale, often
20. Keep out
21. *The Joy Luck Club* author Amy ___
23. *Show Boat*'s "Can't Help Lovin' ___ Man"
25. Big ___ Conference
26. "20/20" network
27. Butter portion
30. Type of store
34. Cooks leftovers
36. Entomb again
37. Clock standard: Abbr.
38. Parable
39. Certifies
40. Directly
41. Ancient reference marks
42. Balkan native
43. Caught
44. Heckler
45. Commonplace
47. Telephone part
48. Capitol title: Abbr.
49. H1N1
50. Altar avowal
51. Driver's lic. and others
52. Come together
53. Beseech
56. Banded stone
60. "___ Baby Baby" hit song by Smokey Robinson
62. "La Bohème," e.g.
64. Twangy, as a voice
65. Carpentry tool
66. Silo contents
67. Greenhouse threat
68. Carry on
69. Offspring

DOWN

1. Strike-breaker
2. ___ podrida
3. Black, as la nuit
4. Blah-blah-blah
5. Moves quickly
6. ___-on-the-spot
7. Wonder
8. Bluecoat in Belgium
9. "...that saved a ___ like me"
10. "For ___ a jolly ..."
11. ___ and outs
12. JFK overseer
13. Take a 747
22. Ethereal
24. Encourage, as a crime
27. Bill settlers
28. Potsdam Conference attendee
29. Casual top
30. Understands
31. Idolize
32. Moon of Uranus
33. Reins in
35. Put in
37. Destroy the interior of
40. *Real Housewives* or *Duck Dynasty*
41. Winemaker's science
43. Embellish
44. Green gem
46. Off course
47. To a great degree
53. Bridges of Los Angeles County
54. Ancient name of Ireland
55. Jets or Sharks, e.g.
56. Prescription notation
57. Breach
58. ___ Wednesday
59. *Clueless* character ___ Frasier
61. Nocturnal predator
63. Ace

21

ACROSS

1. Little lie
4. Beanies
8. Mainstay
14. Worth copying
16. Capture
17. Paint container
18. Niche or nook
19. Level
20. Produce
22. Bug
23. Often discriminatory attitude or belief
24. Investigate
25. Plus
26. Take up a substance
29. ___ Minor
30. Margarines
31. Moon of Neptune
33. Rock concert venue
36. Freon, e.g.
37. *Phantom* ___, 2017 film by Paul Thomas Anderson
38. Do a holiday chore, perhaps tableside
39. ___ race
40. People on their way to somewhere else
44. Defeat
45. Indian metropolis
46. Clod chopper
47. Back muscle, familiarly
48. Emblem
49. Coastal raptors
50. Brings out
52. It's all in the family
55. Nonessential amino acid
56. Currencies used in Greece
57. Goes where angels won't, as it were
58. Finished an email
59. ATM use requires one

DOWN

1. Boxing-related
2. Mischievous
3. Galley of yore
4. Islet
5. First principles of any subject
6. Kids' domain
7. Imminent graduates
8. Bathroom item
9. "I ___ you so!"
10. Parenthesis, essentially
11. Kingdom of organisms that are neither animals, plants, or fungi
12. Cleansing
13. Kind of ears
15. Toni Morrison's ___ *Baby*
21. *Chicago* lyricist Fred ___
24. Pretentious sort (UK)
25. Bob Marley backer
27. Fair-to-middling
28. Hip bones
31. They may have abs of stone
32. Amble
33. Most static
34. Sewing machine part
35. Framework
36. Fine wool
38. First day of the month, in ancient Rome
40. Darling
41. Scampi protein
42. Art of dwarfing plants
43. Toadies
45. Amounts of medicine
48. Be inclined
49. Addis Ababa's land: Abbr.
51. K-Dee, Sir Jinx, and Ice Cube, collectively
53. Calphalon product
54. Halloween month: Abbr.

ACROSS

1. Melody
5. Northeastern Indian state
10. Like a stuffed shirt
14. ___ Minor
15. Machete
16. "My ___": 1998 Foo Fighters hit
17. Magazine middle
19. Assortment
20. Bring up the rear
21. Pitcher
22. Clock sound
23. Bother
25. It takes two
27. Not moving
32. Informant
35. Three-point line
36. Plane, e.g.
38. Render harmless
39. Anita Brookner's *Hotel du* ___
40. Blue wildflower
42. "To" homonym
43. Swelling
45. Benjamin Disraeli, e.g.
46. "Dig in!"
47. Dotty
49. Berate
52. Hot stuff
54. "My boy"
55. Gull-like bird
57. Whip
60. Anxiety
64. *Beowulf* beverage
65. Entirely
67. "I'm ___ you!"
68. Close call
69. Ballet move
70. Attendee
71. Breviloquent
72. ___ lily

DOWN

1. Boor's lack
2. ___-friendly
3. *All My Children*'s Cliff and ___
4. Restaurant activity
5. Patriot's Day month: Abbr.
6. Call at home
7. Falling flakes
8. Lace tip
9. Chennai, formerly
10. Football formation used for passing
11. Makes better
12. Acid related to gout
13. Icky stuff
18. Brio
24. Box office take
26. It may be proper
27. Corporate department
28. Barter
29. Emphasize
30. ___ of the above
31. Add up
33. Dalmatian, e.g.
34. Be theatrical
37. Turkish currency
40. Battering wind
41. "___ for the poor"
44. Scenic balcony
48. Enter the army
50. Big pig
51. Chronicles
53. Fred Astaire talent
55. E.P.A. concern
56. Casino game
58. Antares, for one
59. Possessive pronoun
61. Delight
62. Smeltery refuse
63. Dittography, e.g.
66. "Fancy that!"

ACROSS

1. Cash dispenser: Abbr.
4. "Follow me!"
8. Quaint contraction
13. ___ constrictor
14. Diamond Head locale
15. Fisher with a net
16. Sticker
17. Hotel amenity
19. Imitating
21. Drag
22. ___ *Captain and the World of Tomorrow*
23. Venezuelan coin
26. Capture
28. "All right!"
29. Big show: Abbr.
31. Bold
35. Hunted
36. Computer whiz
37. Correspondence accompanying a résumé (UK)
42. Luxury watch brand
43. French Sudan, today
44. Church part
45. Fraction of a newton
46. Works in the garden
50. Wet, as morning grass
52. Push or force out
54. Infomercials, e.g.
57. Black forest or wedding, e.g.
59. Old Roman port
60. Party
64. *Monty Python* network
65. Foreign dignitaries
66. Actors
67. 1969 Peace Prize grp.
68. Having a cupola
69. Ballyhoo
70. Drops on blades

DOWN

1. Estate of a churchman
2. Wig
3. Boat basin
4. Literally, "dwarf dog"
5. Infamous chairman
6. Interjection of surprise
7. Deaden
8. "Endless" national park of Tanzania
9. AIDS cause
10. Cuckoos
11. Adam's apple spot
12. Deuce topper
15. Repeated word in a Doris Day song title
18. Aria, e.g.
20. ___ degree
24. Excellence
25. Beasts of burden
27. Water carrier
30. Diminutive goat breed
32. Not just "a"
33. "Dear" one
34. No's opposite
35. Register beforehand
36. Communication service
37. Bean counter, for short
38. Black gold
39. Big wine holder
40. "Good grief!"
41. Channel
45. Constructed to keep out the sea
46. Eddie Murphy film *48___*
47. Offer more for
48. Like some mushrooms
49. Dugong
51. Tail motions
53. Bakery offering
54. Ancient
55. Example recording
56. Check
58. Carve in stone
61. Golf peg
62. Cow chow
63. Bee Gees' 1987 album

ACROSS

1. Secret store
6. Harlotry
14. ___ *Borealis*
16. Meteorite
17. Move forward
18. Curiosity, 2 wds.
19. Cuts wood
20. Fill-in
22. Hiding place
23. Iranian monarch
24. Southwestern U.S. tribe
25. First showing
29. Oil or bagel type
33. Handler of employees directly involved in production
35. Bygone bird
36. Odd's opposite
37. Victorian, for one
38. Worthy of a "D"
39. "Kapow!"
40. Museum offering
44. Hardened beetle wings
46. Caught
47. Decay
48. Work surface
49. Kind of battery
52. The "A" in ABM
53. Bungle
57. Conformity
59. Partner
61. Metal-bolt hammerers
62. *Full House* surname
63. Echoes
64. Back

DOWN

1. Beanies
2. Halo, e.g.
3. Boast
4. Brewer's need
5. "… ___ he drove out of sight"
6. Compassionate or sympathetic state
7. Pile
8. *Catch-22* pilot who disappeared in combat
9. "The Chicken ___": *Seinfeld* episode
10. Cheers
11. Opera star
12. Cole Porter's "Miss ___ Regrets"
13. Net fabric
15. Tennis great ___ Gibson
21. Bread maker
23. Scottish actor Alastair ___
24. "It's no ___!"
25. Cadet
26. Avis, to Hertz
27. Foe
28. Boyz II ___
30. French romance
31. *Live and Let Die* star Roger ___
32. Dog-___
34. January's birthstone
38. School org.
40. Proportionately, 2 wds.
41. ___ grass
42. Back up
43. Toner
45. Business person
49. Silk garment
50. Final notice
51. In person
52. Piece of a farm
53. Arial or Helvetica, e.g.
54. Debussy's "Clair de ___"
55. Freeloader (informal)
56. European capital
58. After expenses
60. ___ *de deux*

ACROSS

1. Extra inning
6. Pedometer unit
10. Wine holder
14. French for "goodbye"
15. Pigeon's home
16. Eye
17. Kellogg's Tony the ___
18. Eastern pooh-bah
19. Style
20. Thanksgiving days
22. Taro
23. Lodge product
24. Bad look
26. Kind of approval
29. Journey to Mecca
32. Modus operandi
36. Chooses
38. Decree
40. Say "Li'l Abner," say
41. Forced marriages
44. Invaded in 1956
45. Far's opposite
46. Micturates
47. Beetles' front wings
49. "Dang!"
51. Arid
52. Christian Science founder
54. Beanie Babies, e.g.
56. A very small battery
59. Arby's specialty
64. Deaden
65. "That hurt!"
66. Guitar relatives
68. Husk
69. Any thing
70. Digital dough
71. Put on board, as cargo
72. Burns poem "Comin' ___ the Rye"
73. Cantankerous

DOWN

1. Sylvester, to Tweety
2. Redact
3. Approaching
4. Get ready to drive
5. Cry of triumph
6. Bunch
7. Forum wear
8. ___ alcohol
9. Savory puddings (UK)
10. Piece of glass used with a microscope slide, 2 wds.
11. Ancient
12. Slipped
13. Atlantic City attraction
21. Big mess
25. Checked out
26. *Cabaret* director Bob
27. UK advanced deg.
28. Lack of firmness
30. Islamic spirit
31. Gossiped
33. Like a fork
34. Garden tool
35. Chaotic
37. It can be said
39. Binge
42. Encircle
43. Air current
48. Canny
50. Gelcap alternative
53. Beardless one
55. Two, in poker
56. ___ stage (Freudian notion)
57. Halo
58. Among
60. Maple genus
61. Jerk
62. Flight predictions, for short
63. Ending for Oktober
67. Diffident

ACROSS

1. "The Sweetheart of Sigma ___"
4. Peruvian capital
8. Battle-axe?
14. Second imperial Chinese dynasty
15. Bibliographical abbr.
16. News office
17. Outs opposite
18. Joshes
19. Act of disrespect
20. Chest armor plates
22. Dig
23. Belong
24. Amazes
26. Carve in stone
29. Like a bug in a rug
30. Latin for "while absent," 2 wds.
32. Staircase support
34. Corn unit
35. Gusto
38. Density symbol
39. Blubber
40. CD- follower, once
41. Actress de Armas
42. Heeled over
45. Yiddish for "beggars"
47. Crock pot
51. "___ scudding drifts the rainy Hyades": Tennyson
52. Staffs
53. Band
54. Fire-setting
56. Racing vehicle
57. Sheet metal
59. Decree
61. Pairs with a suit
62. Panama and others
63. Coca ___
64. "___ a real nowhere man": The Beatles
65. Cyclic
66. Select
67. Founded: Abbr.

DOWN

1. Heads
2. Persevere
3. Undisturbed
4. Compare
5. French brand of economy hotels
6. ___-Atlantic states
7. YouTube video interruptions
8. Compulsive preoccupations
9. Break
10. Ambitious
11. Producer
12. "I see!"
13. Destroy the interior of
21. "Why me?" sound
22. Demeaning sorts
24. Pyrenees dweller
25. "This means ___!"
27. "Bye now"
28. Do damage to
30. Dissonant
31. Dresden's river
33. "Giovanna d'___" (Verdi opera)
35. Gigantic
36. Creep
37. Ruling and warrior caste of India, once
43. Dusk, to Donne
44. Nerd
46. Bridge positions
48. Hate
49. Australian parrots
50. Best suited
53. Add up
55. ___-automatic firearm
56. Brass
57. Back talk
58. Result of 54-across
59. TV regulator
60. Chit

ACROSS

1. "Poker Face" singer Lady ___
5. Onion, for one
9. Ditch
13. All excited
14. Wicked
15. Type of tots
16. 1960s dance
17. Restoring or improving
19. Quality of certain metal substances
21. Alternative to a convertible
22. Darn
23. Attacked verbally
27. Savage
31. Dork
33. Wet, as morning grass
34. "The," grammatically
39. Court attention-getter
40. Back problem
41. Handrail posts
44. Catcher's finger-waggling
46. Convene
48. "Ick!"
51. Willie Pep was one
55. McDonald's or Burger King store boss
57. Slightly open
58. Our home planet
59. Rant partner
60. California valley
61. Some are private
62. Dangerous time to drive
63. Old World duck

DOWN

1. Angler's hooks
2. Acquiesce
3. Melon and squash, e.g.
4. Acts of increasing prestige
5. Road shoulder
6. Eye layer
7. Diminutive suffix
8. Fair-haired
9. Those known for tolerance of variations
10. Auditory suffix
11. Mitch McConnell, e.g.
12. Unit of energy equal to .0000001 joules
15. Golden Horde member, once
18. Hop, skip or jump
20. Tear-inducing ingredient
24. Traditional Hawaiian food
25. New newts
26. 1993 Frank Sinatra album
28. P.I. in film noir, e.g.
29. Boring tool
30. Alkaline liquid
32. *Transformers: Animated* character ___ Sumdac
34. MCU actor ___ Cheadle
35. Hurricane part
36. Handful
37. Dust remover
38. Bit of color
42. Percolate
43. *Robot Chicken* creator ___ Green
45. Deadlock
47. Show place
49. Contour
50. Scarecrow stuffing
51. Transport price
52. Biblical birthright seller
53. Guns (as an engine)
54. Half a fortnight
55. Charge
56. ___ *Donovan* TV series

ACROSS

1. Court ploy
4. Faux ___
7. Nearly
13. Sapiutan
15. Anger
16. In deep ___
17. Teutonic
19. Bounce on one's knee
20. Revealing
22. Taste, e.g.
23. After expenses
24. About
28. Comparatively nimble
29. Drops
31. Baby powders
32. It doesn't hold water
33. ___ green
34. In-flight info
35. Head turner
37. Chair part
38. Bleed
39. Postal scale unit
40. Roar
42. City of fabled riches
44. 2021 novel by Helen Oyeyemi
45. Back talk
46. *True Lies* actor ___ Arnold
47. British slang for "bothered"
48. A practical approach
51. Rude one
54. They're used as flavoring in the liqueur raki
57. Former Spanish currency
58. Fiction prefix
59. Become unhinged
60. Paint resins
61. Genetic building block
62. "___ will be done"

DOWN

1. Delay
2. "Uno," in English
3. Oft-disputed territory
4. ___ movement (military maneuver)
5. Husk
6. Right hand
7. Extra ingredient
8. Advance
9. Genghis Khan, e.g.
10. *The ___ Couple*
11. "Sun" in Sevilla
12. Stubbable digit
14. Containing ammonia
18. Appraiser
21. Calm
22. Palette knife
25. 1998 film *The ___ Killers*
26. Guided
27. Siouan speakers
28. Cordwood units
30. Genus of shrubs
32. Incomplete rainbow
36. New Zealand reptiles
41. Lads' girlfriends
43. Fish hawk
44. Copper film
49. Done working: Abbr.
50. Soon, once
51. Marienbad, for one
52. ___ Aviv
53. Pose a question
55. Lah-di-___
56. *Mad* magazine feature ___ vs. ___

ACROSS

1. Indonesian boat
5. Nineteenth letter of the Hebrew alphabet
9. Chart anew
14. Deserve
15. Eye layer
16. Outer layer of a pollen grain
17. During
18. Induced inadvertently by medical treatment
20. Hemmed again
22. Turmoil (Scot.)
23. Sound systems
25. Tunicate sea creature
26. Slapstick falls
28. Disease associated with gluten intolerance
32. Provide, as with a quality
35. Per
37. *Now, Voyager* actress ___ Chase
38. Potato or pasta
39. Pond buildup
40. Cut out
41. Cart
42. Book part
43. Clamps
44. Decorate with gold leaf
46. Of a reddish-brown color
48. Three of diamonds, e.g.
50. Narrator of 27-down
54. Against preconceptions
58. South Indian moth species
59. Organic salts compounds
61. App symbol
62. Bad mannered (Australia slang)
63. Eject
64. Hawaiian myrtle tree
65. Top competitors, often
66. Cravings
67. Accepts

DOWN

1. Fruits with white, maybe gritty, flesh
2. Clone's other
3. Come to mind
4. Not known enough
5. Andean super food
6. Egg cells
7. Dogs, cats, etc.
8. Does' mates
9. Wine and dine
10. Representational model
11. *Dracula* heroine
12. Floridian cuckoos
13. Gnome-like creature of Scottish myth
19. Atriplex
21. *The Way We* ___ (1973 film)
24. Commemorative marker
27. Heroic tales
29. Misfortunes
30. Soapberry tree
31. Bounders
32. Increase, once
33. Flat bread of India
34. Dope
36. Bistros
39. Astronaut Buzz ___
43. Spanish for "beam"
45. Herculean dozen
47. Quarterbacks' throws
49. Part of a simple bouquet
51. Manly
52. Anthurium, for one
53. Grannies, to some
54. Bothers
55. "Good going!"
56. Appropriate
57. Spear holder in an opera
60. City govt.-related

ACROSS

1. Taxes
8. Jeans manufacturer Levi ___
15. Powerful opiate
16. Kitchen worker's gear
17. Little Leaguer, e.g.
18. Persuader
19. Appear onstage
20. Ill-gotten gains
22. Be theatrical
23. The Holy ___
24. Enlarges or widens
26. Pithy saying
27. Africa's Lake ___
29. Cambridge sch.
30. Exposed
31. *In medias* ___
32. Toyota, for one
33. Atlas enlargement
36. Long
38. Cave, in literature
40. "___ the season"
42. Prepare for winter takeoff
45. Romanian currency
46. Indigenous language family of Western Canada
49. Package deliverer
50. Comparatively uncomplicated
51. Hide-___-seek
52. One concerned with pitches
54. Artless one
55. Imperial fighter vehicle in *Star Wars*
56. Commemorate in verse
58. City in Sicily
61. Old English courts
62. Here, there, and everywhere
63. Certain tenants
64. Ingeniousness

DOWN

1. Painting technique
2. Short musical composition
3. Pomposity
4. Decline to participate, with "out"
5. ___-Ra, Princess of Power
6. Haberdashery item
7. In a lucid way
8. It helps create a capital
9. Turn golden
10. Saddles up
11. Jack-in-the-pulpit, e.g.
12. Not inclined to talk
13. Make sure
14. Close overlap of fugue voices
21. Animal house
24. A&W competition
25. "At ___, soldier."
28. Chap
32. Greek god of war
34. And others, for short
35. Female giant of Greek mythology
37. Twelfth month of the religious year on the Hebrew calendar
38. Related to the buttocks
39. Drive away
41. Branch of Islam
43. Pointed teeth
44. Makes beloved
47. Feminine sides, to Jung
48. Happened to
50. Cherish
53. Auspices
57. Tappan ___ Bridge
59. Arch
60. "Carry on my wayward ___"

ACROSS

1. Gene Vincent song "Be-Bop-___"
6. "Don't give me that!"
11. "Well, ___-di-dah!"
14. Penalized
15. Amorphous creature
16. "Gimme ___!" (start of an Iowa State cheer)
17. Drain
18. Lively dance
19. Archaeological site
20. Lawman Earp
21. Bend in a pipe
22. Notre Dame Fighting ___
24. Dream ___
26. Abominate
28. Henry VIII's last wife Catherine ___
30. Suffix with critic or alcohol
32. Baja bash
35. Assortment
36. Blotto
38. Igneous rock
39. Soft mud
40. Kind of cycle
41. "Do ___ others as…"
42. Manson Family victim Sharon
43. Build on
44. ___ song
45. Climb
47. Dusk, to a poet
48. Charge
49. Cut out
51. Asian language
53. Brenda ___ comic-strip
55. British singer Adam ___
57. Group of eight
60. Campaigner, for short
61. Speleologist
63. Attendance counter
64. "Is that ___?"
65. Corpulent
66. Island nation east of Fiji
67. Sylvester Stallone's nickname
68. Cheeky
69. Therefore

DOWN

1. Not many
2. Abundant in calcium oxide
3. In a manner showing lack of love for one's country
4. Part of a desk set, once
5. Private chambers
6. *The Umbrella Academy* actor Elliott ___
7. Narrowness of views
8. 2015 Adele hit song
9. Old blood-typing system
10. Yellowstone sight
11. Queen's attendants
12. Short for Anisette
13. Low's opposite
23. Inheriting the Rh protein or not
25. Loses
27. Insult
28. Assignments
29. Object of many prayers
31. Fastener
33. Original "mounted messenger" in Central Asia
34. *Home* ___ 1990 film
37. Destiny
46. *Netflix* series about drug cartels
50. Overhangs
52. Plantain lily
53. Fitness centers, sometimes
54. Cost to cross
56. Deuce topper
58. Aquatic plant
59. "Agreed!"
62. " ___ Daba Honeymoon" (1914 song that became a 1950s pop hit)

ACROSS

1. PC maker
5. Floor pads
9. Disconcert
14. Idle
15. Biblical twins ___ and Jacob
16. Object
17. *Clueless* catch phrase, 2 wds.
18. Songs for the deceased
20. Restaurant list
21. One losing it
22. Black Sea port city
24. Send back
27. Caught in the act
28. Central, for short
30. Ghost's interjection
31. Converted liberal, informally
33. Artillery burst
35. Sundae staple
39. Toothbrush trees
40. Opposite of theory
41. Aloof
42. "The Raven" writer
43. Pocket billiards
45. More intrusive
48. Temper, as metal
51. *Black-ish* actor Anthony ___
55. Data
56. Bacterial skin infection
58. House
59. Sleep on it
60. One teaspoon, e.g.
61. Radial, e.g.
62. Cities with piers
63. Chooses
64. Coaster

DOWN

1. San Antonio landmark
2. Checked out
3. Online mags
4. One denied permission to emigrate
5. Antifreeze additive
6. Far from ruddy
7. Blackens
8. Cooking fat
9. Dig, so to speak
10. Obscure
11. Friendly
12. "So ___ me!"
13. Sixty min. periods
19. Doofus
23. Blinds, in falconry
25. ___ Scotia
26. Bad end
28. Wavelike design
29. South American civilization
32. Crime boss
33. Heir
34. Destructive felons
35. Conceited
36. Gasoline giant
37. Chronic pessimist
38. Vast extents
42. Get ready, for short
44. Vegetarian soup staple
46. Atlas enlargement
47. Improves writing
49. Prior to, old-style
50. Mooed
52. Change decor
53. Slush
54. Brewer's equipment
56. Telepath's talent: Abbr.
57. Density symbol

ACROSS

1. Apple devices, prefixed by i- or Air-
5. Beside
10. Arch type
14. Airy
15. Eastern wrap
16. Group of bros.
17. Judi Dench, e.g.
18. Sea creature
20. Makes aware
22. Close overlap of fugue voices
23. Strikes from on high
25. Chips in
26. Contemptuous look
27. Coarse file
30. Arid
31. Flowerpot material
33. European raptors
34. Most comfortable
36. Pepper pairing
40. Behavior that benefits one by injuring another
45. Mammalian urine component
46. Check
47. African language
48. Discover
50. Muffling device
52. Defined by an outline
55. Caused some confusion
56. Generator
58. ___-a-dope
59. New Mexico art community
60. ___ on the cake
61. The "U" in UX
62. At one time, at one time
63. Rigid
64. Department store department

DOWN

1. Downloadable audio show
2. Iridescent
3. Coy one
4. Villain, at times
5. Alphanumeric code acronym
6. Facility that's on the quarter system
7. Crumb
8. Brings home
9. Cabbage
10. Football side
11. Bad-weather vehicle (UK)
12. Not western
13. Distinguishing attributes
19. Roman or Victorian, e.g.
21. Fergie's first name
24. Some *Saturday Night Live* sketches
28. Wrinkle fighters
29. Left-lane highway maneuver
32. Police
35. Himalayan region
36. Having deep furrows
37. Like an iris part
38. Building add-ons
39. Most sharp
41. Childish fit
42. At hand
43. Fall more precipitously
44. Slays
49. Conjunction used with "neither"
51. The 'L' of XXL
53. Condo, e.g.
54. Dash
57. Element "Sn" on the periodic table

ACROSS

1. Eat
5. ___ Rouge
10. Interjection of concern
14. Jewish month that marks most mornings with the shofar
15. Green
16. Tom, Dick, or Harry, e.g.
17. Vermin
18. Earthen water jars
19. Ruler's title, maybe
20. After-bath powder
21. Articles made of trees for domestic use
23. Colorless, flammable solvent
25. E.T.-pursuing org.
26. Encircled
28. Bathroom fixture
33. Bipolar, once
38. *Beowulf*, e.g.
39. Command to a horse
40. "… happily ___ after"
41. Daydream, e.g.
44. Inventor Nicola ___
45. Salmon that have spawned
46. ___ Fyne, Scotland
50. Boat basin
53. Multicolored gemstone
58. Elliptical
59. About
60. Navigational aid
61. Actress Gilpin, of *Frasier* fame
62. Casting need
63. World's second-most populated country
64. Classes
65. Central point
66. ___ and crossbones
67. Dermatologist's concern

DOWN

1. Atlanta-based airline
2. ___ artery
3. Study of atomic cores
4. Kind of engineer
5. Cognition
6. Ring of light
7. Czech director ___ Forman
8. Circumvent
9. Change, as a clock
10. Again
11. Dalai ___
12. British boxer ___ Khan
13. Arid
22. Penpoints
24. *GMA* network
27. Adjudge
29. With unchanging entropy
30. With intent to cause disagreement
31. Dec. 24 and Dec. 31
32. Tenure
33. Convene
34. Chapel part
35. ___-Wee Herman
36. *Succession* actor Alan ___
37. Fleeting
42. Oil source
43. ___ mode: pie option
47. Desert sight
48. Dull sound
49. Majority religion of 63-across
51. Informers (slang)
52. *Crème de la crème*
53. Conflicted
54. Sundae topper, perhaps
55. Utilized
56. Lady Macbeth, e.g.
57. Claw

ACROSS

1. Bloodhound's activity
8. Arachnophobe's worry
15. Fish tanks
16. Islington-based F.C.
17. Blunting
18. Leaves for lunch
19. Ancient Italians
20. Clung
21. Train schedule info, for short
22. Dieter's goal
23. Holier-than-thou type, maybe
27. Destroy the interior
28. 1977 bodybuilding documentary *Pumping* ___
29. Integrates
31. Health ___
34. Mailed
35. Rings
36. Above
37. Tic-tac-___
38. January's birthstone
39. Like rams and roosters
40. Day before Sun.
41. Develops
43. Royal blue ornamental mineral
47. "___ we having fun yet?"
48. Bakery treat
49. Silverback
53. Designated flying route
54. Adult doodlebug
55. American boxer ___ Crawford
56. Least newsworthy
57. Composed of horizontal laths
58. Center of a roast

DOWN

1. Staffs
2. "Barbie Girl" band
3. On top of the heap, 2 wds.
4. Dweller
5. Marcel Duchamp's "Fountain," essentially
6. Number of lives, for a cat
7. Makes "it"
8. Shallon
9. Simplifies for easy understanding
10. Narrow strip of land
11. Gear catch
12. Accustom
13. Track events
14. Coasters
22. Funny
23. Atomizer output
24. Bestselling cookie
25. Restlessness
26. Prophet
30. Delight
31. More dignified
32. ___ dancing
33. 1968 film *Planet of the* ___
36. City in Texas
38. Chivalrous
40. Old-time helmet
42. Scottish cloth
43. Beats it
44. Architectural projection
45. Grain sorghum
46. Cornered, as certain prey
49. Cut
50. Suspecting
51. Daft Punk 2013 hit "___ Yourself to Dance"
52. Initial stake

ACROSS

1. Court figures
5. Approach
9. Door beams
14. Bridge toll unit
15. Arab League member
16. In conflict with, with "run"
17. Fast-moving card game
18. ___ mortals
19. Romance, e.g.
20. Bromance or Labradoodle, e.g., 2 wds.
23. Brown ermine
24. Clay pot
25. Small salmon
27. Species of orchid
32. Digital dough, once
36. Subcontinental prefix
38. Publisher Henry ___
39. R and R
41. In a cordial manner
43. Amounted (to)
44. *Schindler's* ___
46. Uneven
47. Bryce Canyon rock formation
49. Light bulb unit
51. Santa ___, California
53. "H," phonetically
57. Dotage, maybe, 2 wds.
63. Purple shade
64. *Casablanca* cafe proprietor
65. Grapelike palm fruit
66. Fragrant organic compound
67. Skin-soother
68. Eggy holiday drinks
69. Tiny
70. The "M" in MYOB
71. Some jewelry stores

DOWN

1. Coarse file
2. Departed Montréal team
3. "Bat an eye"
4. Begin
5. Common soup or sauce
6. Prayer ending
7. Comic drawing
8. Prepare to propose?
9. Luxury auto
10. Not many
11. Like old recordings
12. Vice president under Jefferson
13. "Rosebud" in *Citizen Kane*
21. Too masculine
22. Cool
26. LP player
28. Blacken
29. Bindle bearer
30. Misfortunes
31. Eye affliction
32. Carve in stone
33. Italian for "bye"
34. BBs, e.g.
35. Lentil, e.g.
37. Graph info
40. Kind of insurance
42. Malodorous
45. Language in which "simba" means "lion"
48. Cantankerous
50. Turned state's evidence
52. Emergency shutdown of a nuclear reactor
54. Acknowledge
55. Après-ski drink
56. "Georgia on My Mind" composer ___ Carmichael
57. Old World duck
58. *The Wiz*'s "___ on Down the Road"
59. Adorable
60. Roast host
61. Emblem
62. Bad-mouth

ACROSS

1. Long ago
5. Musk-secreting creature
10. First man
14. A superhero's uniform
15. Goodbye, in Paris
16. Skin hole
17. Gulf south of Yemen
18. Brazilian Formula One driver Ayrton ___
19. Brownish purple
20. Order to attack, with "on"
21. Cow chow
22. African antelope
24. Centers of activity
27. Necklace item
28. Abounding
29. Faintest
32. Infielder
35. ___ Spumante
36. Steinbeck novel ___ of Eden
37. *M*A*S*H* setting
39. Individual unit
40. Like Jeff Bezos
41. Mary or Larry, e.g., 2 wds.
43. Petal peddlers
46. Hammer part
47. Lots
48. American alternative
51. Faucet
53. Sis's sib
54. Ottoman officer
55. St. Louis landmark
56. Allowed for container weight
58. Clobber
59. Bearded animal
60. Head to Vegas, maybe
61. "I had no ___!"
62. Cobblers' tools
63. Artist's stand
64. Interjection to quietly attract attention

DOWN

1. Digital dough, once
2. AM/FM device
3. Involving spectroscopy
4. Big ___ Conference
5. Place that might honour cheques
6. "Don't get any funny ___!"
7. Covered with ivy
8. Poet's "still"
9. Berber people
10. Belonged
11. Unfair things, 2 wds.
12. California gas brand
13. Docile
23. "A likely story!"
25. Patrimonies
26. Online financial transaction: Abbr.
27. *Orange Is the New Black* writer ___ Kerman
29. Large-eyed lemur
30. Check
31. "Pencils down!"
32. Bondman
33. Acclaim
34. Ancient British settlements
38. Meadows of the ancient Greek underworld
42. With 31-down, a golf date
44. 1969 Peace Prize grp.
45. Couch
48. Brunch offering
49. Fits
50. African capital
51. It's a long story
52. Figurehead's place
53. *Super Mario* ___
57. Gulf of Mex. state
58. Immerse briefly

ACROSS

1. Arise
6. Fraternity letters
10. Boxing promoter Bob ___
14. Carried
15. Trig term
16. Georgian currency
17. Jump for joy
18. Swamped
20. Laborer
22. Expels again
23. Military unit
27. Fair-sized musical group
28. Removals
29. Destroyers: Archaic
30. Extricate
32. Prune (UK)
33. Oil holder
34. Discontinue
38. Constructs again
40. Accustomed
44. Feudal domains
45. Dug up
46. Wettest
47. Latin for "I have sinned"
49. *Billboard* item
50. Treatments for mental illness: Archaic
53. Flips through
56. The Kennedys, e.g.
57. Foretell (UK)
58. Not affiliated with major companies
59. Heel over
60. Fungal spore cases
61. Grave marker

DOWN

1. Honor from the queen: Abbr.
2. *Friends* actor Courteney ___
3. Closely adhering lichen
4. Unimpeded: Archaic
5. Teach new skills
6. 23rd letter of the Greek alphabet
7. Ancient Hebrew unit
8. Bury
9. Samoan coin
10. Cottonwood trees
11. Nubby fabric
12. Canal
13. Centers
19. North Macedonia currency
21. Formed in a fluid through precipitation
23. Wrongs
24. *The Last King of Scotland* dictator
25. Accustom
26. Fern
29. Clocks again
31. Engender
34. Terminal
35. Traitor
36. Mineral deposits
37. Attention-getter
38. Fortification
39. Orange-flower oils
40. 1983 Clint Eastwood film *Sudden ___*
41. Black ornamental alloy
42. Written in capitals
43. Fresh
46. Cirrus clouds, e.g.
48. MasterCard alternative
51. Computer
52. Baleen whale
54. Chick-___-A
55. Mediterranean or Baltic

ACROSS

1. "What are the ___?"
5. ___ Guard
10. Bindle bearer
14. Discontinue
15. Spirited vigor
16. Adequate, once
17. Ideas, in Platonism
18. Charging too much interest
19. Phoenician trading center
20. Female element of a flower having separate carpels
22. Earliest versions
24. London art museum
25. Coconut fiber
26. Certain diver
29. Pertaining to an image
33. Reveals, as a secret
35. Rip off
36. Holds up
37. Grammar topic
39. Love's opposite
40. Chooses
42. Amazon lily
44. Excuses for nonappearance in court (UK)
46. Type for titles
47. Chick's sound
48. Barbie or Ken
49. French expressionist Henri
52. Ammonia molecules
56. Japanese herbs
57. Musical repeat signs
59. Hunt for
60. Attempt
61. Bring out
62. "Encore!"
63. Japanese cassettes
64. Loudness units
65. Backwater

DOWN

1. Ancient theaters
2. Big bore
3. Extinct bird
4. Scientists that study the interaction between matter and electromagnetic radiation
5. Gracious considerations toward others
6. Zygotes
7. Central Asian river ___ Darya
8. Dapper
9. Surgeries to remove a butterfly-shaped gland
10. Sexes that reside in different individuals
11. Black stone
12. Inferior diamond
13. Indebted to
21. East Indian mulberries
23. Gain alternative
26. Blender button
27. Organic compounds
28. French clerics
30. Maldives coin denomination
31. Relating to a convulsion
32. Kind of board
34. Reply envelope: Abbr.
38. Counsel
41. Associations
43. Stems used for thatching and bedding
45. Big name in bathing suits
49. Essential
50. Common childhood diagnosis: Abbr.
51. Captured
53. Glowing gas
54. Mysterious (var.)
55. ___-Ball
58. Weapon

ACROSS

1. Round things
5. Way, way off
9. John Fowles's novel *The* ___
14. African mancala game
15. Challenge
16. Accustom
17. Membranous tissue
19. Roman robe, ankle-length
20. Bearing
21. Jamaican soccer player ___ Murray
22. Related to obstetrics
24. In a rude manner
28. Primordial matter
29. "Where the heart is"
30. Strong monobasic compounds
34. Separate piece of news
35. Wood nymph
37. Plane reservation
38. Powerful permanent-magnet alloys
40. Like Sunday morning, in song
41. Booty
42. Part of a board
45. Molecule that represses the expression of gene
49. Barricade
50. German for "housewife"
55. Pet name for Christophe
56. Child sponsor at baptism
57. Cloudless
58. American runner ___ Wilson
59. Ancient theaters
60. Barbs of a feather
61. Atomizer output
62. Impresses

DOWN

1. Didn't have enough
2. Titian's *The* ___ *of Europa*
3. Cup part
4. Locale
5. Radical, in biochemistry
6. Arson, for one
7. All excited
8. Coastline feature
9. Covered with metal
10. Dissects (UK)
11. Solzhenitsyn's *The* ___ *Archipelago*
12. Arrow poison
13. Glacial ice formation
18. Crones
21. State of matter
23. Cornice molding
24. ___ Pet®
25. Unit of weight
26. Prayer conclusion
27. Mutation that produces more than fifty percent—but not complete—mortality
30. Cries of regret
31. Tidy
32. Effortlessness
33. Eye affliction
35. Opportunities, so to speak
36. Anatomical network
39. Office machines
42. Eighteenth letter of the Hebrew alphabet (var.)
43. Hoarse, in Glasgow
44. Latin for "bear"
45. Joseph Heller's ___-22
46. Early French coin
47. French for "to grate"
48. Japanese room divider
51. Cleaving tool (var.)
52. Change
53. Again
54. Hagen et al.
56. Leg, slangily

ACROSS

1. Leak through
5. Twelfth king of Argos, in Greek mythology
9. Strong fiber
13. Kingdom in Indian epic literature
14. Beaver skin
15. Plural of giga
16. Jail (UK)
17. "Me neither"
18. Common sense
19. Having a normal physical response to an antigen
22. Bootlickers
23. Locale within a larger locale
24. Spanish for "robe"
25. Indigenous peoples of the Brazilian Amazon region
26. Come to mind
27. DRC, once
28. Minor player
31. Mets, Jets, or Nets
32. Law school class
33. Departed
34. Masthead names, briefly
35. Soil or ground (UK)
36. Drug dealer or trafficker: slang
37. Unclean
38. Muzzle loader
39. Charge
42. Plumbing, more or less
43. Qualities of rambling tediousness
45. Desktop pictures
46. Freudian topics
47. *Austin Powers* character ___ Me
48. Silk garment (var.)
49. Wings
50. December 24 and 31
51. Pigeon-___
52. Appraiser
53. Birdhouse?

DOWN

1. Arrowhead-shaped leaf
2. Infatuated (UK)
3. Obsessions with oneself
4. Malaria
5. Sleep problem (UK)
6. Voting groups
7. Relating to flight
8. Speedo products
9. Regional populations
10. Earthwork
11. Excel
12. Anatomical roofs
15. Spore-bearing parts of puffball fungi
20. "Good going!"
21. Pleased cat noises
25. Quality of soil that is loose or crumbly
27. Bacteria found in wastewater (UK)
28. Capable of eroding by abrasion
29. Cancer-causing genes
30. Person who studies the size and shape of the earth
32. Having melody and harmony
33. Athletes
35. Treat badly
36. Back of the neck
37. Chiefly Southern curse variation
38. Car wash device
39. Disparager of seniors (var.)
40. Chocolate source
41. Ten million rupees
42. Loin muscles
44. Hideous

ACROSS

1. Not just one
5. Clumps (UK)
9. Adjective for some orange juices
14. Odd (UK)
15. Brightly colored fish
16. Convex molding
17. Alliance
18. Recorded, as a copyright
20. Eighteen-wheelers
22. White Sands National Park feature
23. Laser light
25. Jaguarundi
26. More squishy
29. Buttonhole
34. Blockers
36. Grable's co-star in *The Dolly Sisters*
37. African plant
38. Intestinal
40. Samoan coin
41. Botch
43. Foods produced by bacterial fermentation of milk (UK)
45. Begin
47. Big waves
48. Kingfisher, e.g.
50. Japanese for "unevenness"
51. Barometer that records its readings
56. Trig functions
59. Anomaly
61. *Peter Pan* dog
62. South American vine and antidote for snakebites
63. Greek mountain between Pelion and Olympus
64. Stravinsky ballet
65. Scarecrow stuffing
66. Hasenpfeffer, e.g.
67. Stitches

DOWN

1. Bounces about
2. Heraldic border
3. Brass musician
4. Owner of a *hacienda*
5. A craggy hill
6. Kind of column
7. Maker of early photographs
8. Freshly minted
9. Gift-giving feast practiced by indigenous nations of the Pacific Northwest
10. Eye layer
11. Desolate
12. Argued
13. Astrological aspect formations
19. Italian for "evening"
21. Stuffing ingredient
24. 2008 comedy *Zack and ___ Make a Porno*
26. Adjusts with a wedge
27. Mischief-maker
28. Evasive
30. Australian slender trees
31. Supervise excessively
32. Estonian for "cents"
33. Lock of hair
35. Slumps
39. Bud
42. Get too big for
44. Burden
46. Japanese codeword used to report complete surprise
49. Spanish for "data"
51. Captures
52. Adjoin
53. Back
54. Boat in *Jaws*
55. Gardener's gear
57. Enough: Archaic
58. Without
60. Informal no

ACROSS

1. Ballfield covering
5. Travels on whitewater
10. 1990 World Series champs
14. Affirm
15. Amazon download, e.g.
16. Hip bones
17. Exec's note
18. Golfing term for a certain type of lead
19. The die is ___
20. The big dance
21. Salad veggie
22. Dictatorial
23. Seize
25. Wobble
26. Bar, at the bar
27. Severe
29. Bambi's kind
30. Impudent
31. Italian astronomer
33. Current strength
36. Acorn Computers OS
40. Brooklyn or Queens
41. Nervous
42. Curie discovery
43. Actor
46. "Smart" ones
47. Again
48. ___ *Karenina*
49. Jerk
50. Ammonia compound
51. Laundry quantity
52. Daughter of Queen Elizabeth II
53. Common bar food
54. *Moscato d'*___
55. Medical advice, often
56. Barely beats
57. Clairvoyant

DOWN

1. Buccaneers' home
2. Maintained
3. Compunction
4. Publicize
5. Bag handler
6. Circa
7. Visible as a line branching across the sky, 2 wds.
8. Heavy reading
9. Celestial sphere
10. Cannoli filling
11. Protein that allows skin to stretch
12. Analyze
13. Debaucher
22. Turkish strait
24. Dazzlingly beautiful
25. Bind
28. Disturb
30. Football foul indicator
32. Boxing promoter Bob ___
33. Marine rock-clinger
34. Bondoni fonts
35. Spike for a candle
37. African antelopes
38. Prickly
39. Salt of cyanic acid
41. Jewish woman
42. *M*A*S*H* character "___" O'Reilly
44. Beat around the bush
45. Low point
47. During
50. Reverence

ACROSS

1. Igneous rocks
8. Trousers
14. Caught short
15. Nicki Minaj's music style
16. Post
17. Bodies
18. Funambulist
20. Appearance
21. Affirmative votes
22. Attempt
26. Takes off
28. Dangerous dive
31. Crackers
36. Fit
37. Train unit
38. Mischievous person
39. Beatings
40. Leg bone
42. Nuisance
43. ___ gin fizz
47. Cut like a baby?
50. Absence of concern
56. If nothing else
57. Libya neighbor
58. Chews on
59. Without a hitch
60. Protein ___
61. Backpackers' alternatives

DOWN

1. Burst of wind
2. 2016 Rihanna album
3. Act the blowhard
4. *Little Women* character
5. Indian side or condiment
6. Bad smells
7. Overview
8. Kangaroo court, 2 wds.
9. Turkish currency
10. Answer a Help Wanted ad
11. Require the Heimlich
12. Divided since 1945
13. Boxes
17. Intestinal pouches
19. Drudge
22. David Bowie was one
23. Spanish appetizer
24. Affectation
25. Alliance

27. Agitated state
29. Clash
30. Decorousness
32. Berth place
33. Bad marks
34. Badgers
35. Formerly
37. Put back on
39. Bavarian brew
41. Drummer's contribution
43. Hut
44. Indian police officer's club
45. Acrylic fiber
46. Swelling
48. "___. My name is Inigo Montoya."
49. Barely beats
51. Chance occurrences
52. Drink order detail
53. Sea-eagle
54. Pie perch
55. "___ who?"

ACROSS

1. ___ *profundo*
6. Cabbage salad
10. Medieval brew
14. Scout's mission
15. Prefix with chute or legal
16. Bullets, briefly
17. "He's ___ nowhere man," 2 wds.
18. The sincerest form of flattery
20. Cheap
21. High-water indicators
22. Sesame or poppy
23. Biden pre-VP or POTUS
24. Diesencumber
25. Choral warmup
27. Quick breads
31. 1942 Hitchcock thriller
34. Kind of chop
35. Folk singer DiFranco
36. ___ Aviv
37. Triangular sail
38. Explosive inits.
39. Slice of meat
41. It's wind-driven
43. Deli offering
44. Breathing problem
45. Soda unit
46. Dust remover
47. Falls behind
51. Atlas
55. Iraqi port
56. It's teeming with craters
57. "___ we meet again."
58. ___ fruit
59. Long, long time
60. Lilac, e.g.
61. After-bath powder
62. Acclivity
63. Range rovers

DOWN

1. Kindergarten disrupters
2. Cliffside dwelling
3. Brouhaha
4. No-goodnik
5. Roy Orbison's "___ the Lonely"
6. Catty
7. Layered
8. Bone-dry
9. Lake sport
10. One who accepts charges
11. Ruler
12. Wildly
13. Gets into
19. Friendly
23. Coach for overnight
26. Foot props
28. Alliance acronym
29. Sicilian peak
30. Paving block (UK)
31. Bursae
32. Indonesian wild ox
33. President before and after a George
37. Tokyo native
40. Concise
41. Mexican shawls (var.)
42. What's left in the account
48. Daisylike bloom
49. Daily drudgery
50. Preserves, as pork
51. Obscenity
52. Forum wear
53. Wrapping paper quantity
54. Sorcerers
55. "Here We Go Round the Mulberry ___"

ACROSS

1. Small basin for holy water
6. "Fernando" quartet
10. Cut down
14. Gout deposits
15. Günter Grass's *The Tin* ___
16. Blunted blade
17. Fatty liquid
18. Mediterranean appetizer
19. Polynesian carving
20. Tranquilizing drugs
23. A thing to pass
24. Knock down, in Britain
25. Resembling a copper-zinc alloy
29. Barrel downhill
32. Polish statesman ___ Walesa
33. Untruthful type
35. Short stack topper: Var.
36. Assortment
37. Dry
39. Six on a die
40. Drunken
42. ___ Inch Nails
43. Waste of unevenness
44. Avenue crosser
46. Sailors who determine depth of water
48. Banned apple spray
49. Inuit for "house"
50. Anti-allergy compounds
57. "Have you ever seen the ___?"
58. Good, in Scotland
59. Ketone that is also an alcohol
60. All there
61. Blue Bonnet, e.g.
62. Blink-182's ___ *of the State*
63. Engines: Abbr.
64. Figure (out)
65. Convened again

DOWN

1. Short straight stick
2. Lacquered metalware
3. Airy
4. ___-bang
5. Dry red wines
6. Acknowledgment
7. Swimmers are known for them
8. Gossip
9. Foreign heads of state (var.)
10. Irrational devotions
11. Outermost layer of a nerve
12. West Flanders (Belgium) town
13. Island wreaths
21. ___ Dyke (Scotland)
22. Campaign funders, for short
25. Splotches
26. Found a new tenant for
27. Converting iron into steel
28. Boundaries between land and water
30. Capital of Bolivia
31. To wean (Scotland)
34. Spanish for "renegades"
38. Camelot, to Arthur
41. Sure
45. Spanish for "wheats"
47. Small, sub-Saharan antelope
50. Behind, in Britain
51. Indian bread
52. Lt. Hikaru ___ of *Star Trek*
53. Reality TV personality ___ Leakes
54. Romantically involved
55. Dog command
56. Bed board

ACROSS

1. Ado
5. Sites for studs
10. Altar's end
14. Fish-eating eagle
15. Circumvent
16. Thump
17. Skin art, slangily
18. Fill up
19. ___ Fyne, Scotland
20. Short, erect tail
21. *Sambucus*
23. Mexican American
25. ___ giant hornet
26. Plump
27. Fanciful yarn
30. ___ board
31. Intro
32. Walk through water
33. Hit hard
34. Junkyard dogs
38. For better or ___
39. Bringer of bad luck, to sailors
40. Bamboo musical instruments
44. Heavy silk fabric
45. Pungent ingredient
46. Hurly-burly
47. Bart Simpson's ride
51. Carbon compound
52. Boor's lack
53. People who oppose
54. Number of innings to play
55. Husk
56. Incline
57. Alexander, e.g.
58. Channel
59. Abnormally active
60. Congers

DOWN

1. Part of a machine or motor
2. Eye disease
3. Sensed
4. Spa treatment
5. 1985 Tom Cruise film
6. Convex molding
7. Lyric poet
8. Trim around the lawn
9. Psychic
10. Best qualified
11. Bradley University site
12. Holy
13. Acetylene
22. Soothing substance
24. "___ day now…"
27. Bridge support
28. Bang-up
29. Kind of bulb or TV
31. Tiny opening
33. ___ culture
34. Get going
35. Organize workers
36. Sensible
37. Peanut preparers
38. Dine partner
39. Glass vessel
40. Done by mail
41. Turkey part
42. B vitamin
43. Pot that holds a half-gallon
44. Soap opera
46. Balderdash
48. Big blowout
49. ___ *Murders in the Building* streaming series
50. At the peak

ACROSS

1. Major Florida city
6. Caught in the act
12. Egg-shaped items
14. Mexican cent
15. Pinkish rash
17. Deprives of gender
18. Band member
20. Stem part, maybe
21. Recipe quantities
24. "___ in sight," 2 wds.
25. Suffix for journal or skeptic
28. Ear inflammation
31. Formerly known as Ceylon
33. Fixed, as a coat
35. First-rate
36. Unusually cruel
38. Heir's concern
39. ___ Gawain and the Green Knight
40. Two-dot punctuation mark
42. Female sheep
43. Brain membrane, 2 wds.
46. Dictatorial political system
52. Ape
53. Cheapen
54. Regulated substance, in pro baseball
55. Deals with loose laces
56. Cordwood units
57. Keisters

DOWN

1. Beverly Hills 90210 actor ___ Spelling
2. Shakespeare, the Bard of ___
3. Forest growth
4. Sanctimonious
5. Beautify
6. Absorbent clay
7. Takes a load off
8. Pedestal part
9. Cab
10. Prime-times
11. Biblical verb
13. Offensive pejorative
14. Wrasses
16. Prayer ending
19. God of love
21. Appliance connectors
22. Development areas
23. Pablo's wife in For Whom the Bell Tolls
25. Acquired relative
26. Get by
27. Some bays
29. Vaccinate
30. Unmarried women, in Madrid
32. Substitute
34. Enlarging instrument
37. Profound unconsciousness
41. Aromatic ancient ointment
43. Tinder user, e.g.
44. Ranking
45. Overhangs
46. Server's income
47. Bypass
48. Food sticker
49. Hip bones
50. Cooking fat
51. Ruin

ACROSS

1. Buddhist temples
5. Adjust
10. Cakewalk
14. Halo, e.g.
15. Electron tube
16. Therapeutic plant
17. Modern-day Persia
18. Excellence
19. Catastrophic
20. Acts for declaring someone holy
23. *Consumer Reports* employee
24. Novice (UK)
25. Best quality
28. Pretty good
32. Arises
34. Food fight site
36. Hawaiian tuber
37. Famous archer
38. Respiratory organ
39. Extends
41. Christmas delivery
42. Robin Hood heroine
43. Exasperated sound
45. Ballpark figure
47. Car window adornments
50. Renter's fee
55. Brews
56. Best
57. Cotton type
58. Commuter line
59. Jungle climber
60. Cut, maybe
61. Deeply
62. Facilitates
63. Adjusts, as a clock

DOWN

1. Midsection
2. Plural of 14-across
3. One that conveys a title
4. Piously
5. Look up to
6. Willingly
7. Musician ___ Amos
8. Decree
9. Hired, as a lawyer
10. Instruments used to detect emissions from space
11. Assortment
12. Neil Diamond's "September ___"
13. Urinates
21. Bills featuring Hamilton
22. Bring (out)
26. Drudgery
27. Cassettes
29. Disregard, 2 wds.
30. Hokkaido native
31. Hammarskjold, et al.
32. Check
33. Spanish for "cut down" (a tree)
35. Seek indirectly
37. Biblical hymn
40. Asian ox
41. Army vehicle
44. Moisture overload results, in plants
46. Stripe (as in skin)
48. Calculus calculation
49. Sports data
50. Silk wrap
51. Brio
52. Cover an upper surface
53. Affirmative votes
54. Hamlet, e.g.

ACROSS

1. Clash
5. Asian nurse
9. Clickable image
13. Spoke (up)
15. Apple variety
16. Back of the neck
17. Make-up tool
19. Attracted
20. Transferred Kirk and Spock
21. Aims
22. Grasslands
23. Love's opposite
25. "___ give you the shirt off his back."
26. Swimming appendages
30. Ann ___, MI
33. Heavy hydrogen
34. *Fleabag* actress ___ Clifford
35. Antlered herbivore
36. Biblical wise men
37. Transferable
40. Like a fork
41. Nautical flags
42. Ballpoint ___
43. ___ bean
44. Card game
48. Bogus
50. Some theater workers, once
53. Basil or thyme
54. Versions
55. Ashtabula's lake
56. Achy
57. Balloon probe
58. Live wire, so to speak
59. ___ as nails
60. Home, informally

DOWN

1. Arguments
2. Lab tube (var.)
3. Big name in computers
4. Text necessity, often
5. Seaweed cultures
6. *The Bourne Identity* actor ___ Damon
7. ___ vera
8. Construction worker
9. Quality of being vague
10. Reddish-orange
11. Kind of column
12. Intelligence
14. Big or Little in the sky
18. Attended by both sexes
24. ___ of Enlightenment
26. Brings down
27. Gospel writer
28. Olympic sled
29. During
30. "By yesterday!"
31. Stir up the sediments
32. Akin to a double boiler (French)
33. Balance sheet item
38. American photographer ___ Goldin
39. Pain
40. Beliefs
42. Prefix with normal or medic
44. Waxed, old style
45. Backgammon piece
46. Inclines
47. Money in the bank, say
48. Abandon
49. Batman, for one
51. Ancient colonnade
52. Frau's partner

ACROSS

1. Aquatic plant
5. Deep sleeps
10. Formerly known as Christiania
14. Fail miserably
15. Legislate
16. Its quarter says "Birthplace of Aviation Pioneers"
17. Biblical birthright seller
18. Hindu queen (var.)
19. Speech problem
20. Work behind a bar
21. Gives an incorrect account
23. Field worker
25. Corn ___
26. Egghead
29. Expedia offerings
32. Military academy trainee
33. Bright red in the middle
35. Source of milk, lately
36. Shot putter title
40. "___ we having fun yet?"
41. Autumn tool
42. Attack
43. Element No. 39
46. Autumn blooms
47. "___ Lang Syne"
48. Again
49. Showing off
53. Smooth a shirt
57. Footnote shorthand
58. Bridge positions
59. Tipple served hot or cold
60. Zero, on a court
61. Found a new tenant
62. Grow weary
63. Bad look
64. Coasters
65. It may be grand

DOWN

1. Aid and ___
2. Ditch
3. FBI agent, slangily
4. Arabic for "Father of Gazelle"
5. Composite material
6. Broadcasting
7. Staffs
8. Maple genus
9. Like many Christmas card skylines
10. Tea type
11. Large working equine
12. Santa's aid
13. "My bad!"
22. Hawaiian dish
24. Aces
26. Aerosol
27. Argus-eyed
28. Kind of state
29. At liberty
30. Electric dart shooter
31. Proofreader's notations
33. Enlarge, as a hole
34. Genesis vessel
37. Those who plod along
38. Pinocchio's notable feature
39. Straightens
44. Nautical steering device
45. UN labor agency
46. Acute anxieties
48. Chipped in
49. Animated series *King of the* ___
50. Woodwind
51. Mexican actor ___ García Bernal
52. Place for a castaway
54. Commuter line
55. Gumbo vegetable
56. Margosa

ACROSS

1. Cut
5. Be theatrical
10. Kojak, e.g.
14. J. S. Bach wrote three concertos for it
15. Mooed
16. Assortment
17. Decorated
19. Stew
20. Sound system
21. Grabs
23. Sitcom ___ and a Half Men
25. Certain tribute
26. Business abbreviation
30. Correspond
34. Disgrace
36. Flax fabric
37. "My man!"
40. Uneasiness
43. Mandela's org.
44. Buckwheat cereal
45. Merry-go-round figure, to a child
46. Body of good conduct
47. African antelope
48. Big mess
52. Even if, briefly
55. Board game
59. Electric resistance
64. Units of work
65. Dismissed lightly
67. "Hogwash!"
68. Poisonous when unripe
69. Amount of work
70. "Fishy" story
71. Bank holds
72. Novice

DOWN

1. Tons
2. Help a criminal
3. Achy
4. Prince William, e.g.
5. Bend
6. Cow sound
7. Admits, with "up"
8. Nirvana's "Smells Like ___ Spirit"
9. Icelandic text
10. Fab
11. Gene Vincent's "Be-Bop-___"
12. Bar stock
13. Accomplish, as thou might
18. Poker move
22. Gallic
24. Wise
26. Conclusion
27. Father of Balder
28. Specialized computer: Abbr.
29. Boil stuff
31. Vedic poet
32. "Actually…"
33. Actress Leoni
35. Cosmetics
37. Ethiopian currency
38. Like Santa's cheeks
39. Black stone
41. Skin art, for short
42. Also
48. Refine, as metal
49. Bucket wheel
50. Ohtani, in his MLB debut
51. *Cabaret* (1972) director
53. Aspirations
54. "Look here!"
56. Iridescent gem
57. Centers of activity
58. Bind
60. Periodic shedding
61. Call to a mate
62. Car show *Top* ___
63. Taro root
66. One who lays

ACROSS

1. Fastener
6. Snowboarding trick
10. Celebrity
14. Inmate who's never getting out
15. Anger
16. Didn't pay enough
17. Single-member district
19. Word preceding "warrior" or "trip"
20. Michelle Obama's autobiography
21. Fourth letter in the Greek alphabet
22. "Fe" on the periodic table
23. Encourage
26. Ice over
29. Setting for pastoral poetry
33. PC linkup: Abbr.
34. Forever (archaic)
36. Catchall: Abbr.
37. Open
39. Squeezing (out)
40. Isaac's son
41. Earned
42. Bible giver
44. Gangster's gun, slangily
45. Football formation used for passing
47. Slander
49. The "Hot 100" in *Billboard*
51. Writer Murdoch
52. Very fast
55. Italian almond biscuits
59. Beasts of burden
60. British soap opera ___ *Street*
62. Arm bone
63. Captures
64. Inclines
65. Perfect scores
66. "Let it stand"
67. Cereal killer

DOWN

1. Association
2. Ancestry
3. Buff
4. Guadalajara guys
5. Advance
6. Beam
7. Cooktop
8. Mariana crow
9. *Fresh Prince of ___-Air*
10. Tom, Dick, or Harry
11. Missing from the Marines, say
12. Cold cuts, e.g.
13. *Ragnarok* setting
18. Fired at a funeral
21. *Back to the Future*'s ___ Brown
24. Bird that catches fish by plunge-diving
25. ___ calendar
26. Con artist doings
27. Indian chief
28. ___ duck (Chinese dish)
30. Revolting
31. Bartender Washington on TV's *Love Boat*
32. Sharp
35. Free from, with "of"
38. Greek wines
43. Recount
46. Pan, e.g.
48. Calorie counter
50. *Beetle Bailey* character
52. Beat badly
53. Bridge toll unit
54. Two-time Oscar-winning Sean
56. Lion's share
57. ___ list
58. The "I" in M.I.T.: Abbr.
60. *60 Minutes* network
61. Quaker grain

ACROSS

1. Congress coverer C-___
5. Basilica area
9. Bay of Naples isle
14. Ethereal
15. Intl. oil org.
16. Fits
17. One of the main iron ores
19. Kidney-related
20. Flower
21. Historical record
23. Mounted on
25. Netting
26. Go furtively
28. Emblem
31. Ventilation structures
35. "I ___ you one"
36. Corn holder
37. The ___ of the storm
38. ___ bit
39. ___ *Maria*
40. Fortresses
45. Arthur Golden's *Memoirs of a ___*
47. Animal in a roundup
48. *Wheel of Fortune* choice
49. Slanted typefaces
53. Crew of cons
57. Chart anew
58. Beginning of a conclusion
59. Tray feeder
61. Gastric woe
62. Jacob's twin
63. Nonexistent
64. Grace word
65. Kind of store, once
66. Close, as an envelope

DOWN

1. Brazilian dance
2. Rings
3. Lingo or slang
4. Norwegian language form
5. Fake user
6. Earthquake hot spot
7. "Amphetamine" lead-in
8. Maple genus
9. Belonging to actor Art of *The Honeymooners*
10. Certain discrimination
11. Festive centerpiece
12. *The ___ Ghostbusters* animated show
13. ___ of Man
18. Remy's older brother, in *Ratatouille*
22. Trans-Siberian Railroad city
24. Prefix for agree or respect
27. Lays out
29. Indebted to
30. Bottom of the barrel
31. Heroin (slang)
32. "Shake a leg!"
33. Bow or curtsy
34. Metric mass measure
40. Fight mementos
41. Bite
42. Secret agent parody ___ *Smart*
43. Coward's lack
44. City saved by Joan of Arc
46. Seasons
50. Permeate
51. Arum lily
52. Hex
53. Great Lakes fish
54. Hot spot
55. At rest
56. Legally pending
60. Owed

ACROSS

1. Apple TV's ___ *Lasso*
4. Fink
8. Bacterial source of some food poisoning
13. Brews
15. 60 minutes
16. Bicycle part
17. Instrument for "Lara's Theme"
19. Some sorority women
20. Imaginary creature
21. Merciful
23. Common request: Abbr.
24. Marathoner's need
25. 7 on a sundial
27. Dresden's river
29. Second word in *A Tale of Two Cities*
30. "Superfood" berry
32. Aden's land
34. Alpine transport
38. Beach, basically
39. A hand
40. Don Juan, e.g.
41. ___ bag
42. Actresses Faris and Kendrick
44. Time long past
45. Holiday drink
47. During
49. Good's opposite
50. Number one on a diamond
53. Conservative (UK)
55. Carnegie Hall offering
56. Prep for exercise
59. City in central New York
60. Collectibles
62. City in Lombardy
63. Coconut fiber
64. ___ lamp
65. Distinctive manner
66. Bills featuring Hamilton
67. When it's broken, that's good

DOWN

1. Forbidden: Var.
2. Brio
3. Belladonna, e.g.
4. Acutely
5. Mint
6. Arctic bird
7. Flower base
8. Dermatitis type
9. Science of matter
10. Like Cheerios
11. Tarzan's favorite means of transportation
12. R&D site
14. Bursae
18. Zero, on a court
22. Bowling green
24. Business workshop
25. Gigantic
26. United Nations flight agency
28. Pinto or Kidney
31. Indistinguishable
33. Wax-coated cheese
35. Pitfall
36. Halo
37. Velvet Underground artist Lou
42. Turkish leader (var.)
43. Child minders
46. Fuel rating number
48. Quad building
50. ___ four
51. How a *persona non grata* might be greeted
52. Bumper sticker word
54. Casting need
55. Jamaican exports
56. ___ splints
57. Champagne alternative
58. Try, as a case
61. Macabre author

ACROSS

1. Cleanse, quaintly
5. Beehive
9. Intensifies, with "up"
13. "Don't bet ___ ___," 2 wds.
14. Data
15. "Just ___ ___," 2 wds.
16. Rum cakes
18. Catches on
19. Copenhagen native
20. The cruelest month, per Eliot
21. Diffidence
23. Most authentic
25. Load of laundry
26. Spired
29. Aspersion
30. Popular mottled eyeglasses material
32. Attempt to hurl
33. Ethiopian emperor (1930-1974)
41. *Cogito ___ sum*
42. Parts of some car deals
43. ___ Smith apple
45. Disney's dwarfs and others
47. Legally requires
50. Surrounding glows
51. "___ we forget"
52. Chorus member in *The Producers*
53. Starbucks offering
54. At liberty
55. Cut made by a saw
56. Fastened a knot
57. Walk of Fame symbol
58. Bump off
59. Like Sunday morning, in a Commodores song

DOWN

1. Pneumonia type
2. Metrical foot
3. Singer's quavering
4. Internet store, once
5. Most comely
6. "Trick" joint
7. New newts
8. Postulate
9. Available for summing
10. Expressing sorrow
11. Ringlet
12. Brace
17. Icy rain
22. Rear
24. Fern-to-be
27. Banana oil, e.g.
28. Release
31. Color
33. President before Franklin
34. Asian lake that was once the world's fourth largest
35. Firestarter
36. Short's opposite
37. Calyx part
38. Place
39. Inactivity
40. Will subjects
43. Plays a round
44. Pulls at
46. Down at the heels
48. Old Chinese measure
49. *The Snowy Day* author ___ Jack Keats

ACROSS

1. Supernatural life forces
6. Bindle bearer
10. Chooses
14. Bond, for one
15. Face-to-face exam
16. ___ *Harry Met Sally…*
17. Recipe verb
18. Crossword component
19. Pianist and singer ___ Simone
20. Cakewalk
22. Beer quantity
24. Account
25. Double
27. Making a place more city-like
31. Affectedly creative
32. Old Chinese unit
33. Flamenco band ___ *Kings*
34. Force upon again
36. In's opposite
37. Navy junior rank: Abbr.
38. Streetwear brand
40. Diner order: Abbr.
43. Water-logged
44. Pauses in poetry
46. "Farewell, mon ami"
49. Calcium-rich soil
50. Anatomical nerve network
51. Mrs. Maisel's occupation
53. Any thing
54. Trophy
55. Cereal grain
56. Hyperbolic function
58. Amer. fliers
60. Calf-length skirt
63. Chocolate substitute
66. Unload, as stock
67. Coffee unit
68. Famous 1883 banquet held at Cincinnati's Highland House restaurant
69. Byzantine despot ___ de' Buondelmonti
70. Bothers
71. Electronic instrument, for short

DOWN

1. More, in Madrid
2. Classic kitchen range
3. Nerve inflammation
4. Opposite word
5. Check
6. Monopolize
7. NHL star Bobby ___
8. Siberian lake
9. Ancient
10. Possess
11. *Futurama* protagonist ___Fry
12. Mortise insertions
13. Knotty
21. Annoyed
23. Lively Baroque dances
25. Container weight
26. Small songbird
28. Coarse file
29. Tailgate recyclable
30. Clearasil target
35. Fake
36. Breakfast choice
39. Make, as money
40. Fellow members
41. Early's opposite
42. Abound
43. Tiny
45. ___ tract
46. Charge
47. Puts out
48. African antelope
49. Specialty
52. Poets' feet
57. *Hamlet* has five
59. H1N1, for one
61. NFL quarterback ___ Prescott
62. ___ and outs
64. Thomas Moore's "How ___ Has the Banshee Cried"
65. Word paired with "humbug"

ACROSS

1. Draconian
6. All excited
10. Spanish for "OK"
14. Boredom
15. Aspersion
16. Father of Balder
17. Muffler
18. Aggregates
20. Refused to go along
22. Priestly garb
25. Gets used (to)
26. Add sounds (to a video)
29. Furnace output
31. Bubkes
32. Comparison
34. Car
35. Fed. construction overseer
36. Comfortably warm
37. Aggravate
39. Accumulated mins.
41. Pen's point
42. Backbone of a mountain range
45. Pigeon sound
47. Their 1980s logo was known as "the worm"
50. Altogether
51. Calif. airport
52. Falling flakes
53. Alkaline liquid
54. Traveling performers
56. Grayish-brown
57. Benedictions
60. Keep apart
63. Poetry's metric lines
67. "La donna è mobile," e.g.
68. Hawaiian strings, for short
69. Kind of insurance
70. Like custard
71. Bakery buy
72. Beat

DOWN

1. ___ Just Not That Into You (2004 bestseller)
2. Mandela's org.
3. Vaccine component
4. Irrational number
5. Music maker, once
6. Flabbergast
7. Spherical collection of stars, 2 wds.
8. Exterior
9. Most bleak
10. Cancel
11. Cutting tool (var.)
12. Deception
13. Typesetting measures
19. Skin blemish
21. Be a rat
22. "I get it now!"
23. Romanian currency
24. CBS Late Show bandleader Jon
26. Break up
27. The max.
28. "Single Ladies" singer, to fans
30. Bit of statuary
33. Principal pipes
38. Touchy (UK)
40. Most sudsy
42. "Cool" amount
43. "___ calls?"
44. Part of an alimentary canal
46. Beast of burden
48. Former French coin
49. Barley bristle
55. World's Fair location of 1970
57. Farm call
58. Knack
59. Ad headline
60. RSVP aid
61. Fraction of a joule
62. Band booking
64. CBS sitcom starring Anna Faris
65. Excellent song, slangily
66. Altar vow

ACROSS

1. Prefix with surgery or transmitter
6. Neck accessory
11. "Father and Son" singer-songwriter ___ Stevens
14. Literally, "for this"
15. Bakery supply
16. Legendary Bruin
17. Italian wine
18. Like a dryer trap
19. Jane Smiley's 1995 novel
20. Acclimates again
22. Plant affliction
23. Automobile sticker fig.
25. "That's enough!" 2 wds.
26. Comic Daniel ___
27. Clearing the throat
29. Equip to new specs
30. Selena's 2002 greatest hits album
31. Financial loss symbol, 2 wds.
33. *The Simpsons*, e.g.
35. Ditch for runoff
36. Classic article?
37. Cast out
40. Counterparts of faunae
42. Compact
43. Call at first
45. Flower oil
47. Hogwash
48. Nitwit (UK)
49. Eyelid ailment
51. ___-dimensional
52. Perennial garden bloom
53. Metal worker
55. Science fiction publisher ___ Books
56. Mold and mildew, for two
57. Beamy
60. Potato feature
61. Fictional agency in the DC Comics universe
62. Clear, as a chalkboard
63. One less than tres
64. Assail
65. Nutritious beans

DOWN

1. Partners for Pa's
2. Altar avowal
3. Acting ambassador
4. Amble
5. Arctic or Atlantic, e.g.
6. Burning
7. Faux pas, of sorts
8. Devise
9. Beginnings
10. "Don't give up!"
11. The second Monday in March (UK)
12. Excite
13. Fidelities
21. Nerd
22. Iggy Pop's band
23. The red planet
24. Utterance expressing relief
28. Cereal grasses
32. *The Matrix* character
34. The "H" in HMS
36. Laces
38. House
39. "TEH," e.g.
41. Ecstasy
42. Barber's job
43. Acted maliciously
44. Arid region's watercourse
46. Back up
50. Begets
54. Novice (UK)
56. Marvelous, in slang
58. Fed. property overseer
59. "Absolutely!"

ACROSS

1. Snoozes
5. Prefix with China or Pacific
9. "___ in the balance"
14. City on the Yamuna River
15. Type of tide
16. Anticipate
17. Times to be judged
19. Football play
20. Outs opposite
21. Do some knitting
22. Gang
23. Assigned to a different category
26. *Doctor Who* villain, with "the"
27. Sweet cherry
28. High degree
31. Expectoration
33. Festival held in Ancient Greece in honor of the goddess of love and beauty
36. Actionable words
38. Store convenience, for short
39. Concerning
40. City in Egypt
43. "Bro"
44. Jon Anderson, Chris Squire, Peter Banks, Tony Kaye, and Bill Bruford, collectively
45. Spanish painter Joan ___
46. Shuttlecock
48. Joyous diversions
52. Kind of kick
55. Digestion aid
56. Bluecoat
57. WWI French soldier
58. Arrange differently
60. Bartender's supply
61. American sportscaster ___ Andrews
62. Gulf off the coast of Yemen
63. ___ preview
64. Fraction of a newton
65. "I must lose myself in action, ___ I wither in despair" (Tennyson)

DOWN

1. Low point
2. Past, to past poets
3. Forbids
4. *Three Billboards Outside Ebbing, Missouri* actor ___ Rockwell
5. Thin, membranous coverings (Latin)
6. Approaches
7. Brazen crime
8. Missions, for short
9. Ecuadoran estate
10. Cy Young, e.g.
11. Bust maker
12. Demoiselle
13. Eye affliction
18. Bridge measure
22. Italian for "hello"
24. Glove material
25. 1938 Physics Nobelist
28. Plain language description of an algorithm
29. Back
30. Anniversary, e.g.
31. Cut down
32. Bundle
34. Man with a mission
35. Large lemur
37. Politician with limited power, 2 wds.
41. "Blue" or "White" river
42. Marine rock-clinger
47. Any thing
48. Eyelashes
49. Castor bean poison
50. Honkers
51. All in
52. ___ out
53. Midday
54. Trig function
58. Cabernet, e.g.
59. Buddy

ACROSS

1. Bread rolls
5. Gut areas
9. To the rear
14. *Salome* solo
15. ___ and terminer
16. Striped mammal
17. Connect
18. Rex Stout's detective ___ Wolfe
19. Ruler (var.)
20. Crackpot
22. Copies
24. Bashful
25. Email
27. Drag
28. Annoyance
33. Equips (var.)
38. Call to a mate
39. Charlemagne's domain
42. Carbon compound
43. Pencil pusher
44. Falling star
47. Back
48. Arctic
51. Boil stuff
54. Country bordered by Panama
58. Pursuit in which nothing is going on
60. Kind of group, in chemistry
61. Conical dwelling
63. Animated show ___ *Teen Hunger Force*
64. Big trucks
65. Bring (out)
66. Vice president under Jefferson
67. Related maternally
68. Alluring
69. Aug. follower

DOWN

1. Healing ointments
2. Dickens's Heep
3. Fool
4. Hector Hugh Munro's pen name
5. Musical work
6. ___ of Horus
7. Daughter of Saturn
8. Bouquet
9. Flowering shrub
10. Altar
11. Aid a criminal
12. At liberty
13. Blackens
21. French romance
23. "Blech!"
26. Appears
27. Chemist with a gas law
29. Flavor
30. Leg part
31. Folk stories
32. Looker
33. (Clears throat)
34. Ice cream vessel
35. Coagulate
36. Back stabber
37. Animal catcher
40. Calvin Klein fragrance
41. Abyssinian outcry
45. Be absorbed gradually
46. Spice mix for ribs
49. Deck posts
50. Former Congo
51. Arouse
52. Appropriate
53. Brainy
54. Beer buy
55. Sign
56. Andes capital
57. "Will do!"
59. Small amounts, as of cream
62. Caused by *Variola* viruses

ACROSS

1. Boardroom illustration
6. Messy dresser
10. Digestion aid
14. Isuzu model
15. Ames's state
16. "Comme ci, comme ça"
17. Deflect
18. Card game, 2 wds.
20. Knee cartilage
22. Copenhagen coins
23. Boutique
24. Shift, e.g.
25. Interpret wrongly
29. Dostoevsky novel *The ___*
30. Cool
31. During
35. High-five, e.g.
36. Blow
38. Bananas
39. An inflorescence
40. Certain digital watch face, for short
41. Argentina capital Buenos ___
42. Scraps
45. Adele and Cher, e.g.
47. Flatbread served with dal
48. Early computer
50. Inflexible
54. Lamb's lettuce, 2 wds.
56. Lack of muscle firmness
57. Oklahoma city
58. Lady of Lisbon
59. Taboos
60. Gym sets
61. Iridescent gem
62. Composer and musician Reznor

DOWN

1. Fat unit
2. Amble
3. Yemen port
4. Sub apparatus
5. Ace
6. Ab strengtheners
7. Estimates on weather forecasts
8. Middle of IOU
9. Broke
10. Irish lads
11. Religious images (var.)
12. Channel
13. Appraiser
19. Joshua ___
21. Pro's opposite
24. Big bore
25. Assorted, in brief
26. One way to stand by
27. *The King and I* setting
28. Heavy footsteps
31. One causing estrangement
32. Neil Diamond's "September ___"
33. Style for coffee or tea
34. Bed down (UK)
36. City of fabled riches
37. 1990 World Series champs
41. Inflexible
42. Singer Redding
43. Like one battery terminal
44. Bother
45. Hoisted, nautically
46. Domain
48. Maple genus
49. *The ___ Ranger*
50. SNL alum Carvey
51. Sound
52. Knowing, as a secret
53. Dermatologist's concern
55. Chop (off)

ACROSS

1. Cats, dogs, fish, and birds
5. Fountain locale
10. "___ ___ no good," 2 wds.
14. Indian nanny or maid
15. More abundant
16. Surplus fiber
17. Archaic name for a giraffe
19. Peel
20. Lively intelligence
21. Housetop materials
23. Alliance
25. Performs, as Jay Z
26. Fuddy-duddy
29. Battering device
32. Bloodsucker
35. Not much
36. Assembly rules
38. "___ close for comfort"
39. Confederate soldier, for short
40. Well-groomed (var.)
41. Blouse, e.g.
42. More, en España
43. Set aflame
44. "OK"
45. Demonstrated
47. African antelope
48. Category
49. Approaching
51. Hurting
53. Woody
57. Ballgame ration
61. "Will do!" 2 wds.
62. NASA explorer, 2 wds.
64. Unit of pressure
65. *Animal House* wardrobe
66. Once more, to Twain
67. Deeply
68. Hoodwinks
69. Fly, e.g.

DOWN

1. Clip
2. Fledgling bird
3. Pack (down)
4. Cold dessert
5. First: Prefix
6. Back talk
7. Way, way off
8. Abysmal test score
9. Eagerness
10. Green
11. Flower displayed at Christmas
12. Bell sound
13. Former G.M. make
18. Flower displayed at Easter
22. Bogus
24. 1961 Roy Orbison song
26. Cultivates
27. Form of West Indian spiritual practice
28. Gay Nineties ideal
30. Emulsifying agent
31. *Rigoletto* locale
33. Delaware senator Chris
34. Aspirations
36. Swamp
37. ___ bit
40. Burn
44. Carnivorous plant
46. ___ mix (weather forecast)
48. Hack
50. Legions
52. Kind of board
53. French novelist Pierre
54. Knowing, as a secret, 2 wds.
55. Quentin Tarantino's *Once ___ a Time in Hollywood*
56. Kind of palm
58. Chief official of Venice or Genoa
59. Kimono sashes
60. Chap
63. Avian cry

ACROSS

1. Burglar's accessory
8. Singing
14. Monster-like
16. Deprived of oxygen
17. Hugeness
18. Spit
19. Brother
20. Bad look
22. Do-nothing
23. Allocate, with "out"
25. More than just talkers?
27. Having wings
29. "___ be my pleasure"
30. Snake's sound
34. Condescend
35. Catch
36. Portent
37. Arp's art
38. Cheerful little earful
39. "___ ___ snuff," 2 wds.
40. Daughter of Robert Carradine
41. Advil target
42. Fold
43. Cleave
44. Strummed inst.
45. Core groups
46. Funny bone
48. Cancels
49. Express
52. Tyler Durden manufactured and sold it
54. Civil rights icon Parks
57. Bridge answers
59. One of a kind
61. Periphery
62. Like traditional Catholic mass
63. ___ spinner
64. Bracelets

DOWN

1. Check
2. Atlantic City attraction
3. British heavy metal band
4. Small-scale farming
5. Cash dispenser: Abbr.
6. Dirty
7. "High as a ___"
8. Duct, to your doctor
9. Broadcasting, 2 wds.
10. Ignoring, 2 wds.
11. Angle between leaf and branch
12. In person
13. *The Lion King* villain
15. Inveterate, 4 wds.
21. Spin
24. X number
26. Irascible
27. Calculator, at times
28. Bequeath
31. Cold
32. Bristles
33. Snobs
35. Perverse people
38. Slap on
42. Opposite of bellum
45. Per ___
47. Pigeon's perch
49. Composer Carl
50. Prefix with -scope or -helion
51. Footnote note
53. Kuwaiti, e.g.
55. Fill
56. Brews
58. Undertake, with "out"
60. Beefeater, e.g.

ACROSS

1. Ices
5. Atlantic cod relatives
10. Curtain call actions
14. Hold up
15. Caribbean spiritualism
16. Layperson
17. Container weight
18. Old Toyota
19. Gumbo ingredient
20. Copyreading (UK)
22. Deed hearing
23. Directly
24. Passe slang for "cheat"
26. Manage
30. TV meteorologist Ginger ___
31. Wildebeest
34. *Mensa et thoro*, 2 wds.
37. Bacchanal
38. It's a wrap
39. Royal flush, e.g.
40. Place for an announcement
45. Blue
46. Embrace
47. Bull, at times
48. English for "adios"
49. Cap with a kilt
50. Expression used to drive animals away
53. Powerful stellar explosions
60. *The Bridges of Madison County* setting
61. Crossbeam
62. Pie perch
63. Swear
64. Acquiesce
65. *The Wiz*'s "___ on Down the Road"
66. Advance
67. Clairvoyants
68. Lento

DOWN

1. Chooses
2. "Mrs." in Berlin
3. Sunflower, e.g.
4. Racetracks
5. Stocking stockers
6. Adjoin
7. Visored cap
8. Make, as money
9. One who caught 10-down, once
10. Ball hit just over the infield
11. Like certain whites
12. Electronic transfer service
13. Lasting mark
21. Two-in-one
25. Assenting vote
26. Spills
27. ___ firma
28. Urged on
29. Clear from mist
30. Ornamental holders for hot drinks
31. Colossal
32. Present
33. Over opposite
35. Humorous wordplay
36. Functional holders for hot drinks
41. Introverted
42. Spanish for "slopes"
43. Menu section
44. Horse with a flecked coat
48. Get on
50. Igneous rock
51. Hoisted aboard
52. *The Virginian* author ___ Wister
54. Advocate
55. Reduce, as expenses
56. 2021 stuck ship ___ *Given*
57. Small container
58. Likewise
59. Batch

ACROSS

1. Intoxicating Pacific island beverage
5. Circuit
10. *Spider-Man: No Way* ___
14. *Marley & Me* star ___ Wilson
15. Seabird fertilizer
16. "Fine"
17. Mouth part, 2 wds.
19. Advocate
20. Top
21. Out of bed
22. Aforementioned
23. Euphrates' counterpart
25. "At any ___…"
27. Polish president ___ Walesa
28. Western New York county
32. Movie beverage
35. Translucent
36. It glows in the dark?
40. Fuel source, 2 wds.
41. Caught in the act
42. Climber's need
43. Dump
46. Bits of binary code
47. World heritage site designator: Abbr.
50. "In ___ of…"
53. Richard Wright's ___ *Son*
55. Persian, e.g.
57. "Neither snow nor rain nor heat nor gloom of night…" org.
58. Make worse
60. Arctic sight
61. Tender spots
62. Hot box
63. Come clean, with "up"
64. Belt
65. Sandra Bullock film *While You ___ Sleeping*

DOWN

1. Eye liner
2. Anticipate
3. "The Four Seasons" composer
4. Plus
5. Common mushroom
6. Stubborn
7. Bleats
8. Rescued by Rambo
9. Pedicure target
10. Like fish, they stink after three days?
11. Vegetable served in stews or fried
12. Wise men
13. Checked out
18. Reduce, as expenses
24. British greenhouses
26. After-bath powder
29. Bad marks
30. Houston university
31. Crater near Las Cruces, New Mexico
32. Advertisement
33. Youngstown state
34. Pineapple purveyor
35. Prefix for teen or med
37. Loudness measure
38. Vigor
39. Earliest recorded form of Low German, 2 wds.
43. Infomercial device
44. Be bullish
45. Bad look
48. Desire
49. Exterior
50. Sail into the wind
51. ___ of Wight
52. Body of verse
54. Purple tuber
56. Kelly who sang in the rain?
59. Arrow pairing

ACROSS

1. Use an ax
5. Cicatrix
9. Puts a stop to
14. ___ hoop
15. Leafy green
16. "Famous potatoes" state
17. Not "fer"
18. Not made more desirable
20. State southwest of 16-across
22. Farm machine
23. Nickname of painter Domenikos Theotokópoulos: El ___
24. Asian palm tree
25. Units of work
29. Garden need
31. Invitation notation
33. They linger
38. Pass during the NFL playoffs
39. Scrooge's interjection
40. Funky-smelling fruits
41. "Stairway…" band ___ Zeppelin
42. Sticker
43. People who establish
45. Long-legged bird
47. Classic game show ___ *That Tune*
48. Psychic
49. In perfect condition
52. Clear
56. File
58. Online newsgroup system
59. Wladimir Klitschko and Volodymyr Zelenskyy, e.g.
63. Approaching
64. Athletic events
65. Pivot
66. Rabbit fur
67. Eucharist containers
68. Bowlers
69. Carbon compound

DOWN

1. Twin brother of Eng Bunker
2. Even more vast
3. Antipasto morsel
4. Verve
5. Gull-like bird
6. Beverage holder
7. Accused's need
8. Chart anew
9. Bring on
10. Loves
11. Head, for short
12. Genuine article
13. Ground cover
19. Fetal sac
21. All-out
24. Approaches
26. One hundred kopecks
27. More cheerful
28. Coasters
30. Certain doubles
32. Surmises
33. Middle East political figure
34. Early 20th-century French painter
35. Pang
36. Be in session
37. Corrupt
44. Singer ___ Trent D'Arby
46. Come up with
50. Like Liam Neeson or Saoirse Ronan
51. African antelope
53. Electrolysis particle
54. Music notation
55. ___ alcohol
57. Fail to see
58. Manipulations
59. Person in a mask
60. E or G, e.g.
61. Oedipus ___
62. Cashew, e.g.

ACROSS

1. "All for one and one for all," e.g.
6. Archaic word for "count"
11. Characterized by the absence of life
14. Nonsensical singing syllables
16. Spanish for "cent"
17. Unkempt
18. Biblical herbs
19. Low-iron conditions
20. Bottom line
21. Supreme Court commentator Totenberg
22. Quadruped set
26. Inebriated
30. A share
31. Flat
33. *Matilda* author Roald ___
34. Applaud
35. Dye
36. Lake's landmass
37. Indigenous language of the Japanese archipelago
38. Vulgar expression for wanton women
39. Appear
40. Wavelike design
42. Nonunion workplace
44. Blockage
46. Backstabber
47. Kabul currency
50. Awakening
55. Fashions
56. Series of related rock formations
57. Stretched to the limit
58. Indigenous arctic peoples, once
59. Charger
60. Lilac, e.g.

DOWN

1. Airspeed ratio
2. Follow orders
3. Anchovy containers
4. Little ones
5. Good-for-nothing
6. Having a rhythmic beat
7. Primly fastidious, once
8. French Sudan, today
9. "Guilty," e.g.
10. Wee amounts
12. Urges
13. Beauty expert
14. Go from Russian to English, say
15. Indian royal
22. Big sheet
23. Muscat native
24. Acquire again
25. Fill the tank
27. Leisurely walk
28. Lug
29. Primordial matter
30. Ponzi scheme, e.g.
32. Catches
41. Flying high
43. Baby announcement birds
45. Eleven, basically
47. *Hamlet* has five
48. Fingerboard ridge
49. Characteristic carrier
51. Acid that causes gout
52. "___ here"
53. Unknown author: Abbr.
54. "___ we forget…"

ACROSS

1. Messy dresser
5. Buddhist who has attained enlightenment
10. Big fishhook
14. Money in Dhaka
15. Money in Lagos
16. Be a monarch
17. Offbeat
19. Impulse transmitter
20. Less of a mess
21. Asset for an actor
23. Hose site
26. Chic, for today
27. Numero uno
31. Worn by "King-Size Homer" in *The Simpsons*
33. Finger ____ (NY region)
35. Eclipse, for one
40. Eye doctor
42. Consist of
43. Call into question
45. Addiction
46. Heir's concern
48. Allocate, with "out"
49. Off the mark
53. Admiral who explored the Antarctic
55. Wet
57. Places to sleep
62. Vexes
63. Deflection
66. Chill
67. Dalmatian, e.g.
68. Data
69. Gym set
70. Swelling
71. Great Lakes fish

DOWN

1. Bowl over
2. Channel
3. Luffa
4. Thai currency
5. Anatomical cavity
6. "Go team!"
7. That guy
8. Bone-dry
9. Reserved
10. Annoy
11. Plant hormone
12. Genesis narrative
13. Boggy
18. "Sure"
22. Frequent cast auxiliary
24. Ought not
25. Nipper
27. Alliance
28. A head
29. Gull-like bird
30. Snitch
32. A half
34. Mum
36. Brickbat
37. Rapper/actor Ice ____
38. Mine entrance
39. Anatomical nerve network
41. Old Roman coin
44. Blah-blah-blah
47. Slips
49. Hinder
50. Blush
51. Assemble hastily
52. Pack animals
54. Nickname for an MD
56. Doofus
58. Auditory suffix
59. Hyperbolic function
60. Bean curd
61. High-hatter
64. Enemy
65. Aries astrological sign

ACROSS

1. Oil amt.
5. Assumption for the sake of argument
10. Bite off, with "at"
14. Command to a dog
15. Like some walls
16. Hot spot
17. The Platters' "___ You (And You Alone)"
18. Sheer fabric
19. Christmas season
20. Whistle blower
21. It began after 1945
23. Scandinavian rug
24. Brook
26. Tuesday food, maybe
28. Most glistening
32. Go by, as time
35. French bean stew
37. English county
38. Dealing with
39. Aphorism
41. Ballyhoo
42. Mixer with quinine
44. Slide subjects
46. Feline hybrid
48. A bit
49. Arctic sight
50. And plus
51. "For Me and My ___"
53. Budget
57. WC
60. Impulse transmitter
62. West Indies native
63. Hawk's opposite
64. Pivot
65. Convex molding
66. Ancient
67. Basil, e.g.
68. Describing some letters
69. Vega's constellation

DOWN

1. God with a hammer
2. Italian for "OK"
3. Baker's shortcut
4. Carry on
5. Tile alternative
6. *Austin Powers* villain Dr. ___
7. Attention
8. Cat call
9. Biologically attached
10. Camera ___
11. Study of the brain and behaviors
12. Comrade in arms
13. "Not guilty," e.g.
21. Muse of history
22. Breathing noise
25. Firmly establish, as values
27. They're nuts
28. "Great ___!"
29. Asian capital
30. High-five, e.g.
31. Bush country
33. Brown shade
34. Latin for "he/she may leave"
36. Novice
40. Devoted son
43. "Neato!"
45. Diner order, with "patty" or "tuna"
47. Converted liberal, maybe
51. Cut
52. Shaft
54. Surfing need
55. Boast
56. Alternative to acrylics
58. Assert
59. Sacred Hindu writings
61. Colo. neighbor
63. Legume dish

ACROSS

1. High-quality sound: Abbr.
5. Trick-taking card game Oh ___
10. Booty
14. Knowing a secret, 2 wds.
15. Bring up
16. By way of, briefly
17. Vitreous quality
19. Holds up
20. Membranes
21. *Show Boat* classic "Can't Help Lovin' ___ Man"
22. "Thanks ___!"
23. Urban area
25. Occupations
27. Wiry-coated terriers
31. Dead-end jobs
32. Mister, in Dortmund
33. Artless one
35. Simmer in liquid
38. Advocate
39. "Super Six" automaker
41. Polar perch
42. Bounded
44. Container weight
45. Kitty's call
46. Tide type
48. Lamps of old
50. Blast furnace
53. Forecast extremes
54. Cost to cross
55. Butter holder
57. Sweethearts
61. Central shaft
62. Nonpartisan
64. Appearance
65. Found a new tenant
66. Barely beat, with "out"
67. Fly, e.g.
68. End
69. Blown away

DOWN

1. Elevated
2. Deeply
3. Froth
4. Camper's need, 2 wds.
5. Untouched
6. Spanish for "saint"
7. Hightailed it
8. ___ tea
9. Veer toward the sunset
10. Between Sicily and Calabria, 3 wds.
11. Warehouse owner
12. Day to celebrate trees
13. Blows
18. Agitated state
24. Bakery supply
26. Pendulum weight
27. Jewish house of prayer
28. A river in southwestern France
29. Cell bodies
30. Kind of rug
34. Not domesticated
36. Masked critter
37. Chops
40. Rock within a rock
43. Ink: Abbr.
47. Early explosive device
49. UK slang for an annoying person
50. Express displeasure
51. Daring
52. Indian coin
56. Gaucho's weapon
58. Boat with an open hold
59. "At ___, soldier"
60. Coaster
63. Affranchise

ACROSS

1. Avoid
5. With a bow
9. Judo exercises
13. Privilege
15. Dog-eared
16. Final, e.g.
17. Dior creation
18. Brightly colored fish
19. Abounding in certain trees
20. High-fives
21. Cocktail twist
23. Foursome
25. Theater offering
26. Ringed, anatomically
29. Edema
33. Cow or sow
35. Papal court
36. Wise men
39. Cancels
41. Closed fist, in a game
42. Wrecks
44. Leg bones
46. Asexual
48. Individuality
52. Yemen port
54. Big hit
55. Similitude
60. Chip away at
61. Centers of activity
62. Libyan football club Al-___ S.C.
63. Bacon unit
64. "Oh, my aching head!," e.g.
65. Advocate
66. Monopoly purchase
67. EPA concern
68. Cooking fat
69. Like a busybody

DOWN

1. Cascades peak
2. Cry out loud
3. Eastern Catholic
4. Like a charity, 3 wds.
5. Truant, as a G.I.
6. ___-a-dope
7. Constrain
8. Postponed, 2 wds.
9. Stay calm, 4 wds.
10. Bridge toll unit
11. Dull
12. ___ nitrate
14. Flea market deal
22. Bust maker
24. Angry outburst
27. Drawn tight
28. ___ Island (New York landmark)
30. Ace
31. Latin for "thus"
32. Talk, talk, talk
34. Dresden's river
36. American cartoonist Scott Adams has one: Abbr.
37. Month before Sept.
38. Fed. procurement agency
40. Bank deposit
43. "Which ___ are you on?"
45. All over again
47. Big count
49. City north of Lisbon
50. Golden ___
51. Extremely
53. ___-Gandhi political dynasty
55. "___ for the poor"
56. Come into view
57. UN flight agency
58. Stuffing ingredient
59. Invalidate

ACROSS

1. Gets hard, as bread
7. Final: Abbr.
10. Eastern music
14. Flight
15. Donation request encl.
16. Test
17. Bewitch
18. Myanmar monetary unit
19. Add-on
20. Espresso vessels
22. Ending with bi- or tri-
23. Believer in a strong centralized government
24. Medical advice, often
26. *The Last of the Mohicans* character ___ Munro
28. Join forces (with)
32. Kind of dealer
36. After-bath powder
38. American lizard
39. Building block, 2 wds.
42. Essential flower oil perfume
43. Fit
44. Start of a play in football
45. Walked over again
47. Concrete section
49. Grandiose verse
51. Tapestries
56. Madam
59. Climate controller
61. Maple genus
62. Bit
63. Carve
64. By way of, briefly
65. Work unit
66. Cherry-pitting device
67. Appear
68. Budget letters for a homeowner
69. Agree out of court

DOWN

1. Outbuildings
2. Article of faith
3. Blue-headed lizard
4. Calculus calculation
5. Arousing
6. Circus Hall of Fame site
7. Mailing letters
8. Cake part
9. Afternoon service
10. Chemicals
11. Bridge toll unit
12. Show shock
13. Andy's radio partner
21. Large valley
25. Caribbean and others
27. Assumed name
29. Phobos, to Mars
30. Arm bone
31. Chick's sound
32. Way, way off
33. Automatic
34. "Heinz 57" dog
35. Paradiddle producer, 2 wds.
37. Apprehend
40. Discontinue
41. Aviation safety statistic
46. Like some lines
48. *Jane Eyre* author
50. Lamb Chop's pal ___ Lewis
52. Scarf
53. Restrict
54. Artist's stand
55. Timber measure
56. Belfry residents?
57. Advil target
58. Lead-in to wolf
60. Irascible

ACROSS

1. Departed
5. ___ shooting
10. Argued
14. All fired up
15. Dissect
16. Back
17. Turned right
18. Decrease
19. "At ___, soldier."
20. Particle predicted in 1933
22. Deuce topper
23. Tappan ___ Bridge
24. Pop hit
25. Wards (off)
26. Flipper
29. Census datum
30. Mandela org.
31. Variant
38. Fed. med. research agency
39. Reeler
40. Scandinavian rug
41. Madagascar jasmine
43. Gun, as an engine
44. Tofu source
45. ___ public
47. Acquired relative
50. Ground cover
53. Satirical magazine founded in 1952
54. Advent air
55. Make poor
59. Ganges step
60. Dolphins' town
61. Perry Como's "___ Loves Mambo"
62. Zero, on a court
63. ___ wrench
64. Auditory
65. Pitcher
66. Chaotic
67. Adam's apple spot

DOWN

1. Around the bend
2. Kitchen need
3. Philosopher who originated the *Übermensch*
4. Whirlpools
5. Fighting word
6. Shish ___
7. A muse
8. Bar
9. Young'un
10. Excuse
11. Discover
12. Alleviated
13. Squirrels' nests
21. Carnival feature
25. Chilling
26. Beach shades
27. "Will do!"
28. Compensate
29. Draft holder
32. Florida politician ___ DeSantis
33. Cow call
34. Final, in brief
35. Expose to rays
36. Court type
37. Blue shade
42. Prayer book
46. Atlantic game fish
47. Fireplace
48. At all, slangily
49. Bequeath
50. Photographer's request
51. Milky gems
52. Some stadium features
55. Leads prayers in a mosque
56. Covered with ivy
57. ___ & Span
58. Commit a computer crime

ACROSS

1. "Pipe down!"
6. Jerks
12. Actor Nicolas Cage's real last name
15. Braided bread
16. Egg part
17. Pasture
18. Exulted
19. Aluminum discoverer Hans Christian ___
20. Possession
22. Female rower
28. Big Mama Thornton hit in 1952, 2 wds.
34. Jewish mysticism
35. Forget
36. Tech's valley
37. Consisting of two
38. Also called thoroughworts
39. More majestic
41. Entrances
47. Endurance
52. Museum show
54. Scammed
55. Exalt
56. Inferior imitator
57. Piled
58. Northwest Malaysian state
59. Largest city in West Yorkshire, England

DOWN

1. Slang for "heroin"
2. Finnish poet and translator Anselm ___
3. Cellist's stroke
4. Brush off
5. Mr. Simpson, to Marge
6. Diploma
7. Henry VIII's last wife Catherine ___
8. Priestly garb
9. Bed board
10. Ancient sorcerer
11. Abandon
13. Bad look
14. Etcetera
15. Cathedral section
21. Beldam
23. Corduroy feature
24. Eastern ties
25. Defensive spray
26. "Thanks ___!," 2 wds.
27. Bobbsey sister and photographer Goldin, et al.
28. Activity centers
29. Kool & the Gang's "Get Down ___ ___"
30. Arm bone
31. Drink order
32. Defy
33. Construction process, 2 wds.
36. Certain horses
38. Beseech
40. Absurd
42. Departure
43. Bar
44. Because
45. Scooter alternative
46. Evaluated, with "up"
47. Increase, with "up"
48. Bind
49. Like, with "to"
50. Prefix with phone
51. Knowing, as a secret
53. 1991 sequel *Bill & ___ Bogus Journey*

ACROSS

1. Intensifies, with "up"
5. Attention ___
9. Bucks
14. Get-out-of-jail money
15. Justice Black
16. AM/FM device
17. Hatches
19. Coldly
20. Four-legged animal
21. Allots, with "out"
22. Call, as a game
23. Avow
25. Grab bag: Abbr.
29. Blocks
34. Literally, "for this"
36. Expansion
37. Italian Renaissance polymath, 3 wds.
40. Corncrake, 2 wds.
41. Eventually become
42. Most soporific
44. Exercise establishments
45. Staffs
46. Battering device
49. White, in Marseilles
52. Age of dinosaurs
57. Reason
58. Indecisiveness
59. Blackberry drupelets
60. Song and dance, e.g.
61. Indian bread
62. "That's it!"
63. Terrier type
64. Advance, slangily

DOWN

1. Not much
2. Challenge for a barber
3. Ancient Scot
4. Aspersion
5. Contour
6. Delay
7. Ancient
8. Discouraging words
9. Upsurge in lawlessness, 2 wds.
10. Injuring
11. Passageway
12. Stephen King's *The Green* ___
13. Some beans
18. Keep out
23. Dry
24. Sail constellation
25. Shopaholics' destinations
26. Archetype
27. Excelled
28. Excoriating
30. Adulated ones
31. Famous aviator "Lucky ___"
32. ___ *tenens* (Latin for "place holder")
33. Hand shears
35. Raw meat dish
38. Drops from the sky
39. Fizzles out
43. Reliable
47. Come to mind
48. "Welcome" sign we step on
49. Give away
50. Centers of activity
51. Slang for "against"
52. *The* ___ (1979 film starring Steve Martin)
53. ___-culottes, radical French revolutionaries
54. Break
55. Formed in 1947 under the auspices of the UN
56. Copper
58. Possesses

ACROSS

1. Astrophysicist and author ___ Sagan
5. "I want it!"
10. Feed bag contents
14. Chill
15. Suffix with sect
16. Flutter
17. Bluster
18. Balloon probe
19. It's ___ ___ good cause
20. Coronavirus variant
22. Fellow
24. Single guy's home, 2 wds.
27. Bird that builds a hanging nest
28. Kind of cycle
33. Cat's scratcher
37. Annoying
39. Caring
41. Products of glaciation
42. Turnpike
46. Fourth of the canonical hours
47. Heraldic band
48. Hirsute
50. Fantasizing
56. Digit
60. Shrub of the barberry family
61. Greasy
62. Greenfly, e.g.
65. Furrows
66. Excursion
67. Linen fabric
68. Get ready
69. Ballyhoo
70. Senior
71. Half a matched set

DOWN

1. Chocolate substitute
2. Collection of early Buddhist texts
3. Having secret meaning
4. Creep's craving
5. Fuels
6. Magnetite, e.g.
7. Time div.
8. ___ cow disease
9. Formerly known as "clyster"
10. Ices
11. Very much, 2 wds.
12. Container weight
13. Bandy words
21. Gun, as an engine
23. Do-nothing
25. Done working: Abbr.
26. Soup holder
29. A Swiss army knife has lots of them
30. Mi, for example
31. Visa alt.
32. Medical advice, often
33. One who makes orders
34. Sumptuous
35. Band's rigs
36. Word in title after *Star* or *Storage*
38. Non-minister who conducts some services
40. Destitute
43. Quiet
44. Large amount of money
45. Unit for a frequent flier
49. Yes, in Fargo
51. Winged
52. Change shape
53. Accustom
54. Fertilizer ingredient
55. Short pants
56. Does, the old way
57. Breezy
58. Cut short
59. Sort
63. Cambodian dictator ___ Pot
64. Holed up

ACROSS

1. Super garb
5. Remove, as a hat
9. Cons' opposites
13. Way, way off
14. Semirural settlement
16. Goddess of youth
17. Catch, in a way
18. Andrea Bocelli, e.g.
19. Not much
20. Iffy, 3 wds.
22. A deadly sin
23. Interference
24. Blacken
26. Ganges step
29. Charioteer constellation
32. Docking spot
36. Bed head
38. Nurse
39. Magical wish granter
40. Slog
41. Bandwagon joiner
43. Like a gnat
44. Heat
45. Sort
47. Arctic native
48. Stellar
53. FedEx, say
55. Writing desk
59. Peewee
60. Actress Sophia ___
61. Bolted
62. Units of work
63. Bluish gray
64. Open a crack
65. Batman Adam
66. Kind of page
67. Big name in chips

DOWN

1. Supermarket vehicles
2. Happening
3. ___ New Guinea
4. At attention
5. Rip off
6. "Oregon Trail" purchases
7. Back financially
8. Jumper
9. Shorebird
10. New entombments
11. Eastern ties
12. Paving block
15. Heavy fabric with a woven design
21. Low's opposite
25. Airline's home base
27. Intended to fill a pause
28. 2020 Christopher Nolan film
30. Understand
31. American Girl doll ___ Walker
32. Hay unit
33. Fledgling bird
34. Alerts
35. Psychoanalyst
37. Breezy
39. John and others
42. Trophy
43. ___ control
46. Hurt
49. Add up
50. Red wine of Spain
51. Variety
52. Bad looks
53. Old World duck
54. Bring on
56. Role played by Ford and Ehrenreich
57. ___-shoot
58. Anatomical nerve network

ACROSS

1. Bite
5. "That's a ___!"
9. Practice boxing
13. Under's opposite
14. Serf
16. Bat's home
17. Index digit
19. Like a desert
20. Represent with restraint
21. Stationer's stock
22. ___ *Chef* reality competition series
23. "Not only that…"
25. Sask. neighbor
28. One who commemorates
34. It may be revolutionary or civil
35. Renouncer
36. Burned
39. Free from, with "of"
40. Exalt
41. Checked
44. "___ boom bah!"
45. Came across
47. Word with "bath" or "welcome"
48. Goes quickly
49. *Book of Mormon* actor Josh ___
51. Tech. detail
53. City in New South Wales, 2 wds.
60. French novelist Pierre ___
61. Weakening
62. Song and sculpture, e.g.
63. Film units
64. Language spoken chiefly in South Asia
65. Nets or Mets
66. Bottom of the barrel
67. Forest growth

DOWN

1. Good source of protein
2. Shakespeare's river
3. Sheldon Cooper, e.g.
4. Receive
5. Speak quietly
6. ___-a-car
7. Water plant
8. Pablo Neruda, e.g.
9. Shoulder blades
10. Mutuality
11. All fired up
12. Warren Beatty's 1981 epic
15. Fearful
18. Gift tag word
24. Bet
25. Cognizant
26. Burdened
27. Italian appetizer
29. Excellence
30. Express
31. Less polite
32. Balkan capital
33. Assignation
37. Ancient school of logic
38. False's counterpart
42. Echo
43. Neutralize
46. Black birds
50. Experiment number
51. Bed board
52. ___ over
54. Figure skater's jump
55. Butter on roti
56. Battering wind
57. Copter's forerunner
58. Zeus, Odin, e.g.
59. Rectum

80

ACROSS

1. Old streetlight, 2 wds.
8. Foot-operated vehicle
15. Like an iris part
16. South American river
17. Baby carrier
18. *En* ___ (capture of a pawn)
19. Azerbaijan's capital
20. Badge of honor
21. Erase
22. Hotel amenities
23. Blue hue
25. Artless one
26. If-___ (conditional statements)
31. Pillbox or porkpie, e.g.
32. Beethoven's birthplace
33. Dugong, 2 wds.
34. Shipping hazard
36. Buttercup family member
37. Mucus
38. Bleak, as an outlook
39. Assent indication
40. Class
41. David, e.g.
42. Ask
43. "No kidding"
45. Dim ___
46. Having a will
49. Staid
51. High flyer, 2 wds.
52. Harder to come by
55. Life-everlastings
56. Golden
57. In an inappropriate fashion
58. Razzed

DOWN

1. Breach
2. Kuwaiti, e.g.
3. One by one
4. "Hey, good ___!"
5. For all to hear
6. "More" in Madrid
7. Prior to
8. Complain
9. Delete
10. Disrespect
11. Research place: Abbr.
12. Checked item
13. Bad marks
14. AI game competitor
20. Drops from the sky
22. Caroled
23. Erik Estrada TV show
24. Marina sight
25. Standard
27. ___ and cheese
28. Thrifty
29. Taboos
30. Jenny Lind, e.g.
32. Bringing forth
33. Barber's motion
35. ___ canto
36. Military force
38. Battering wind
41. Precious
42. Ran as engines should
44. Badger cousin
45. Extra
46. Unit of pressure
47. Big show
48. Scrape, as the knee
50. Allocate, with "out"
51. Fiddle stick
52. Word preceding Francisco or Diego
53. Remind
54. *Little* ___ *Riding Hood*

ACROSS

1. Beach material
5. Anxiety
10. Cart
14. Chill
15. Daniel of the frontier
16. ___ brat
17. Shoot
18. Chopper blade
19. *Mad ___*
20. Animate
22. "The dole"
24. *___ of Eden*
26. Cassia plants
27. Darts
31. About to explode
33. Controversial issue
35. Forms a residue
39. Borehole
40. The "one" in a one-two
41. Certain
42. Implied
44. Based on hearsay or rumor
47. Native New Zealander
49. Election decider, at times
50. Appearances
53. Clip
55. Blimp
57. Cornmeal concoction
62. Agitated state
63. Dress material
65. Mastercard alt.
66. Amazon native
67. Absurd
68. Brood
69. ___ work
70. Ratty place
71. Slaloms

DOWN

1. Call at first
2. Opposite of fer
3. Nonexistent
4. Moore or Lovato?
5. *Au courant*
6. Middays
7. Caught
8. Falling flakes
9. Nobel-winning "Mother"
10. Wrestling hold
11. Suffix with sect-
12. Dark area
13. Dissolves, as cells
21. Kill, in a way
23. ___ *Make a Deal*
25. Huge
27. William Shatner's nickname: "The ___"
28. 2022 Oscar-winner for Best Picture
29. Suffix with dich- or symbi-
30. Seeing the glass half full
32. After-bath wear
34. Spanish for "to tear"
36. Ford, for one
37. Five-time U.S. Open champ
38. "To thine own ___ be true"
43. Dash gauge
45. Bing Crosby or Rudy Vallée, e.g.
46. Copy
48. Egyptian god
50. Kilns
51. Barracks decor
52. Balderdash
54. French wine region
56. Window part
58. Machine parts
59. Crazily
60. Visored cap
61. Former spouses
64. Deviation

ACROSS

1. Cut short
5. Kind of song
9. Coffee order
14. Better
15. Spanish painter Joan ___
16. Be of use
17. Ballpark figure
18. Like some cheeses
19. Audacity
20. Ancient Roman magistrate
22. Avower
24. Everyday
26. Least tainted
27. Future flower
29. College servant (UK)
30. Indonesian island
31. Pre-op procedure
33. Speech study
38. Contribute
39. Cheer
40. Kidney-related
41. Old-fashioned, 2 wds.
43. "Haste makes waste," e.g.
44. Central point
45. Apprehend
47. ___ Orleans
48. Get a payoff
51. Actor's incidental activity
53. Straighten out
55. Bag handler
58. Bear
59. ___-ran
61. Carpenter's groove
62. Bounty
63. The Kennedys, e.g.
64. Multi-tools have many
65. More rational
66. Some male dolls
67. Confined, with "up"

DOWN

1. Offensive move in pro wrestling
2. Frown
3. Betrotheds
4. Basil use
5. Excessively flattering
6. Hairpiece
7. "He's ___ ___ nowhere man…": The Beatles
8. Acceptances
9. Nimble
10. Not really that good
11. ___ blanche
12. Busy places
13. Argus-eyed
21. Street musician, 2 wds.
23. Between two points
25. Estimated: Abbr.
27. Laser light
28. Annul
30. ___-on-the-spot
32. Bad luck
34. TV's *Hee* ___
35. Be that as it may, 3 wds.
36. Hamster's home
37. Killed
42. Crosspiece
46. Kitchen wear
48. Crescent features
49. Bone cavities
50. One may be taken to the cleaners
51. *Beauty and the Beast* protagonist
52. Make sense
54. Dearth
56. First president of Somalia ___ Adde
57. Announce
60. Europe's ___ Marino

ACROSS

1. Belt
5. Short for "officeholders"
9. Drummer Ringo
14. By way of, briefly
15. Assist at the gym
16. Asian rice dish
17. Goals
18. Easily maneuverable, as a vessel
19. Development areas
20. Alliance
21. Longtime Big Brother host Julie ___
22. Ascended
23. Angel
25. Marathon
27. Feudal lord
29. From above
34. "The Overcoat" author Nikolai ___
37. Soviet spy Alger ___
39. Annul
40. Biological rings
42. Riot act relative
44. Functions
45. ___ carotene
47. A question of ownership
48. Amount to be taken
50. Drive
52. Mine access
54. Experts
58. Brush off
62. ___ and bolts
64. Achy
65. Insert symbol
66. Overabundance
67. Aspersion
68. A deadly sin
69. Channel
70. CNN host Lisa ___
71. High-pitched
72. Units of work
73. Bind

DOWN

1. Runs through
2. Snow White's "Whistle ___ You Work"
3. Metal wear
4. City on the Black Warrior River
5. Analyst's concern
6. Brightly colored fish
7. Danger for sailors
8. Court figure
9. Plant that gives us latex
10. South American monkey
11. Brews
12. Pink, as a steak
13. Archaeological site
24. Tablet
26. TV series ___ Bridges
28. Clarified butter
30. Cruelly
31. Data
32. Bothers
33. Star Trek android
34. Cheap trinket
35. Italian for "bear"
36. Orders to plow horses
38. Did laps, say
41. Lying, maybe
43. Blown away
46. Like some heads
49. Sinclair Lewis's Elmer ___
51. Affixes in a scrapbook, say
53. Fireplace
55. Salk's conquest
56. Luggage compartment
57. Twilled fabric
58. Lasting mark
59. Window filler
60. Advocate
61. Netflix executive ___ Hastings
63. ___ oil (varnish ingredient)

ACROSS

1. *Carmina Burana* composer Carl ___
5. Street fleet
9. Outfit
14. Baklava dough: Var.
15. Chill
16. Charm
17. Lou Gehrig, on the diamond
18. Ballistic missile type, for short
19. Easy runner
20. Get a higher grade, in a way
22. Self-centered type
24. *Lulu* composer
25. Motown band ___ Earth
26. Dodge pickup model
29. Latte dispenser
30. A cry for help
33. Lyric poem
34. Ill-gotten gains
35. Cottontail's tail
36. Between universities
39. Lentil, e.g.
40. Comrade in arms
41. Avoid
42. Nth degree
43. Get-up-and-go
44. Certain camera support
45. Attends
46. ___ & Span
47. Distance between digits on a dial
50. Buttonholes
54. Asian capital
55. Gumbo vegetable
57. Good, long bath
58. Assume
59. Dried fruits
60. In doubt
61. Beguiling behavior
62. Fingerboard ridge
63. Fill

DOWN

1. Ices
2. Brawl
3. Chimney channel
4. Presaged
5. Smartphone feature
6. Getting on
7. Sticker
8. Respectively
9. Aplenty
10. Be theatrical
11. Amazonian
12. Exercises
13. Chipper
21. *The Last Picture Show* director Bogdanovich
23. Blooper
26. Belief in God through reason
27. Breathing problem
28. Big name in pads
29. Quartet member
30. Diving duck
31. Best
32. Charger
34. Dispose of quickly, 2 wds.
35. Pneumoconiosis
37. Insert symbol
38. Suffix with "tele" or "photo"
43. Is appropriate for
44. Directed skyward
45. Inclination
46. Platoon nickname
47. Become friendlier
48. Dry riverbed
49. Carbon compound
51. Chesterfield, e.g.
52. President who became a Supreme Court chief justice
53. ___ terrier
56. White wine aperitif

ACROSS

1. Source for appetizers and entrees
5. Experienced
9. Bias
13. Impulse transmitter
14. Asian nurse
15. Egyptian peninsula
16. "Ol' Man River" composer
17. ___ mortals
18. Go downhill, maybe
19. Diffusing by absorption
21. Goes off
22. Dangerous situation
24. Hallowed place
27. Coal carrier
28. Ms. Knowles, to fans
31. Have an impact
32. Beam
34. Battering wind
35. Ancient alphabetic character
36. Sidekick
37. ___ probandi: burden of proof
38. Dry
39. Airport pickup, for some
40. Bluish gray
41. Acquire
42. Water-logged
43. Lots
44. Cantankerous
47. Bordeaux product
50. Inaction
54. Any living or extinct member of the Hominidae family
55. It can be a bargain
56. Jordanian Princess ___ bint Faisal
57. Representative or spy
58. Clue
59. Characteristic carrier
60. Suffix meaning "knowledge, truth, or wisdom"
61. August 3, e.g.
62. Units of work

DOWN

1. Ocean menace
2. Bruce and Demi, e.g.
3. *Cheers* stalwart's nickname
4. Blending in, maybe
5. Extreme shortage
6. Correct, as text
7. The "L" of XXL
8. Punk rock band ___ Clash
9. Word with City or Falls
10. "Sack" starter
11. ___–West Schism of 1054
12. Mental keenness
15. New England catch
20. Hyperbolic function
21. Black
23. Safari sight, for short
24. Scarecrow stuffing
25. Beautiful maiden
26. Altercation
28. Far from fresh
29. Rinse, as with a solvent
30. Affirmatives
32. Southern breakfast dish
33. CD follower, once
34. The best of times
36. Traction aid
40. Exclusive
42. Extract
43. Flattened at the poles
44. O. Henry device
45. Eyelashes
46. TSA request
47. Neighbor of Libya
48. Apple's apple, e.g.
49. Financial page heading
51. Appraiser
52. Caroled
53. The Beatles' "___ Leaving Home"
55. High degree

ACROSS

1. Express pain
6. Roughly
10. Name on a Woodstock poster
14. Collectible art print
15. Merriments
16. Not home
17. Bloodless
18. Apartment
19. Bulgarian bucks
20. Bundle
21. Paid tribute in music
23. High-ranking person in India
25. Farm young
26. ___ Bell
29. Luxury watch brand
33. "Stop right there!"
37. Dry land
39. They cross Sts.
40. Let in
41. Glacial deposit
42. Platinum anniversary
44. ___ nitrate
45. Pretty flower from South Africa
46. Curb, with "in"
48. Paving block
50. Last place
55. Subsurface currents
60. Dressing material
61. Good vantage point
62. Indian nurse
63. Stereo port, perhaps
64. Demoiselle
65. ___ list
66. Go viral
67. Abounding in certain trees
68. Agitated state
69. Facilitates

DOWN

1. Window material
2. Hindu poet
3. Additional
4. Get ___ in life
5. Like some yogurt
6. Opposite of ons
7. Be a monarch
8. Devour
9. Pertaining to the manipulation of bones
10. Russian instrument
11. Blown away
12. Church part
13. Pair
22. Artless one
24. Gunfire sounds
27. Basic monetary unit of Ghana
28. Abalone
30. Fat unit
31. Prize since 1949
32. Old Chinese measure
33. Door fastener
34. Maintain
35. Counterclockwise
36. African danger
38. Baptism, for one
43. At no time, poetically
47. Cancel
49. Evergreen also called Christmas berry
51. Mrs. Bush
52. Illumination units
53. Nitrogen compound
54. Mangles
55. Advocate
56. Knot of wool
57. Quad building
58. Dry riverbed
59. Attempt

ACROSS

1. Beardless one
6. Couch
10. The "I" in M.I.T.
14. Embryo sacs
15. Young salmon
16. Company originally known as Blue Ribbon Sports
17. Decorated with panels
19. Start your turn
20. Loudness measure
21. Inhabitants of the Horn of Africa
23. Soundness of mind
25. Hot drink
26. Ancient stone
29. Hemingway's "The ___ of Kilimanjaro"
33. ___-relief
36. Postulate
37. High-altitude region in Asia
38. Arm bone
40. Present
42. Breezy
43. Forearm bandage of support
45. League members
47. Census datum
48. Representative
49. Abet, as a fugitive
51. Olympic event
53. African whitewood
57. They often point toward Mecca
62. Conceited
63. Ad ___: off the cuff
64. Incapable of combining
66. Mine opening
67. Checks
68. Alimentary canal part
69. Brings home
70. Coin opening
71. Far from sterile

DOWN

1. Bawls loudly
2. Berkshire Hathaway's home
3. Kind of jack
4. Australian beer can
5. Possesses
6. Advance, slangily
7. Pledge
8. Cargo carrier
9. Eagerness
10. Armpatch, e.g.
11. Philippine thatch material
12. Peel, as a fruit
13. Addition column
18. Sri Lanka, formerly
22. Announce
24. Spinning toy
27. Change taking place at constant temperature
28. Skin problem
30. Eastern ties
31. ___ the Millers starring Jason Sudeikis
32. Charon's river
33. Boom alternative
34. Comrade in arms
35. Cut
39. Wall Street workers
41. Adorn in relief
44. Bond
46. Blubber
50. Bad-mouth
52. Southern breakfast carb
54. Highland Games pole
55. Where blood vessels enter an organ
56. Foe
57. Agenda
58. Carnival attraction
59. Not much
60. Boss on a shield
61. Essence
65. Butt

ACROSS

1. Blocks
5. Bounces about
9. Literally, "for this"
14. Mine passage
15. Brawl
16. First: Prefix
17. Impose, as a tax
18. Annul
19. Charged
20. Cave diver
22. Smart ___
23. Clothing
24. Calcium-rich soil
26. "Shotgun!"
29. Go-getter
33. Big mess
37. David Petraeus, e.g.
39. Wicked
40. Zero, on a court
41. Concise
42. Email command
43. A Swiss army knife has lots of them
44. Successor
45. Pack animals
46. "Big ___," a WWI German cannon
48. Deaden
50. Words to swear by
52. Beat to the tape
57. Choir section
60. Element variant, as graphene to carbon
63. Elementary particles
64. Cambodian currency
65. Discover alternative
66. Control ___
67. Italian for "silk"
68. Server's list
69. Glove material
70. "Zip it"
71. Miniature sci-fi vehicles

DOWN

1. Corkwood
2. Proficient
3. Fix firmly
4. Needles
5. Country on Borneo
6. Farm call
7. Be an omen of
8. Attack
9. Queen's home
10. Subtle quality of some humor
11. Better
12. Auditory suffix
13. Prepare to fire
21. *Lingua franca* of Pakistan
25. American Girl ___ Walker
27. Cheese on crackers
28. Arrive, as darkness
30. Ancient greetings
31. Coal site
32. Auto founder Ransom
33. Yarn irregularity
34. Proboscis
35. Declare
36. Bedecked
38. By way of, briefly
41. Excellent
45. Adjoin
47. Annoyance
49. Cabbage
51. Draconian
53. Bum
54. Beau
55. Defeat
56. Connection
57. Rock equipment
58. Hawaiian feast
59. Build strength
61. In ___ of
62. ___ *All Sing With the Chipmunks*

ACROSS

1. Mimicking bird
5. Pitch
10. Lying, maybe
14. "D"
15. Postal scale unit
16. Jaywalking, e.g.
17. Arkansas governor Asa ___
19. Urging word
20. Afflict
21. Qualified
23. Devote, as time
26. Squirm
27. Glacial deposit
28. Hale
29. Over there
33. Assent
34. Swampy lowland
36. Grave marker
37. It changes
39. Withdraws
41. Poker declaration
42. Challenges
44. "Who ___?": Saints fans' chant
45. Footnote word
47. Cooking meas.
48. Destiny
49. Mollify
51. Got along
52. Ringlet
55. Battering device
56. Ceremonial dance
57. Sheer
62. "___ ___ to ask"
63. Bristles
64. Arm bone
65. Characteristic carrier
66. Swelling
67. Fastener

DOWN

1. Dashboard abbr.
2. "___ rang?"
3. "___ a chance"
4. Esoteric
5. Dirt
6. "___ intended"
7. Extra leaves (as for a table)
8. Intestinal bacteria
9. Clemency
10. Peoples of antiquity
11. Fail miserably
12. Carbon compound
13. Exhausted
18. Holed up
22. Paranormal presences
23. Airport aide
24. Spanish dish
25. Inbox items
26. Tech magazine
28. ___ Tuesday (Mardi Gras)
30. Cedar tree
31. Dissolved matter
32. Sang
34. Cassava
35. Trigger, for one
38. Belie
40. Energy
43. Olympian, e.g.
46. Pudding-like dessert
48. Celebrated
50. In a corner
51. Near's opposite
52. Catch, as flies
53. Light-colored
54. Religious image: Var.
55. Perlman of "Cheers"
58. Cap
59. Final: Abbr.
60. African antelope
61. "We've been ___!"

ACROSS

1. Send to the canvas
5. Band jobs
9. Go after
14. Prize since 1949
15. Romantic interlude: Var.
16. Alternative version
17. Shoestring
18. Immature cell stage
20. Exodus figure
22. Frames
23. Alliance
25. Afflict
26. Cane material
30. ___ of attrition
32. Simple
36. Broadcasting
37. Ant, in a UK dialect
39. Bleat
40. Cocktail that goes boom
42. Corrosion-resistant metal
44. Short order, for short
45. Shell out
47. Man with a mission
48. Brand, in a way
50. "Before" prefix
51. One of Henry VIII's Annes
52. ___ Framed Roger Rabbit?
54. Real howler
56. "The Blue Danube" composer
60. Manacling
65. Grove grower
67. Carbon compound
68. The Importance of Being Earnest author
69. Fledgling bird
70. Arm bone
71. Asparagus unit
72. Breathe hard
73. Turned blue

DOWN

1. Food for sea urchins
2. Asian nurse
3. Pool site, maybe
4. Deed hearing
5. Richard Gere movie American ___
6. Lana Turner's birthplace
7. High school dance site, maybe
8. Coaster
9. Early spring blooms
10. Badger
11. ___ nitrate
12. Locale
13. Angelina and Brad, e.g.
19. One without scissors, perhaps
21. Cancels
24. Welsh for "valley"
26. Strikes out
27. American lizard
28. Gozo Island is part of it
29. High school class, for short
31. During
33. Bear
34. Cousin of the needlefish
35. Chinese official's office
37. "… happily ___ after"
38. Alert
41. Resist
43. Legume dish
46. ___ Brunswick, Canada
49. Burundi neighbor
51. Most azure
53. Even more vast
55. Arctic or Pacific, e.g.
56. Farm females
57. Excursion
58. Breathing noise
59. One of 12, at A.A.
61. Clash of clans
62. Deeply
63. ___ of the above
64. Garden bloom, informally
66. Deep-pile Scandinavian rug

ACROSS

1. Haul with tackle
6. Report
10. Bad look
14. Canton neighbor
15. Long, for short
16. Arm bone
17. Current
18. Seriously
20. Medieval confederation, 2 wds.
22. ___ nitrate
23. Dinner bird
24. Cut into a slope: Var.
28. A deadly sin
31. River in Germany
32. Coward's lack
34. Slog
38. Cave, in literature
39. Word after "zinc" or "nitrous"
40. Chevy, for one
41. Puts in stitches
42. Come again
43. "Hold it!"
44. Beer buy
45. Castrato
47. Fine thread
51. Prepare an onion
53. Drugs used to treat despair
60. Leveled off
61. Amazon download, e.g.
62. Ad headline
63. Mountain goat's perch
64. Bit of color
65. Appraiser
66. Blood pigment
67. Posture problem

DOWN

1. Rubber ducky habitat
2. Southern vegetable specialty
3. Small songbird
4. Princes, e.g.
5. Ingratiate
6. Accord
7. Need for pie a la mode
8. Board member, for short
9. One hundred dinars
10. Kind of cycle
11. Mournful poem
12. Come later
13. Critic, at times
19. Deprived, poetically
21. Ancient jar
24. Units of work
25. ___ as shooting
26. Dog with a blue-black tongue
27. Song and dance, e.g.
29. Language heard in Pakistan
30. Sound systems
33. Donald and Ivana, e.g.
34. Stooge
35. Maui party
36. Auditory suffix
37. "The lady ___ protest too much…"
44. Formally surrender
46. Angers
47. Run out, as a subscription
48. Dental filling
49. Flat
50. Carafe size
52. Beat around the bush
54. A head
55. Untainted
56. Not much
57. Jaywalking, e.g.
58. Like some orders
59. Beehive

ACROSS

1. Pork portion
5. Alliance
9. Pants
14. Witching ___
15. Bananas
16. Form of spiritualism
17. By its very nature
19. Rocket fuel ingredient, for short
20. Latin hymn about Judgment Day
21. Early explosive device
22. Bubbly beverage
24. Governmental overthrows
28. Flat floater
32. Boredom
33. Dissociable
35. E. B. White's *Stuart* ___
37. One imposing a tax
38. They hang around
42. Alternative to a convertible
43. The "O" in SRO
44. Fast food quality, perhaps
46. Iditarod vehicle
47. Wardrobe
51. Artists' boards
56. Devastation
57. Beach house arrangement, perhaps
58. Soul
59. Auditory suffix
60. Advocate
61. Organ part
62. Musician Kanye
63. Secretary, e.g.

DOWN

1. Reproved
2. Pueblo-dwelling people
3. Yorkshire river
4. Opposite of cons
5. Honked
6. Neighborhoods
7. Group of eight: Var.
8. Pigeon's call
9. Dead duck
10. Somewhat
11. Rossini's *La Scala di* ___
12. Young salmon
13. Wearing footgear
18. Capable of being split
21. Pansy piece
23. Blast
24. Quartet member
25. Part of "the works"
26. Ending at
27. Caulking material
28. Deep black bird
29. Bear
30. Pests
31. Graceful fliers
34. Lives
36. Part of a horse's hoof
39. Work unit
40. Break
41. Sandwich meats
45. Blue-ribbon
46. Stick-on
47. Crack, in a way
48. Channel
49. *Ars amatoria* author
50. *Brave New World* cure-all
52. Fall follower
53. Container weight
54. Plural of 39-down
55. Hunt for
57. Haul

ACROSS

1. It shares a common base with Hindi
5. Completed a tax return
10. Crafts' partner
14. Booty
15. It may cause serious food poisoning
16. Touch
17. Remark
18. Rice wine used in cooking
19. Betting game
20. Constitutional add-on
22. "___ see that coming!"
23. Litigant
24. Adhesive
26. Conviction
29. Feeble
32. Wicked
33. Deep cavity
37. Spanish title
38. Chaim Potok's *My Name Is Asher ___*
39. Entangle
40. *Sister Act* chorus member
41. Arduous journey
43. Malay religion
44. Actress Gilpin, known for *Frasier*
45. Boardwalk activity
47. Remained
49. Seducer
51. Turned gray, maybe
52. Burn the midnight oil
54. Timepiece
59. Novice
60. Dutch cheese
61. Yoked bovines
62. About, 2 wds.
63. Opposition bloc
64. *Downton Abbey* mother
65. Dampens
66. Exams
67. "Sack" starter

DOWN

1. Arm bone
2. Hotel unit
3. Spoil, with "on"
4. Part of a place setting
5. Alluring woman
6. Less cordial
7. Desolate
8. A-list
9. Constant noise
10. Attached
11. Cash, 2 wds.
12. Beach bird
13. Coin opening
21. Directly
22. *Mad Men* antihero ___ Draper
25. *Cortaderia selloana*
26. Wallops
27. Flip
28. Spreadable sausage
30. Accustom
31. Dog or wolf
34. Famous
35. Assent
36. Add up
42. Spiral-horned antelopes: Var.
44. Locker protection
46. Actress Myrna
48. One-year-old sheep
50. French wine region
51. Sit in on
52. House
53. Radial, e.g.
55. Opposite of ins
56. Impulse transmitter
57. Italian for "evening"
58. Become unhinged
60. Gun slang

ACROSS

1. Messy dresser
5. Boss on a shield
9. Picturesque caverns, for short
14. Bantu-speaking people
15. Washington locale, with "the"
16. Accelerate sharply
17. Not much
18. Slog
19. Upper crust
20. Stick-on
22. Teetotaler
24. Contradict
26. Favor
27. Famed sharpshooter
32. Suitors
33. Assent
34. Dennis Mitchell's dog
38. Pain
39. California airport
40. Divided Asian peninsula
41. Bind
42. Statehouse VIP
43. Guesstimated
44. To-the-letter meaning
46. Home type
50. Newspaper column
51. Clerics
54. Evening hour
58. Edit
59. Newspaper section
61. Counterclockwise
62. *Eraserhead* actor Jack ___
63. Civil War navy ship USS ___
64. Mineshaft
65. More fitting
66. Belt
67. Its motto is *Lux et veritas*

DOWN

1. Certain herring
2. Garage job
3. Suffix with neur- or symbi-
4. Flammable hydrocarbon gas
5. Person in a mask: Abbr.
6. Asian peninsula
7. Amorphous mass
8. Poet Sharon
9. ___ spoon: diner
10. Kindled anew
11. Like Bo-Peep's charges
12. Student getting one-on-one help
13. Whale type
21. Apprehensive
23. Angry, with "off"
25. Discouraging words
27. Partner of far
28. Canceled
29. Breakfast area
30. Jack
31. Nova, e.g.
34. Simple song with a refrain
35. Advocate
36. Charges
37. In things
39. Auction offering
40. Cabbage-like vegetables
42. Bronx cheer
43. Breach
44. Storage spot
45. Forum platforms
46. Life force in yoga
47. Chart anew
48. Javelin, e.g.
49. Parry
52. Drops off
53. Attracted
55. Sacred Hindu writings
56. "The root of all ___"
57. Legal tender
60. Be in session

ACROSS

1. Office software
5. Ballgame souvenir
9. Gentlemen callers
14. Allege
15. Musician's quality
16. Dior creation
17. Corporate document
19. Heat-resistant glass
20. It's usually capitalized
22. Cashless deal
23. Howl
24. Morphine, e.g.
26. Underground worker
27. Gambit
29. Paving block
30. Financial penalty
32. Another kind of exam
33. Gaudy state
37. Hamlet
41. One of the Fates of Greek mythology
42. Colony member
43. One-seeded fruit
44. Take a leak
46. Furniture wood
47. Cemetery
50. Crawl
52. St. ___ of Hippo, author of *Confessions*
53. Ever
54. Algonquian language
55. Carbon compound
56. Wuss
57. Half a matched set
58. Farmer's place, in song

DOWN

1. Currencies, once
2. Cover
3. Get back on the horse
4. Liquid bead
5. Begin
6. One thousand kilograms
7. Annul
8. Actor Bridges, known for *The Fabulous Baker Boys*
9. Small bun or roll (UK)
10. Mythological heaven
11. Radio medium
12. Like leftovers
13. Portmanteau for Dr. Ruth, e.g.
18. Back
21. Present occasions
25. Hammer part
27. Allots, with "out"
28. Sculpture and song, e.g.
30. Come to light
31. ___ skirt
32. "Say ___"
33. Higdon hat
34. Lizard constellation
35. Grecian
36. Biblical coins
37. Indicated
38. Iridescent
39. Another name for vitamin A
40. Find a buyer beforehand
42. Romeo's "two blushing pilgrims"
44. Insistent one
45. Rakes
48. Per
49. Fix
51. Single layer

ACROSS

1. Benito Mussolini, e.g.
8. Easily recite
15. Epithet of Greek goddess Hera
16. Bedroom furnishing
17. Train unit
18. Splashes around
19. Hatter
21. Cups: Fr.
22. Peachy
23. Philip K. Dick's "___ the Dull Earth"
25. Name of a famed nun
28. Dispatches
33. Meanings
36. Be a busybody
37. Affirm
38. *Metropolis* director ___ Lang
40. Central points
41. Kind of position
43. Like tumblers
45. Start of a refrain
46. Disburse
47. Bud Fisher's ___ *and Jeff*
49. Luxurious
52. Religious teachers
56. Software that simulates
60. Online workshop
62. Capable of bringing together
63. Garden-variety
64. Ready
65. Like some mail
66. Horseshoes players

DOWN

1. Kind of team
2. At full speed
3. Grin
4. Michael Mann's 2004 Tom Cruise film
5. Firebrand
6. *CODA* filmmaker ___ Heder
7. Container weight
8. Slang for "brilliant"
9. Muse
10. Equips with flood protection
11. Arcing shots
12. Alternative to acrylics
13. At liberty
14. Come clean, with "up"
20. Take up farming
24. Bakery offering
26. Call, as a game
27. Absorbed
29. Arouses
30. Booty
31. Centers of activity
32. ___ & Span
33. Flat floater
34. "Happily ___ after"
35. Greek cheese
39. Menagerie
42. Layered
44. Hooligans
48. Grammar topic
50. Attendance counter
51. Hang
52. Did laps, say
53. "___ Only Just Begun"
54. Encourage
55. Bog
57. Essential
58. Golden rule preposition
59. Cincinnati's team
61. Spanish for "net"

ACROSS

1. One with a razor?
6. A Swiss army knife has lots of them
10. Event attended by Cinderella
14. ___ apso: dog breed
15. Slang for "excellent"
16. UN aviation agency
17. Pint-sized
18. Bolted
19. Locale
20. Floor it
21. Christmas decoration
23. Actress Betsy ___, known for *Breaking Bad*
25. Chippies
26. Keep out
28. Usher hit, in 2004
29. Not me
30. Swedish sheep
31. Spanish for "mushroom"
32. Agents making busts
36. Thousand ___, CA
38. Auto damage
41. Feline with a mane
42. Blind followers
44. Arab sailboat
46. African antelope
47. It goes with chips
49. Binge
50. Computer storage unit, informally
51. Christmas decoration
54. Washington city
56. Try again
58. Infield protectors
61. ___ of access
62. Crime genre
63. Intestinal bacteria
64. Ancient greetings
65. Yorkshire river
66. Bavarian river
67. Certain salmon
68. Allows
69. Demands

DOWN

1. Cutlass maker: Abbr.
2. Small piece
3. Bamboo thicket
4. Information booth visitor
5. Distress calls
6. Current
7. Stenographer
8. Make
9. Constant
10. Attraction to people of either gender
11. Blackberry drupelets
12. Coffee order
13. Fertile soil
22. Object in the night sky
24. Call for
26. Boys
27. Nurse
33. Complex procedure
34. Ice cream vessel
35. Like a bug in a rug
37. Most calm
39. Where Shakespeare is shown (UK)
40. Good, long bath
43. Brad from *Thelma and Louise*
45. Like an unlisted candidate
48. Carbolic acid
51. Cause, as havoc
52. Plunder, old style
53. Studio furniture
55. Twin crystal
57. Grimace
59. Appealed
60. Guys

ACROSS

1. Hoax
5. Fastener
9. Chris Hemsworth's Marvel character
13. Bindle bearer
14. Song
15. Cross your fingers
16. Sci. school
17. Not much
18. Fare for Oliver Twist
19. Methane compound
21. Going on and on
22. TV franchise *The ___ Housewives*
23. Cafeteria carrier
25. Find a space
26. Propagated
31. Agreements
32. Lop
33. Hit Ctrl-S
34. Prefix with -matic or -biography
35. Annoyed exclamations
36. Cole ___
37. Commoner
38. Chill
39. Bride's attendants
40. Avoids
42. Yorkshire river
43. Agreement
44. Soothing salve
45. Seeming
49. Contrary contentions
53. Deprive of courage
54. Passage
55. Carbon compound
56. Romantic interlude
57. Beat it
58. Houston university
59. Lacquered metalware
60. Apprentice
61. Boat with an open hold

DOWN

1. Level
2. Better
3. Synoptic
4. Pregnant, 3 wds.
5. Drag one's feet
6. Slang for the subway, in London
7. Continuously
8. Ascertains
9. Through: Abbr.
10. Sixty minutes
11. Kind of column
12. Depend
18. Nell ___, mistress of Charles II
20. Gabs
24. Goals
25. St. ___ Girl: beer
26. Theatrical skill
27. Assailants
28. Supernatural
29. Circumvent
30. "Mountain" soft drinks
31. Easy-to-eat foods
35. Computer info
39. Alternative to a fence
41. ___ doctor
44. Broad-winged hawk
45. Bail out
46. Annul
47. ___ nitrate
48. Ad headline
50. Bavarian brew
51. Bananas
52. A bunch

ACROSS

1. Association
5. ___ India Company
9. "The ___": Calgary skyscraper
12. Had on
13. Fill
14. Georgetown University basketball player
15. Old wizard
16. Hip-hop subgenre
17. Appraiser
18. Oust
20. *Gnomenreigen* composer Franz ___
21. Cleaner of clothes or money
23. Haunt
26. Exaggerate
30. Except
31. Convention
34. Fledgling bird
36. Like a hot fudge sundae
37. Achy
38. Butt tosser, often
40. Big jerk
41. Crackers
42. Hematologist's study
45. UK slang for disappear, 2 wds.
49. Drive
52. Promoter's job
55. Detective film genre
56. Affectation
57. Drudgery
59. Hints
60. At liberty
61. Data
62. "If only ___ listen…"
63. Binge
64. Paving block

DOWN

1. Vowel-less Welsh word for valley
2. Amount of work
3. Advocate
4. Retro car
5. Heat
6. Composer Copland
7. Bear
8. Traditional Plains home
9. Word before and after "will be"
10. French for "hear"
11. Dermal development
14. Doris Duke, for one
19. Consumes
20. Counterclockwise
22. Like some muscles
23. Ancient reference marks
24. Join the poker game
25. Sports figures
27. Laugh-a-minute folks
28. Hardy wheat
29. Last in a Greek series
31. Blubber
32. Aretha Franklin's 1975 album
33. Computer storage unit, informally
35. Model-home helpers
36. Got bigger
39. Carbon compound
42. Disagreeable difficulty
43. Rent
44. "The way things are…"
46. To the rear
47. France's longest river
48. Birthplace of K-Pop
49. Creep
50. Grimace
51. ___ Piper
53. ___ of the above
54. Knack
58. Auction offering

ACROSS

1. Apply gently
4. Strong fiber
8. Black birds
12. Greasy
14. Nine ___ Nails
15. Embankment
16. Actress Summer
17. Pineapple giant
18. Winter mountaineering tool
19. Wrap
21. British informer
22. Appraiser
23. Fleshy mushroom
24. Actors
27. Belief that all natural objects have souls
31. Cheap lodgings
34. Applause
36. Stores
37. "Ol' Blue Eyes"
38. Sunburn aftermath
39. Filling with cheer
40. Old TV parts
42. Grant and Lee: Abbr.
43. Arid
44. "Shake a leg!"
47. Spanish title
49. Trimmed
53. Article of faith
54. Born's partner
55. Courtroom word
57. Charm
58. Crazily
59. Break
60. American playwright ___ Hart
61. Mimicking bird
62. Sloth or pride, e.g.

DOWN

1. "What's up, ___?"
2. Affectation
3. Exploded
4. Fussbudget
5. American lizard
6. Eye doctor's white coat?
7. In German, das, der, or die
8. Make some heads roll
9. Affirm
10. Watered-down
11. Census datum
13. Assent
15. Plant supervisor, 2 wds.
20. Go downhill
23. *Captain America: ___ War*
24. Cleanser brand
25. According to
26. Indifference to pleasure or pain
28. Barely beat, with "out"
29. Nonviolent protest
30. Dawns, in verse
31. Cool, once
32. Jitterbug variant
33. Dressing ingredient
35. Bother
41. Excessively flattering
45. Ancient Greek theater
46. Bloody Mary liquor
47. Audition tape
48. ___ *probandi*
50. "___ a chance"
51. Fledgling bird
52. Singer Lovato
53. Cap
54. Comic sound effect
56. Buddhist discipline

ACROSS

1. Chimney channel
5. Show contempt, with "at"
10. Azerbaijan's capital
14. Kentucky Senator ___ Paul
15. Affecting a lobe
16. Declare positively
17. Quality of being heard
19. Safecracker
20. Fakes it
21. Chasers
22. Some beachwear
23. Epidermis
25. ATF concern
26. Fool's hat, 2 wds.
30. Cuff
32. Pennsylvania village for which a wagon was named
33. White wine aperitif
34. Winnie-the-Pooh creator
35. It's a wrap
36. Impropriety
39. Errand runner
41. Exile
42. Commanded
43. Hyperbolic function
44. Volcano feature
47. Money substitute
50. Checks and ___
51. Surplus fiber
52. Fools
54. Data
55. Blood carrier
56. Gull-like bird
57. Freshman, probably
58. "Encore!"
59. Alluring

DOWN

1. Blended coffee drinks, for short
2. Former first lady Bush
3. Lends moral support
4. Bleep
5. Arrows' accompaniment, to Hamlet
6. Common ailments
7. Eastern ties
8. ___ Tuesday (*Mardi Gras*)
9. Oil boil
10. Rifle attachment
11. Ancient greetings
12. They're tapped
13. Advocate
18. Sesame
21. JPEGs, e.g.
23. Bright
24. "Trick" joint
26. 1960 Italian film *La ___ Vita*
27. Breakfast treat
28. Fit of shivering
29. Surname of Henry VIII's last wife
30. ___ row
31. ___ Cooper
32. Child's play
34. Average
37. Delta follower
38. Cut short
39. Pink and grey cockatoo
40. Idiosyncrasy
42. Albania's peninsula
44. Desert bloomers
45. Brought back, in literature
46. Test, as ore
47. Agitated state
48. Ice cream vessel
49. Abounding
50. Cold Adriatic wind
52. Bleat
53. Account

ACROSS

1. Buttonhole, e.g.
5. Gorse
9. Type of vice
14. Spanish for "all"
15. Bindle bearer
16. Form of pneumonia
17. Malocclusions
19. Critical
20. Appraiser
21. Forger's shop
22. Go off script
23. Catalogs
25. Fish that lays a mermaid's purse
26. Asinine
30. Like skim milk
35. Greece neighbor
37. Golden
38. Football lining
39. Comedy club act
40. Atoll features
41. First-rate
42. What Spider-Man's friends call him
44. A funny thing happened on the way there
45. Blue-ribbon position
50. Gloomy
54. Big picture
56. Milk-Bone, e.g.
57. Dissident
58. Canonical scripture in Jainism
59. Holly
60. Victorious goddess
61. Drive away
62. Announce
63. Some beans

DOWN

1. Leaf opening
2. Cherished
3. Archetype
4. They may have abs of stone
5. Blender sound
6. Marriott worker
7. Spain and Portugal
8. Discouraging words
9. Bucks
10. Centers of activity
11. Adjoin
12. Algebra or trig
13. Hunted
18. Mac
21. Astral
24. Cohabitating horses
25. Attack
26. Wainscot
27. Annul
28. Appearance
29. Blocks
30. Certain protest
31. Prefix with -graph and -mobile
32. Mouth, in slang
33. Sloughs
34. Outstanding, slangily
36. Duffel or satchel
43. Elvis's birthplace
44. Kind of position
45. In favor of
46. DC Comics superhero John Henry ___, a.k.a. Steel.
47. Queen's "___ Ga Ga"
48. Cough-inducing
49. Burdens
50. Antares, for one
51. Entreat
52. Ballet move
53. Flimsy, as an excuse
55. Barbershop call
57. Cool

ACROSS

1. Dull
5. Neither hot nor cold
9. Deep cavity
14. Garage job
15. House plant
16. Slow
17. Timeless
19. Kindled anew
20. Canopy support
21. Campus life
23. Mauna ___
24. "Boo-___!"
25. Photoshop purveyor
29. Reddish-gold wildcats
34. Forbidding
35. Sedimentary
36. Arm bone
37. Fare on a stick
38. Shoe bottom
39. Suburban chauffeur
41. Family group
42. Wooden peg used to fasten ship timbers
43. Sheet music direction for soft or smooth
44. Gangster's gun
45. Aircraft compartment
47. Happy refrain
51. Spring flood causes
56. Foreshadow
57. Pantry
59. Amalgam
60. H. H. Munro pen name
61. Warning yelled by golfers
62. Bulrush, e.g.
63. Board member, for short
64. Blemish

DOWN

1. Give away
2. Longtime Arizona basketball coach Olson
3. Lying, maybe
4. Cord fiber
5. ___ Line Is It Anyway? improv series
6. Large artery
7. Scandinavian rug
8. Palindromic language related to Tamil
9. Isaac's father
10. Reared in a specified environment
11. American lock maker Linus ___
12. Whole milk alternative
13. Allocate, with "out"
18. Prod
22. Chocolate substitute
25. Burned
26. Grief
27. Postal scale unit
28. Steady
29. A computer language
30. Tech hardware conglomerate
31. Coral island
32. Spring flower
33. Play part
35. Espresso cup
37. African animal enclosure
40. "Assume the position," 2 wds.
43. Fraction of a newton
45. Penniless
46. Containing gold
47. Checks
48. Be a monarch
49. Ancient
50. Respiratory organ
52. ___ Schulwerk music teaching method
53. April honoree
54. Portuguese for "get out!"
55. *Mergus albellus*
58. Money paid to Uncle Sam

ACROSS

1. Door part
5. Show shock
9. Astute
14. Way, way off
15. Chill
16. Leg bone
17. Religious
19. Lace tip
20. Testify
21. Acetate, alcohol, bromide, and ether
22. Bottom line
23. Kardashian-Jenner matriarch
24. Condiment (var.)
28. Guitar picks
31. Mountain crest
32. *À la mode*
33. *Ant-Man* actor Paul ___
35. *Better Call Saul* actress ___ Seehorn
36. Attack locale
37. Annul
38. Cotton sheet
39. Miles per hour, e.g.
40. Mound
41. Bit of legalese
43. Chick-___
44. Slang for "cheat"
45. Physique, informally
46. Bathtub sound
49. Boss
53. Native Alaskan nation
54. Fabricated
56. Stir up
57. Creep
58. Target's bullseye, for one
59. Steve Cohen, to the New York Mets
60. Oolong and Earl Grey, e.g.
61. Continual change

DOWN

1. The "one" in a one-two
2. Not many
3. French Sudan, today
4. UK native, for short
5. Ceded
6. AARP concern
7. Phoenix NBA franchise
8. Wooden pin
9. Interference
10. Tense
11. Well
12. Cambodian currency
13. Taps
18. Arise
21. At attention
23. *A Fish Called Wanda* actor Kevin ___
24. Engine part, for short
25. Buddhist who has reached enlightenment
26. Choppers, so to speak
27. Capitol
28. It's a snap
29. Chatter
30. Befuddle
32. Box
34. Airhead
36. Mouthing off
40. Language of southern China
42. Club list
43. Twelve in a year
45. Any grape, banana, etc.
46. Kind of palm
47. Farm equipment
48. Boxer Spinks
49. Coal site
50. "A good walk spoiled"
51. Carbon compound
52. Big name in pasta sauce
54. Hale
55. Brined salmon

ACROSS

1. Excitement
6. Prefix meaning "on this side"
9. Darn
13. Fast runners
14. Exhausted, with "in"
15. Hoisted aboard
16. Hot spots
17. Loaded past capacity
19. Bait
20. Lacking courage
21. Mismatched, 2 wds.
23. Noncommittal gesture
24. Blemish
28. Chump
32. Amigo
34. Zero, on a court
35. Fused alumina
37. Convertible furnishing
39. Data
40. Keep out
42. Barflies
43. Batty
44. Affect, 2 wds.
46. Reassurance
52. Deli sandwich filler
56. Egyptian peninsula
57. Large terriers
58. Leftover
59. Catch some Zs
60. Houston university
61. Acquiesce
62. "Cut it out!"
63. Talk, talk, talk
64. Equals

DOWN

1. Hindu loincloth
2. "Boléro" composer Maurice ___
3. "He's ___ ___ nowhere man…": Beatles lyric
4. Bright circle?
5. Evaluated
6. Hide, 2 wds.
7. Krypton, e.g., 2 wds.
8. Wait on
9. Indian staple (var.)
10. Traveled by bike or horse
11. Ancient greetings
12. Addition column
14. Philanthropist
18. Certain digital watch face, for short
22. Bush
24. Ado
25. Brain area
26. Affirm
27. Joins
28. Stated
29. Arm bone
30. Take into custody
31. Bow
33. Kind of ticket
36. Mississippi state flower
38. Jester's headgear
41. What one might be, per Jeff Foxworthy
45. Not those
46. Coal carrier
47. Winglike
48. Dreary sound
49. Accustom
50. Accuser
51. Digs
52. Stationer's stock
53. Brawl
54. Rice-shaped pasta
55. Number two, for short

ACROSS

1. Pots and ___
5. Chowder morsel
9. Boot out
14. Not much
15. Like some hair
16. Edge
17. *Peanuts* character
18. Appearance
19. Aristotelian endgame
20. Flat
22. Job for a dummy
24. *Toy Story* dinosaur
25. Present and future
26. Eyeball benders
28. Eye doctor's white coat
31. Holiday drink
32. Eyepiece
34. Big bucks, briefly
38. "___ rang?"
39. Big-eyed primates
41. Govt. agency involved in the Human Genome Project
42. Discovered by Wilhelm Röntgen in 1895
44. Least crazy
45. Pigeon noise
46. The "fifth element"
48. Express
50. Ancient military hub
53. Alfred E. Neuman's home
54. Heavy
58. Beg
61. Kind of cycle
62. Figurehead's place
64. Facts, briefly
65. ___ squash
66. Chill
67. Heroin, slangily
68. Culinary herb
69. Cattle collective
70. Half a matched set

DOWN

1. Buddies
2. Adjoin
3. Central American nation
4. A hairdresser, sometimes
5. Semicircular basin in a mountain
6. Like flock members
7. Affirm
8. Mimic
9. Book before Job
10. Robin Williams film *Good Morning, ___!*
11. Runs in neutral
12. Intimate
13. Exams
21. Glorify
23. Cordwood units
26. Black stone
27. "D"
28. Silk fabric
29. "Crazy" singer Patsy
30. ___-guided
33. Bill sharer
35. Frequency
36. Dorothy's "cowardly" friend
37. Loafer, e.g.
40. Defeat decisively
43. Part of a sail support
47. Forever, poetically
49. Rather wan
50. Comics sound effect
51. Joey's home
52. Bother
55. Brightly colored fish
56. Advocate
57. Bar order
59. Quite a distance
60. Quentin Tarantino's *Reservoir ___*
63. Lent's start, e.g.: Abbr.

ACROSS

1. Put away
5. Bad
10. Luxurious
14. Brazilian offshore oil field
15. Slang for "money"
16. Remarkable (UK)
17. Reddish apes
19. Walked heavily
20. Elder Earp brother
21. Actors McConaughey and Broderick
23. Stallions
25. Call, as a game
26. ___ pole
28. Bringing on staff
31. Blouse, e.g.
34. As real as Latveria
36. Inconspicuousness
40. Deer fly fever
41. Pairing with chips
42. Depletes
43. Chin indentation
47. "Cool" amount
48. Mock orange
52. Relax
57. Textile fibers
58. Centers of activity
59. Swallows beforehand
61. Fledgling bird
62. Mojave plant
63. Give four stars, say
64. Daily constitutional
65. Range rovers
66. Mucus

DOWN

1. Hot spot
2. City on the Po
3. Abstract art style practiced by Bridget Riley
4. Improvise
5. Charm
6. Shakespearean "know"
7. Froth
8. Arm bone
9. Bringing up the rear
10. Protestant worshipper
11. Crude
12. Boat with an open hold
13. Bricklayers' equipment
18. Copter's forerunner
22. Hackneyed
24. Skincare product
27. Meredith Wilson's 1957 show *The ___ Man*
28. Virus identified in 1983
29. Not yet final, at law
30. Pant
31. Ballet dress
32. Burden
33. Controversial
35. Money in Muscat
37. Mythical serpent with a deadly stare
38. Strumpet
39. Certain theater type, for short
44. Eagles' nests (var.)
45. Attack a CO, maybe
46. Clock watchers
49. Month after Adar in the Jewish calendar
50. Affect
51. Money in the bank
52. Ball of thread or yarn
53. Georgetown athlete
54. Brightly colored fish
55. Advocate
56. Rip
60. Commonly rented item, once

ACROSS

1. Ado
5. Hundredweight: Abbr.
8. Cap attachment
14. Rend
15. Enthusiastic cheering, when doubled
16. European corvine bird
17. Correct a text
19. Pillaged
20. Coming
21. Concealed through sleight of hand
22. Bad look
23. Free from, with "of"
24. Chanel of fashion
27. Severity
29. A head
33. Titter or chuckle
35. Discouraging words
36. Clean
37. Courtyards
38. Baby's first word, maybe
39. Buzzing
40. Earthquake
41. Cool, once
42. Bear
43. Nasal product
44. Buckos
46. Warner ___ movie studio
47. Amigo
48. Blanched
50. Delegate
53. Surpass
57. One who believes in one reality
58. Due date
59. Discordant
60. Beaujolais, e.g.
61. Romantic interlude (var.)
62. Coal tar distillate
63. *Show Boat*'s "Can't Help Lovin' ___ Man"
64. Clerk's call

DOWN

1. At liberty
2. Describe
3. Affirm
4. Prison management student
5. Oregon lake known for its depth
6. Haunt, 2 wds.
7. Word needed with "below" and "belt"
8. Bakery buy
9. "Get ___ of yourself!"
10. Study, say
11. Stringed instrument
12. Ancient
13. High degree
18. Directly
21. Personification (Greek)
24. Category
25. Like Cheerios
26. Antique shop item
28. Like a hot fudge sundae
29. One side of a bygone wall
30. Persian poet ___ of Nishapur
31. Durable fabric
32. Range rovers
34. Second son of Noah
36. ___-relief
44. Fight
45. Egghead
47. Korean port
49. Headed up the line
50. Partially decayed
51. Carbon compound
52. Pungent evergreen
54. All alternative
55. Black stone
56. Bombard
57. Nth degree
58. VHS successor

ACROSS

1. Bursae
5. Ices
9. ___ bit
12. Applaud
13. Excellent: Scot.
14. Leon Uris's 1984 novel *The* ___
15. Arm bone
16. Copy
17. Webpage
18. Period preceding Easter
19. Bob Marley devotee, maybe
20. Auditory
21. Connive
22. Fragrant essential oil
23. Effort
24. Scrabble piece
25. Mount Olympus ruler
26. Butter up
27. Sky sight
29. Dock
31. Coal carrier
32. Escape
34. Ancient greetings
36. Popular family dog
39. Blah
41. Landlord
44. A Muse
46. Cinnamon ___
48. Affirm
50. The "T" in STEM
51. Crawdad habitat
52. Basketball team number
53. Cobbler's focus
54. Full-length
55. Gymnast's feat
56. Excoriate
57. Choker
58. Counterclockwise
59. The W.C., slangily (UK)
60. Flying toy
61. Fledgling bird
62. Assent
63. Feed bag contents
64. Drop

DOWN

1. Carve
2. Adjective when discussing gene mutations
3. Little Italy dessert
4. Paints like Pollock
5. Flattened at the poles
6. Become covered with a layer of ice, 2 wds.
7. Acclaimed 1940 animated musical anthology
8. Have faith in, often with "by"
9. Milky
10. Corrode
11. Kicked out
16. The opposite of saner
17. Pepsi or Sprite
26. Prepare tea or coffee
28. Change
30. Geometrical locus
33. Irrational distrust
35. Snapped up
36. Launches a barrage of insults
37. Biological rings
38. Turkish pastry (var.)
40. Protest tactic
42. Curse
43. Restaged Broadway show
45. He and she
47. Heels
49. Peace of mind
51. Confidence game

ACROSS

1. Lion's share
5. Tail motions
9. Romeo's "two blushing pilgrims"
13. Bring upon oneself
15. Crazily
16. Comrade in arms
17. ___ jacket
18. Balcony section
19. Economical
20. Gasket
21. ___-it-all
22. Diet-minded, in ads
23. Monica's brother on TV's *Friends*
24. Kind of wheel
25. Spore disperser
27. Diploma word
28. Spielberg blockbuster in 1975
29. Class or grade
30. Partner
33. Gospel legend Houston
34. Abounding in certain shady trees
35. Shark species
37. Court figure
40. Punk or metal, to rock, e.g.
45. Camry creator
47. Hunted
48. Spasm sound
49. Hebrew letters
50. Free from
51. Adriatic resort
52. Charge
53. Jersey, e.g.
55. Irish software company
56. Visored cap
57. Clenched hand
58. Lizard
59. Olefin chemical
60. European auto
61. Buzz
62. Anatomical nerve network
63. Level, in London
64. Department store department

DOWN

1. Balearic island
2. Burdensome
3. Deep divisions
4. Goes bad
5. Romps
6. In the middle of
7. Energetic
8. Barbecue rod
9. Babble
10. Gut inflammation
11. Typewriter parts
12. Business buzzword
14. Floor covering
24. Injure badly
26. Henchperson
28. Thin towel (UK)
31. Sommelier
32. Crack
36. Ancient
37. Less decorated
38. Coal tar product
39. Butterfly feature
41. Rebels
42. Rootstalk
43. Apparition
44. Ballpark figures
46. Request
51. Flax
54. Palm thatch
55. Alt. spelling signifier

ACROSS

1. Easy dupes
5. Sour sort
10. Brightly colored fish
14. Adjoin
15. Sound of a rush of air
16. Charge
17. Channel
18. Arctic diving bird
19. Gift tag word
20. Didn't dawdle
22. Large shooting marble
23. Urban blight
24. Communiqués
27. Beer buy
28. Chef's mushroom
29. He snoops
30. More rational
31. Translucent
32. Antonym for "transgendered"
34. *Big* star Tom
35. Dubuque native
36. Wallops
37. Astrological ram
38. Breathing noise
39. Corrective
44. Affirm
45. ___ canto
46. Bank
47. Ghana currency
48. Alas and ___
51. Steelers coach Chuck
52. Dilute
53. Egyptian peninsula
54. Cut short
55. Spiritual, e.g.
56. "In case you ___ noticed…"
57. Red ___ (frankfurters)

DOWN

1. "Rabbit food"
2. Counters
3. Kicks a pigskin
4. Prepare, as tea
5. Semicircular basin in a mountain
6. "___ rang?"
7. Van Morrison's homeland
8. Gal Gadot's homeland
9. Gnaws
10. Outside the frame
11. Made a certain kind of bet
12. Alarm clock
13. Dress finisher
21. Patterned fabrics
25. Kitchen tool
26. Algonquian Indian
29. Type of verb
30. Molding
31. Mended
32. Got on a radio talk show, 2 wds.
33. "Whatcha ___?"
34. Boot
36. Floral leaves
37. Aviator Earhart
39. Discompose
40. Freshwater fish
41. Convex molding
42. Kindled anew
43. Pound sounds
49. "___ you dig it?"
50. DIYer's purchase

112

ACROSS

1. "Oh, ___!"
5. Mint
9. Tried to get home, maybe
13. Cancel
15. Boss on a shield
16. Hamster's home
17. Atlanta-based airline
18. Agitated state
19. Stalk
20. Allegation
21. "My country, ___ of thee"
22. TV, radio, etc.
23. Affectation
24. Rich deposit
25. Cremona violin
26. Highly seasoned beef shoulders
28. Canonical hour
29. Affirm
30. Strengthen
31. Play guitar
35. Agent or congressperson, for short
37. Trash hauler
38. Apple or berry lead-in
39. Accra currency
41. Barbershop debris
43. Literally meaning "winged lizard"
48. Skin problem
49. Breezy
50. Salad ingredient
51. The Dow, e.g.
52. Campaigner, for short
53. "Eat!"
54. Solid fossil fuel
55. French door part
56. Assumed name
57. Khaled Hosseini's 2003 novel *The ___ Runner*
58. Fledgling bird
59. Affect
60. Coaster
61. Buddies
62. Appear

DOWN

1. Like the Marx Brothers
2. Honeysuckle shrub
3. Back biters
4. Whistler or Wyeth, e.g.
5. Client
6. Any which way
7. Tropical birds
8. "___ a chance"
9. Conceptual frameworks
10. Extoller
11. Combusting
12. Captive
14. Cap
22. British parent
24. WC
27. Battering device
31. Performer's routines
32. Lubricant and fuel once sourced from whales, 2 wds.
33. Bad-weather contingency
34. Let out, as a fishing line
36. Nonpareil
37. High school class, for short
40. Arid
42. Bleeding Gums Murphy's instrument
43. Yellow tropical fruit
44. Fence crossings
45. Common pyroxene mineral
46. Eastern Catholic
47. Kidnapper's demand
53. Nobel Peace Prize winner ___ Hammarskjöld
55. Type of talk or rally

ACROSS

1. Whole alternative
5. Wet's opposite
8. Some undergrad degrees
11. 1993 standoff site
12. Small salmon
13. Best-liked, for short
14. Appraiser
15. Engraving tool
16. Holly
17. Predicament, 2 wds.
19. Breezy
20. Catches sight of
21. Campus women, once
23. Computer info
25. Campfire sound
29. Semicircular basin in a mountain
32. "Death, be not proud" poet
34. Skeletal
35. Affirmative votes
37. Bizarre
39. Bank
40. "Concentration" objective
42. Did a blacksmith's job
44. Detachable container
45. Commit
47. TV show ___ Trek: Discovery
49. Impatiently eager
51. Blue blood, briefly
55. Gift tag word
58. Caused to turn
60. Ballet move
61. Bar order, with "the"
62. Neuter
63. Trees with acorns
64. Discovery
65. Carbon compound
66. Wield
67. Cigarette, in Staffordshire
68. Like Santa's cheeks

DOWN

1. Jenny Lind, e.g.
2. Lays out in a ring
3. Freeze
4. Grisly
5. Column style
6. One with a thick skin
7. Over there
8. Indonesian province
9. Affirm
10. Alluring
12. Baby bear
13. Bombs
15. Grant
18. Blues musician ___ Belly
22. Apply gently
24. Loss of bodily sensation
26. "Sack" starter
27. Prefix for "to the left"
28. Checked out
29. An inflorescence
30. Withdraw gradually
31. Actor Damon or Dillon
33. U.S. public health agency
36. Economizes
38. Micromanager's concern
41. QB's cry
43. Truth alternative
46. Back of the neck
48. Fake
50. Offspring
52. Court figure
53. Aristotelian end
54. "Much to my surprise…"
55. Bomb
56. "Get ___!"
57. Like certain trees
59. "Cool, man!"

ACROSS

1. Bronze Age neck ring (var.)
5. Oil source
9. Igneous rock maker
14. Way, way off
15. Chill
16. "It's been ___ ___ pleasure"
17. Imaginary surface: physics
19. Odor
20. Accountant's "closing time"
21. As a milquetoast would
22. Actor ___ Danza or Shalhoub
23. Certain Turk
24. Hinder growth
26. All the rage
27. Become friendlier
31. Brainy
32. Aug. follower
33. Scout's promise
34. Snowman prop
35. Goods
36. *Iliad* city
37. Auditory suffix
38. Crazily
39. If-___ (conditional statements)
40. "Comin' ___ the Rye"
41. Ground cover
42. Erato's realm
43. Mimicking bird
45. Booty
46. Self-serve meal
49. Jauntiest
52. Bread spreads
53. Go to bed, 3 wds.
55. Animal catcher
56. Carbon compound
57. Lacquered metal ware
58. Does' mates
59. Contradict
60. "___ Wanted"

DOWN

1. Tan skins
2. White person (slang)
3. Four-star review
4. Convenience item
5. Bring up
6. Extreme pain
7. Bergman in *Casablanca*
8. *When Harry ___ Sally...*
9. Amplifying device
10. Ready for battle
11. Nerd
12. Place to shop
13. Comrade in arms
18. Attack locale
21. Dog registry rejects
23. Fraction of a ruble (var.)
24. Forger
25. Animal with a snout
26. Biblical king
28. Fast runners
29. Lack of muscle firmness
30. Explanations
31. Advance, slangily
32. Pago Pago's place
35. Coen Brothers' 2001 film *The Man Who ___ There*
39. Canine or molar
42. Santa descriptor
44. Affirmatives
45. Allow to be known
46. Eleven-time NBA All-Star Chris
47. Arm bone
48. Fright
49. Durable wood
50. Loafer, e.g.
51. Short's opposite
53. "___ make a lovely corpse": Dickens
54. *Dragonwings* writer Lawrence

ACROSS

1. Seize
5. Rowan Atkinson creation's surname
9. Abandon
14. French novelist Pierre ___
15. Annul
16. Accustom
17. Feed bag contents
18. Hardboiled genre
19. Adjust
20. Put an edge on
21. Coin opening
22. Dissolves, as cells
23. Small bite
25. Jerk (var.)
27. ___ and crossbones
29. Avid
32. Likely to break down?
36. Handful
38. Formerly Facebook
39. Burned
40. *Vanity* ___
42. Dry's opposite
43. Italian sandwich ingredient
45. Man with horns
47. Accord
48. Mexican magnate Carlos ___
50. Oz-inspired 1975 musical, with "The"
51. Operatic villains, often
55. French writer Émile ___
58. *Schindler's List* extra's role
61. With
62. Holly
63. Tucked in
64. Sage
65. Church part
66. Kind of court
67. Sketches
68. Garden bloom, informally
69. Cry

DOWN

1. *Lento*
2. American lexicographer ___ Webster
3. Reduced
4. Carpellate
5. Bread for a burger
6. Carbon compound
7. Spanish for "bye"
8. ___ blackout of 2003
9. Kind of box (var.)
10. Deeply
11. Sounds of reproof
12. Actress ___ Summer
13. Half a matched set
24. Provide
26. Gozo Island is part of it
27. *Casablanca* pianist
28. Experienced
30. Ladylike state
31. Accomplishable
33. Its movie industry is known as Kollywood
34. Worshipping
35. Certain canine
37. Weaken
41. Sunbeam
44. Black bird
46. Churchill symbols
49. Word in chemistry class
51. Type of fish or guitar
52. Crazily
53. Arias, usually
54. Snob
56. Bulgarian bucks
57. Canceled
59. Ardor
60. Romantic interlude

ACROSS

1. Low islands
5. Colliery entrances
10. Caroled
14. Chemical compound
15. Full-length
16. White House's ___ Office
17. Fruitfully
19. Perry Como's "___ Loves Mambo"
20. Big citrus fruit
21. Big bucks, briefly
23. *The Joy Luck Club* author Amy
24. Blight
26. Dappled
28. "Stop that!"
29. "Best Song Ever" singers ___ Direction
31. Make waves
32. Releases vapors
35. Amuse
36. Information on some dating apps
37. Birdbrain
38. Golf supply
39. Amerada ___
43. Eat
46. Annual reference book
48. Darth Vader's childhood nickname
49. Jamaican exports
51. Smooth, in music
52. Idle
54. Dude with a lot of lines
56. Any thing
57. Valid
58. The ___ Star State: Texas
59. Come clean, with "up"
60. Got out of bed
61. Units of work

DOWN

1. Gently held
2. Arid region's watercourse
3. Naval clerks
4. Least risky
5. Freeway in France
6. ___ test, as for paternity
7. Part of a nuclear arsenal, for short
8. Garden bulb
9. Needles
10. Absorb, with "up"
11. Embodiments
12. Flamethrower fuel
13. Hormone producer
18. Albanian founding father Spiridon ___
22. Blood poisoning
25. "Come in!"
27. "___ here long?"
30. "Snowy" bird
32. Going from gig to gig
33. Baffled
34. Earth orbiter
35. Aims
36. Converts charges
37. Be generous
39. Bargain
40. Bewitch
41. One of 100 in a baht
42. Quick breads
43. Golden State: Abbr.
44. Muslim teacher (var.)
45. Ruler under Islam (var.)
47. ___ in Black (1997 blockbuster)
50. Kind of palm
53. Dash lengths
55. Insult, slangily

ACROSS

1. Fellow crew member
9. Skiff
14. Important role in *Our Town*
15. Tasting more like *vino*
16. Chicago's 312, say
17. Acute anxieties
18. *The Great Escape* baddies
19. Near
20. Eminence
22. Crackpot
26. TV show *Better Call* ___
27. Going to the dogs, e.g.
28. Vigors
33. Preserve, in a way
34. Currency in Berlin or Turin
35. More soiled
40. Boatload
41. Opposed
42. Cuff closer
43. Raw fruit snack
48. Plods
49. Bacon orders
54. Friends
55. ___ dissertation
56. Bring in
57. Basify
58. *Playbill* listings
59. Cut

DOWN

1. Catch
2. Aesop's lost to a tortoise
3. Furious feelings
4. Fool, to a Brit
5. Paving material
6. ___ dermatitis
7. Checklist items
8. "... ___ he drove out of sight"
9. Bezique card game (var.)
10. Anxiety
11. Second-generation Japanese Americans
12. Affect
13. Incendiary crime
15. Crunchy brownie bit, sometimes
19. "See you"
21. Cooking meas.
22. Fail to see
23. Radio/podcast personality ___ Carolla
24. "Blue" or "White" river
25. Bit
29. Messy's opposite
30. Abrupt
31. "*Cogito* ___ *sum*"
32. Before long
36. Park protectors
37. Swallow
38. Flight data, briefly
39. Washington Irving's "___ Van Winkle"
40. Spanish for "slopes"
42. Ink and jet
43. Body of good conduct
44. Bouquet
45. Mounds (UK)
46. "The village ___"
47. Drudge
50. Burrow
51. Julia Roberts title character ___ Brockovich
52. Bring down
53. Coaster
55. Dried legumes

ACROSS

1. Chicken part
7. With 10-across, 2006 Cormac McCarthy novel
10. See 7-across
14. Indecent
15. ___ and cheese
16. Deeply
17. *The Wizard of Oz* prop
18. "Let her ___"
19. What "mansion" and "division" have in common
20. Cutthroat competition
22. Better
23. Chap
24. Like some traffic
26. Blockhead
28. Lung membrane
29. Bring down
30. At sea
31. Chin indentation
36. Liveliness
38. Actress Sigourney
39. Heraldic band (var.)
40. Enclosing structure
43. Anatomical nerve network
44. Realist art movement
46. Between black and white
47. Beauty school subject
50. Effeminate
51. Game ender, perhaps
52. Dionysian's opposite
56. Certain organic compound
57. Actor Affleck
58. Right, in a way
59. *Coriolanus* setting
60. Aircraft compartment
61. Save
62. "Blast"
63. "Dee-lish!"
64. Some lines

DOWN

1. Amorphous mass
2. Aggravate
3. Praises formally
4. Equips
5. Disreputable
6. Addition column
7. HBO blockbuster series *Game of* ___
8. Bob or buzz
9. "Caveat ___"
10. Hindu poet
11. Cause of tears in the kitchen
12. Beside
13. Fraction of a newton
21. Game on horseback
25. Defensive spray
26. Not kosher
27. Decline
28. One layer (of several)
32. Generosity
33. Completely
34. Greek cheese
35. Deuce topper
37. Reverse, e.g.
38. Cyst
40. Nice hat
41. It stands for something
42. Highlander
45. Mange-afflicted
47. Privilege
48. Bouquet
49. Bay entrance, maybe
50. Best vision spot
51. Drove
53. Enrich
54. Chill
55. More than want

ACROSS

1. Durante's "Mrs."
9. Bit of Gothic architecture
14. Handel bars
15. King or queen
16. Beget
17. Giving up
18. "The ___ Daba Honeymoon": 1914 song
19. Bank jobs
20. Workforce withdrawals
24. Orthodontic devices
26. Denials
27. Backers for plasterwork
28. Auspices (var.)
29. Bluecoat
32. Sundae topper, perhaps
33. Analyze, in a way
34. Carnival attraction
35. Fourposter, e.g.
36. Horse's pace
37. Asperity
38. Gobs
39. African trip
40. Bird dog
43. Sushi condiment
45. Caught
46. Improvises
47. Fall out of place
52. "Silly" birds
53. Ludwig Feuerbach or Karl Marx, e.g.
54. "Come in!"
55. Echoed

DOWN

1. Minor player
2. "We ___ the World": 1985 charity single
3. PC linkup
4. Absorbed, as a cost
5. Acid salts
6. Rockcress
7. Psychedelic rock instrument, maybe
8. Clod chopper
9. Environmentalists
10. Sit in on
11. Seventh heaven
12. Advanced
13. Units of work
17. Mozzarella or parmesan
20. Judged
21. Bounce back
22. Captivate
23. Damp
24. Amorphous mass
25. Steakhouse instruction
28. Our "mother"
29. Humidor item
30. Aroma
31. Actress Gilpin, of *Frasier*
33. Eyelid ailment
34. Abounding
37. Snake in the grass
38. Women's ___: dismissive term for a feminist
39. Butt of jokes
40. ___ of Langerhans
41. Bring up
42. Heron
43. "Minimum" amount
44. City in Yemen
47. ___ Beta Kappa
48. Spanish for "wing"
49. Barbecue site
50. Motor oil viscosity number
51. Armageddon

ACROSS

1. Gets rid of
7. Groups of bees
13. Holes in shoes
15. Rotting flesh
16. Filling material
17. Washington capital
18. Depend (on)
19. "Big ___": 1994 song by The Notorious B.I.G.
21. Canine cry
22. Closely related
23. Possesses
26. Swerve
27. Certain rice spirits
32. Accused's need
34. Discouraging words
36. Apprehensive
37. Frost-covered
38. Bottom line
39. Part of a train
40. "Cheers!"
41. Mauna ___
42. Kind of group, in chemistry
43. *Barry* actor Winkler
44. City featured in *The Iliad*
46. Blue
47. Latin rodent genus
49. Stuck-up sort
53. Absence permit (UK)
54. Shake up
58. Aspiring
60. Classic exile site
62. Confident
63. Allergy sufferer
64. Compound in detonators
65. Turned around

DOWN

1. Brand, in a way
2. An inflorescence
3. Not fake
4. Comrade
5. Cribbage piece
6. Mainstay
7. "Rabbit food"
8. Crooked
9. Uniformed group
10. Opportune
11. Churn
12. Become unhinged
14. Russian city on the Dnieper River
15. Endure
20. Ballet twirl
22. With enthusiasm
23. Draconian
24. Equally
25. "Graceland" singer Paul
27. Forever
28. Enlarge, as a hole
29. Auspices
30. Swedish money
31. Church assembly
33. Den denizen
35. Profane insult
45. Day trip
47. Riot
48. Fired, informally
49. Belt
50. Snout
51. Boot
52. Cloud
54. Taunt
55. Rice-like pasta
56. "Hogwash!"
57. Container weight
59. No longer wet
61. Ottoman governor

ACROSS

1. Furnished with shoes
5. Publication: Abbr.
8. Quagmire
13. Champagne alternative
14. Cancels
16. Obviously surprised
17. Eastern ties
18. Brother
19. Glass-polishing compound
20. Instant
21. Forerunner
23. Appropriate
25. Actor Jude
26. Portion
29. Certain herring
33. Grammar, rhetoric, logic: classic Greek education
35. Havana's home
36. Family keepsake
40. Sail constellation
41. Least worldly
42. Poker action
43. TV series ___ John, M.D.
45. Bestseller
46. Stevie Wonder's ___ in the Key of Life
50. Olympic prizes, e.g.
57. Exactly, 3 wds.
58. All excited
59. Pluck
60. Rice-like pasta
61. Full range
62. Actress Rossum
63. Appearance
64. The Playboy of the Western World author John M. ___
65. Census datum
66. Easily maneuverable, as a vessel

DOWN

1. Barges
2. Addiction
3. Like Bo-Peep's charges
4. Karl Marx's 1867 opus
5. "Oh, ___!"
6. Impulse transmitter
7. Bodyguard to the British monarch, 3 wds.
8. Defensive spray
9. Ancient
10. Unusual
11. *Wheel of Fortune* choice
12. Furnace output
15. Dagger
22. Hundredweight
24. Counterclockwise
27. Fix
28. Blackguard
29. Eye surgery
30. Activity centers
31. Adjoin
32. Beaver's work
33. Duke Ellington's "Take ___ ___ Train"
34. "Let's ___"
36. Pipe material: Abbr.
37. Drivel
38. Cool
39. Ancient greetings
43. Animated TV show ___ Simpsons
44. Chain of hills
47. Bucket wheel
48. Astronomer, at times
49. Backgammon piece
50. Comedian's stock
51. White person, in certain slang
52. Describe
53. Dope
54. Dole out
55. Citrus fruit
56. Charon's river

ACROSS

1. Disgusts
8. *Dans* ___
15. Islamic law (var.)
16. Hairstylist's specialty
17. Conjunctivitis
18. Greece neighbor
19. Farm young
21. Small songbird
22. New Orleans Saints fans: Who ___ Nation
25. Registered trademark of the Wham-O toy company
28. Air-conditioning on a hot day
30. Mostly bygone souvenir
31. Coal container
34. Architectural projection
35. Mimics
36. Ancient alphabetic character
37. Small creature
39. Bad-mouth
41. Yemen port city
42. "___ stage": Freudian notion
44. Charger
45. *The Simpsons* neighbor Flanders
46. Like a stuffed shirt
47. Buccaneer's crime
48. Artistic grouping
50. Away
51. Prepare pasta water
53. Blowgun ammo
55. Butcher
58. Easily recite
63. Close to the coast
64. Harvest helper
65. Diplomat's quest
66. Sacred songs

DOWN

1. Death on the Nile cause
2. ___ Beta Kappa
3. Calphalon product
4. Noah's vessel
5. Willingly
6. "Stop bothering me!"
7. Cut or clip
8. Shaquille O'Neal's degree
9. "Is that ___?"
10. All-natural flytrap
11. Cognizant
12. Cram, with "up"
13. Archaeological site
14. Pilot's in-flight guess
20. Speech problem
22. Ridicule
23. Flared, as a skirt
24. Link
26. Take
27. Kiss
28. Brutus, e.g.
29. Yellowstone resident
31. News office
32. Bug
33. Destitute
35. Cancel
36. Vintage word
38. Foot
40. Tire fig.
43. Ancient
46. Farmed fish
47. Wholly
48. Church donation
49. *Garfield* exclamation
51. The "B" of N.B.
52. Brewer's equipment
54. Abound
55. ___-Atlantic
56. *Maus* creator Spiegelman
57. Formerly
59. PC linkup
60. Artist Yoko
61. Gave dinner
62. Swelter

ACROSS

1. Without limit
6. Boring
10. Wal- follower
14. Asian capital
15. Brain area
16. Chill
17. Crosses over
18. Affirm
19. Street fleet
20. Pigeon noise
21. Formally surrender
22. Bagpiper's wear
23. Format for a 1990s audio engineer
25. Vessel for mapo tofu
27. Conjectures
29. Missile type: Abbr.
30. Bags
32. Good times
33. Nod, maybe
34. Shoplift
36. Goggles
40. Penny
42. *The Crucible* setting
44. "Hold it!"
45. Daisylike bloom
47. French composer Maurice
49. "___ bad!"
50. Little sip
52. Eat
53. Semicircular basin
54. Big name in bathing suits
57. Large wine cask
58. Leonard's partner, in Joe Lansdale novels
59. Coal dust
60. Bangladesh currency
63. Grinder
65. Advocate
66. Hybrid work acronym for Tuesday through Thursday
67. C-___
70. Economical
71. Cleanse
72. Cancel
73. Chipper
74. Fledgling bird
75. Rice ___

DOWN

1. Healthcare system (UK): Abbr.
2. Pensioner (UK): Abbr.
3. Law
4. Jaywalking, e.g.
5. Cuts off
6. *Ursus americanus*, 2 wds.
7. Zero, on a court
8. Lying, maybe
9. "… upon receipt ___"
10. Wool coat
11. Once more
12. One hundred kopecks
13. Exams
23. Bangladesh's capital, once
24. Fits
26. Feed bag contents
28. Wrinkly faced pup
31. Word with Caesar or Greek
35. Floats
37. It keeps time in place
38. Bell OH-58 ___ helicopter
39. Defeat decisively
41. Flat
43. Café's offerings
46. Free from, with "of"
48. Camera protector
51. Container that holds two quarts
54. Shape
55. Blender button
56. "Enigma Variations" composer Edward ___
61. Not here
62. Intoxicating Polynesian beverage
64. Arm bone
68. Kind of pie
69. A single layer of toilet paper

ACROSS

1. Contraction
6. Bleat
9. It may have nine lives
12. Buccaneers' home
13. Central point
14. Stern
15. Codeine source
16. Stadium section
17. Annul
18. Over-the-top
20. "Upper": Abbr.
21. Calendar square
22. Kind of dealer
23. Posture problem
24. Cheapest way to buy, with "in"
26. ___ Shadow pulp magazine
28. Shaka was their king
31. "___ and see"
32. Space between
35. Like a start-up business, maybe
39. "___ not!"
40. "Go ahead!"
41. Concise
42. Deck (out)
43. Coarse file
45. Artillery burst
49. He fought against Troy
51. Caught
54. History Muse
55. Capitol
58. Cambodian currency
59. Ditch
60. Related maternally
61. Not much
62. Carbon compound
63. Engraving tool
64. Time div.
65. The Mandalorian's first name
66. Literature exam finale

DOWN

1. Endured
2. ___ New Guinea
3. Accord
4. Cowboy boot attachment
5. "Oh, ___!"
6. Witch's mount
7. Of an early Caesar
8. Cancels
9. One thousand escudos, once
10. Kind of feed
11. Clobber
13. Court employee
14. Kansas's "___ in the Wind"
19. "For Me and My ___"
23. Arrangements
24. Sticker
25. Comfortable with
27. Get a move on
28. A's opposite (UK)
29. Prefix with form or corn
30. Inc., abroad
31. Drenched
32. "Scram!"
33. Delighted cry
34. ___ a trade
36. Nanki-___ of The Mikado
37. Tubular trattoria offering
38. ___ current
43. Badger cousin
44. Can
45. "Beat it!"
46. Excuse
47. Get some extra sleep, maybe
48. Electric unit
50. Singer Mraz or Derulo
51. Thickening agents
52. Old Roman port
53. Itsy-bitsy
55. "Rosebud"
56. Greek goddess of youth
57. Latin for "accountability"

ACROSS

1. Chuck
5. Bottomless pit
10. *Ant-Man* actor Paul
14. "Funny!"
15. Sam the Sham and the Pharaohs' song "___ Bully"
16. Blue Bonnet, e.g.
17. Equal in duration
19. Catch
20. Building levels (UK)
21. Bed coverings
23. ___ cry
24. "Yeah"
25. *Wonder Woman* actress Gadot
27. Bad grades
30. Dwell
33. Crooked
34. Familiarize
37. Ping-___
39. Peke squeak
40. Woebegone
42. Sea urchin eggs
43. Catch
45. Tearjerker
46. Depress, with "out"
47. Close, as an envelope
49. Aug. follower
50. Back talk
51. Eats or runs
54. Get a move on
56. Authorize
59. Bands of colors
63. Pinot ___
64. Plant with showy edible flowers
66. Yorkshire river
67. Pelvis part
68. Boss on a shield
69. *All in the Family* creator Norman
70. Grandmother, in some families
71. Hunt for

DOWN

1. "___ is the end. My only friend, the end": The Doors lyric
2. Hop kiln
3. Dessert made with molasses, 2 wds.
4. Spine-pelvic connectors
5. Not straight
6. Castigating chorus
7. "Silent Night" adjective
8. Cut
9. Slender woman
10. Floral fruit
11. Arm bone
12. Gone
13. Kind of life
18. Concerning this
22. Polish
24. Futile
25. Acting lover of Charles II
26. Operatic solos
28. Cleaving tool
29. Blaze
31. Move twice as fast
32. Boredom
35. "Forget it!"
36. Excursion
38. Hobbling gait
41. Infernal
44. Worker
48. Blue
52. Red Square figure
53. Start of a refrain
55. Stress in a metrical series
56. Carbon compound
57. Grimace
58. Galileo's birthplace
59. Bowl over
60. Fast feline
61. Bumpkin
62. Crazily
65. Envy, e.g.

ACROSS

1. It may be grand
5. Precipice
10. Equips with weapons
14. Counterclockwise
15. Pie cuts, essentially
16. Blue-green hue
17. Affirm
18. Heretofore
19. Anatomical nerve network
20. Mud dauber, e.g.
21. ___ canto
22. Existed
23. Consumes
25. "Awakenings" drug
27. "All You ___ Is Love": The Beatles hit
29. Beg
31. Place for tests
34. Contraption (var.)
35. American symbol
36. Prefix with cycle or brow
37. According to
38. Scandinavian rug
39. Vermont or Florida, e.g.
41. ___ bit
42. Nahuatl speaker
44. Schlepper
45. An IG post
46. Drunken
47. Lying, maybe
48. Do-nothing
50. Crooked
51. Gawk
53. Keep out
55. Facetious
59. Burrow
60. "Whistle ___ You Work"
62. Arm bone
63. Comrade in arms
64. Prolific author Joyce Carol ___
65. Best Buy's ___ Squad
66. Chaps
67. Boot out
68. Farm females

DOWN

1. Cabbage salad
2. Bulgarian bucks
3. Spanish for "birds"
4. Minimal meaningful language unit
5. Grouches
6. Beam intensely
7. Romantic interlude
8. "A pox on you!"
9. Hale
10. Hoisted, nautically
11. Assess again
12. Buddy
13. Snow Day want
22. Guide
24. Darling
25. Bequest
26. Arabic letter
27. Second-generation Japanese Americans
28. In particular
29. More high-spirited
30. Cake part
32. Chipped in
33. Bavarian brew
34. Stare at (UK)
40. Fillpots, 2 wds.
43. Alphabet end
49. Squirrels' nests
50. Yank away
51. Catch, as pop flies
52. Balsam
53. Angler's hope
54. One of the acting Baldwin brothers
56. Spanish for "oil painting"
57. Was aware of
58. Gabs
60. Anguish
61. Leon Uris's 1984 novel *The* ___

ACROSS

1. Twinges
6. Change
10. Deaden
14. Spinachlike plant
15. Board member, for short
16. Obligation
17. Antiquated
18. Former British mandate
20. Fixate
22. 1/500 of the Indianapolis 500
23. Quaint curse
24. Annoyance
26. *Sesame Street* watcher
29. ___ cry
30. Deviation
31. Cool
32. "Come again?"
33. Show fear
35. Cogitate
36. Scapula
41. Explanations
42. Soft palate
43. Pensioner (UK): Abbr.
44. Inc., abroad
47. Account
48. Yearly shareholder to-do: Abbr.
51. Ex, ___, zee
52. Spanish for "creek"
54. Bleat
55. Good, long bath
56. Can't stand
59. Plant-type meaning "hidden reproduction" in Greek
64. Bogus
65. Cashmere, e.g.
66. Bishop of Rome
67. Young chicken (var.)
68. *Spartacus* actor ___ Curtis
69. Agitated state
70. Former name for a Chicago tower

DOWN

1. Lose it
2. Epic film *Lawrence of* ___
3. Egypt's Lake ___
4. UK HS diploma equiv.
5. Spike Lee's ___ *Gotta Have It*
6. Agent: Abbr.
7. Tests
8. "Yum yum!"
9. Eyespots
10. "___ on my watch!"
11. Higher ed.
12. Of city govt.
13. Mad cow disease letters
19. Leak through
21. Wrap
25. Blown away
26. Fall follower
27. Yorkshire river
28. Motown's ___ Supremes
30. The 'Y' in TTYL
33. S&P 500 entries
34. Gun, as an engine
35. Yorkshire mom
36. Country music duo Dan + ___
37. Ballyhoo
38. Depend (on)
39. Red Cross donation
40. Big galoot
41. Word showing shock and awe
44. Bringing up the rear
45. Soldiery
46. Creature on Bhutan's flag
48. Deciduous ornamental shrub
49. Knee-slapper
50. Mums
53. Smaller giraffe with striped legs
57. Bad grades
58. Container weight
59. Hundredweight: Abbr.
60. *Winnie-the-Pooh* baby
61. "Run hither and ___"
62. A single layer
63. London city police dept., with "the"

ACROSS

1. Bungle
6. Wager
9. An arm and a leg
14. Gene Vincent's "Be-Bop-___"
15. Cheer word
16. Dead to the world
17. Lockheed Martin field
19. Lecterns
20. Sleeper ___
21. Doctor's order
23. Bank deposit
24. Whispers sweet nothings
26. Eave attachment
28. Foil
31. Carrot, e.g.
32. Fargo assent
33. Beat
36. Coffee order
40. Light detector
43. Artist's stand
44. Ending for bi-, tri-, and motor-
45. Cap
46. "___ my words"
48. Outcasts
50. Anesthetic gas
53. Do some knitting
54. Shakespearean king
55. Ayes and nays
58. Civil proscription for UK misdemeanors, once: Abbr.
62. Tear open
64. Legal title
66. Seed covering
67. Buddhist discipline
68. Ammonia derivative
69. ___ alcohol
70. Assent
71. Control ___

DOWN

1. Bleats
2. Margarine
3. Gang land
4. Zoological cavity
5. Hath, lately
6. Bonny hills
7. Per
8. Action 1980s TV show ___ ___-Team
9. Back talk
10. B vitamin complex
11. Cry for a corpsman
12. European food fish
13. Affirm
18. For the time being
22. High school sci. class
25. Bunting once eaten as a delicacy
27. Equal
28. Sort
29. "Funny!"
30. "___ next?"
31. Campus military org.
34. Gooey dirt
35. Use diligently
37. Commend
38. Try, as a case
39. Ernest Hemingway's *A Farewell to* ___
41. Boldness
42. Maltreat
47. M.L.K. title
49. Hematologist's study
50. Rinse, as with a solvent
51. Article of faith
52. Draconian
53. Phila. state
56. Like mud
57. Dainty
59. Leg part with splints
60. Dwell
61. European auto
63. Amigo
65. ___-off

ACROSS

1. "Blueberry Hill" musician ___ Domino
5. ___ ___ *Off Place*: 1993 adventure film
9. Scarecrow stuffing
14. CEO, e.g.
15. Ruled by Fidel Castro from 1958 to 2008
16. Caribbean cruise stop
17. Weepily
19. Subtraction word
20. With skill
21. *Little Women* woman
22. Charge
23. Sit in the sun
26. Drive-___ window
29. Guarantee
32. "___ boom bah!"
35. Reality TV pioneer *The ___ World*
36. Risky
37. Anguish
38. Arm bone
39. Doctor's request
40. Percussion instrument
41. Bro, for one
42. Chaired
43. A little lamb
44. Cracker Jack bonus
45. Taking the place (of)
46. Unusual (UK)
47. Goldfish, e.g.
48. Semicircular basin in a mountain
50. ___ ___ song
53. Conceptual frameworks
58. Amused reaction
60. Reckless sort
61. Baffled
62. Ancient greetings
63. Unload, as stock
64. One hundred thousand BTUs
65. *Pee-___ Big Adventure*
66. Deuce topper

DOWN

1. Greek cheese
2. Canned
3. Binge
4. "King's evil"
5. Mark placed above a vowel, 2 wds.
6. At capacity
7. Well
8. 2004 biopic starring Jamie Foxx
9. ___ Cooke, the "King of Soul"
10. Extended family
11. Ancient alphabetic character
12. Adjoin
13. B.C. neighbor
18. "Phooey!"
23. Daredevil's cord
24. Noblewoman
25. E or G, e.g.
26. Believe in
27. Prefix with centric
28. Bounced off
30. Groups of fish
31. Meccan, e.g.
32. Faint
33. Charged
34. Music sign
40. Most morose
42. Get a move on
47. Cell alternative
49. Lent's start, e.g.: Abbr.
50. Apartment
51. ___ of office
52. Con
53. Reliever's stat
54. Spanish for "believe"
55. Affirm
56. Game piece
57. Geopolitical partner
59. Spotlight hog
60. Black bird

ACROSS

1. Wedge placed under a wheel
6. *Lulu* composer
10. Buddy
14. *All My Children* vixen ___ Kane
15. Affirm
16. Adjoin
17. Archer, at times
18. Known for its leaning tower
19. "What ___ God wrought?"
20. Atlanta suburb named for an ancient Greek city
22. Crested bird
24. "You ___!"
25. They put out high-frequency sounds
26. British co.
29. "___ ___ Rosey": 1967 Van Morrison single
31. "Polythene ___": 1969 song by The Beatles
32. Stadium cheer
33. Arise
35. Egyptian emblem
39. Exaggerated
41. Inverse function in trigonometry
43. Small Middle Eastern dish
44. Offensive term for an unskilled worker
46. Handful
47. Haul
49. Smudge
50. Bog
51. Most rueful
55. Troll doll inventor Thomas ___
57. More squeaky, as stairs
58. Ballroom floor markings
62. Baldwin known for *30 Rock*
63. Chow
65. Accustom
66. Amble
67. Coal scuttles
68. Acquiesce
69. Didn't dillydally
70. Too cute
71. Beat (out)

DOWN

1. Caribbean and others
2. Prudish
3. Frost-covered
4. Biting
5. Accumulated
6. Protestant denom.
7. Someone who ejects
8. Plant again
9. Post-deadline blessings
10. Sages
11. Decrease
12. Coach
13. Character
21. Periodic table measure
23. Mauna ___
26. The big dance
27. Cleanse
28. "At the home of"
30. Change
34. Vex
36. Unpleasant smell (UK)
37. Leg joint
38. Axed
40. Went over
42. Whale or dolphin
45. Impose (upon)
48. Boor (UK)
51. Cicatrices
52. Lowest deck
53. *Superman* actor Christopher
54. Asian antelope
56. "In the Summertime" band ___ Jerry
59. Cold-storage candidates
60. At liberty
61. Lentil, e.g.
64. Mad cow disease letters

ACROSS

1. Domed roofs
8. Reached
13. Eating disorder
15. Chicago sports journalist David ___
16. Minuteness
17. Instant ___
18. "I" lid
19. Loafer, e.g.
21. ___ card
22. European auto
24. Swings around
26. French door part
27. Ripped
28. Enter a tournament
30. "___ bad!"
31. Beep
32. Has a litter
36. Hard to get
38. Bodies of knowledge
39. Begin again
40. Dynasty in which Confucianism emerged
41. Atlantic catch
42. Makeshift solution
44. Old Chinese measure
45. Kind of dealer
48. Showy displays
49. Lined with a certain shade tree
50. Cock-a-___: designer dog
51. Bawdy
52. Grammatical case: Abbr.
53. Cup holder
55. Charging
60. Offspring
61. Blood cancer
62. Animal in a roundup
63. Excuse

DOWN

1. Kitty
2. Sea urchin
3. Heavy
4. Brooks Robinson, e.g.
5. Advanced
6. Can
7. "___ boom bah!"
8. Butter on roti
9. Pensioner (UK)
10. City on the Arkansas River
11. "Encore!"
12. Culinary herb
14. Appropriate
17. Dalbergias
20. Cool, once
22. Aquatic mammal
23. *His Family* author Ernest ___
24. Kind of hunt
25. Balcony section
26. Spy
29. By way of, briefly
31. Cotton fabric
33. What you may adjust your watch to after a flight
34. Intro
35. "It pains me to say…"
37. Temps
38. Rebuked
40. At the tail
43. Black bird
44. Afternoon service
45. Orbital point
46. Certain tribute
47. Cursor mover
51. Bad look
52. Doris or Patty
54. Nod
56. Fleshy mushroom
57. Blackguard
58. Eighty-six
59. Gun, slangily

ACROSS

1. Physics units
5. The "one" in a one-two
8. Big ape
13. Adjoin
14. Affirm
16. Euripides drama
17. Attendee
18. Artifice
19. Bar fight
20. Chevy, for one
21. Pepper pairing
22. Not a Dem.
23. "Cut it out!"
24. Public health org.
25. Dine at home
28. Consumes
31. Coll. hoops competition
33. Carpenter's groove
34. Amused
39. Coal container
40. Chipper
41. John Hamm drama ___ Men
42. *Nestor notabilis*
43. Account
44. "Uh-huh"
45. Off the avenues
48. Obnoxious type
50. Cashew, e.g.
51. Cool, once
52. Volcanic rocks
54. Atlantic catch
56. Lake in Winter Haven, Florida
60. U2 hit "With or Without ___"
61. Often formed by esters, ketones, and aldehydes
63. Clarified butter
64. Blender sound
66. Baltic capital
67. Symbolic gift on *The Bachelor*
68. Postal scale unit
69. Declines
70. *Star Wars* actor ___ Guinness
71. Ham and ___ (average Joe)
72. "___ a chance"
73. Coordinate

DOWN

1. Indian melodies
2. Circa
3. Because of
4. Poem part
5. It had a 1983 3-D sequel
6. Bird-related
7. "La Sonnambula" composer
8. Dying technique
9. Brushed up on
10. Not fixed
11. "What's ___?"
12. "For Me and My ___"
15. Considers again
26. Dope
27. Fools, in Australia
29. ___ race
30. One may be taken to the cleaners
32. Choppers, so to speak
34. Pharaoh's land
35. Micronesian country
36. Epitomizing
37. Evidence providers
38. "Truth or ___"
46. British school attendee
47. Bit of wit
49. Aerospace measure
53. More likely
55. Pooch, informally
57. Wild Asian dog
58. Affirmatives
59. Bloodsucker
62. Leonardo's "The ___ Supper"
64. Anguish
65. Embrace

133

ACROSS

1. Snares
6. Age-determining stat.
9. Close, as a door
13. Charged
14. Ad headline
15. Taboo
16. Final inning, mostly
17. Queso or fondue, e.g.
19. Gunk
20. Dig like a pig
21. Beauty shop offering
23. Gecko, e.g.
27. As a whole
28. Not following suit on purpose (var.)
29. *Amigo*
31. Find a fix
33. Cousin of a loon
34. Distant
36. Fare reductions
38. Auction cry
39. Observant one
41. Red-spotted creatures
43. Tina of *Baby Mama*
44. Fighting
46. Noted blind mathematician
48. ___-Lorraine
49. Filleted
51. Box-office buy
53. Muffler
55. Like Pope Francis, e.g.
58. Hockey rink insult
59. Attendee
60. Blown away
61. As a leaf's edge
62. Mars's Olympus ___
63. Barbecue tidbit
64. Crowded

DOWN

1. Anchovy containers
2. Stirs
3. Decimates
4. Coal miner
5. Frameworks
6. "Hurray!"
7. Margarine
8. Retro car
9. Allergy sufferers
10. Coal carrier
11. Prefix with cellular or form
12. ___ hat
14. Moving downscreen
18. Singapore ___: cocktail order
22. Slog
24. When one begins to distinguish right from wrong
25. Money in Moscow
26. Industrious (UK)
28. Amplified, online
29. Distinctive bear
30. In conflict with, with "of"
32. Victory sign
35. Storytellers
37. Ballgame souvenir
40. Castor bean poison
42. Pie-eyed
45. Ambrosia accompaniment
47. "More!"
49. Star in Cygnus
50. Gown, e.g.
52. Fuzzy fruit
54. At liberty
55. Shareholder gathering: Abbr.
56. *Winnie-the-Pooh* pal
57. X or Z, e.g.: Abbr.

ACROSS

1. Cattle chews
5. ___: *Love and Thunder*: 2022 Marvel film
9. Brindled cat
14. European auto
15. "All right!"
16. Spanish for "advertisement"
17. Drop
18. Demolish (UK)
19. "The face that launched a thousand ships"
20. Disinfect with an antiseptic (UK)
23. Ethnic slur
24. Agitated state
25. Muslim pilgrimage (var.)
28. Chinese ornamental tree
33. British parent, familiarly
36. Opinions
39. Arm bone
40. Swellheaded traits
44. Ox of India
45. Church assembly
46. Poker move
47. Moisture overload results, in plants
50. Dirty
52. Johns
55. Amusement park in Portland, Oregon
58. Biases
63. ___ it up: celebrate noisily
65. Breathing noise
66. Lady Macbeth, e.g.
67. Hopeful start?
68. Ten cents
69. Russian assembly
70. Office stations
71. Romantic interlude
72. Betelgeuse or Polaris, e.g.

DOWN

1. Conclusion
2. Defeat
3. Atlanta-based airline
4. "Jingle Bells" conveyance
5. Phoenician trading center
6. Bucket of bolts
7. Kilns
8. Bonn's river, auf Deutsch
9. Polynesian island
10. Ancient greetings
11. Digestion aid
12. Indian stock exchange: Abbr.
13. "Hither and ___"
21. Italian wine
22. Butt
26. Noise
27. *West Side Story* faction
29. Cashew, e.g.
30. Pat
31. ___ deep
32. Kiln for drying hops
33. Ankara appetizer
34. Ancient
35. Defunct antiwar org., with "the"
37. Crooked
38. Breaks a commandment
41. ___ *laude*
42. Murmur
43. Going to the dogs, e.g.
48. Hebrew letters
49. Blue
51. Glasgow landowners
53. *Rigoletto* composer
54. Composed
56. Russian whip
57. King arrest site (1965)
58. Cookers
59. Comedian Chris
60. Well shaded by certain trees
61. Casting need
62. Mark
63. Large amount of money
64. Get a move on

ACROSS

1. Give away
5. Flattens
10. Barter (UK)
14. Took a bus or bike
15. Acquired relative
16. Chinese dynasty
17. Goals
18. Dig, so to speak
19. Gym sets
20. *Habeas corpus*, e.g.
21. Some fundraisers
23. Dictionary
25. Cap
26. Small carpet
27. Cheat
29. It's a wrap
32. Wake-up call
35. Bummed out
36. Blanched
37. Be a monarch
38. Fold of skin
39. Ancient alphabetic character
40. Ancient
41. Lascivious sort
42. Like London Tube pricing
43. Chicken ___
44. Rubberneck
45. Census datum
46. Except
47. Beholdings
51. Unethical tact
55. Modern-day French Sudan
56. *Peter Pan* dog
57. Some hairstyles
58. Ancient greetings
59. Gross
60. Take back
61. After-dinner selection
62. High-ranking Turks
63. Back
64. American fashion designer Arianne ___

DOWN

1. Bar fight
2. ___ Valley: French wine region
3. Blend
4. Roused to action
5. Kind of box
6. ___ a high note
7. Coagulate
8. Go-___
9. Flowering vine
10. Curtain fabric
11. "This is fun!"
12. "I goofed"
13. Boil stuff
22. Sunshine unit
24. Trophy
27. Camera sound
28. "That hurt!"
29. Mr. Tumnus, e.g.
30. Arm bone
31. Casting need
32. ___-shoot
33. German aviator ___ Sperrle
34. Holly
35. Exploded
36. Close
38. Creature named for its flat feet
42. Tappan ___ Bridge
44. Destroy the interior
45. Device that keeps motors and generators running together
46. Acts like an ass
47. As yet
48. Belly button
49. Flash of light
50. Actress Spacek
51. Carp and minnows
52. Black
53. French for "bridge"
54. Yorkshire river
56. Pen point

ACROSS

1. ___ & Span
5. Palm roofing
11. Join securely
13. Daring display
14. Conciliatory
16. Armed
17. A little of this, a little of that
18. Students
20. Large amount of money
21. Deck (out)
23. Ancient country in present-day northeastern Iran
25. A funny thing happened on the way there
27. Gull
28. Berth place
31. Comparatively cockamamie
33. Butts
35. UK health org.
37. Colo. neighbor
38. ___-tac-toe
40. "She Loves ___": The Beatles tune
41. Blouse, e.g.
42. Indian staple dish
43. Chill
45. Another name for *jai alai*
47. Faithful, in Scotland
49. Apprehend
51. Anglo's partner
52. Depleting
55. Enthusiasm
56. Discouraging words
58. Trust
60. Fleshy mushroom
62. Aluminum hydrate
64. BLT need
66. Acquires the film rights to
67. Word before "park" or "slide"
68. In a dishonorable way
69. Beach bird

DOWN

1. Upper drug, for short
2. ___ cavity
3. Set in stone
4. Pro's counterpart, as on a list
5. Garbage
6. Accident
7. Frank acknowledgment
8. Oft tinned fish
9. Debit's opp.
10. "We've been ___!"
12. Barely beat
13. ___ bandits
15. Trophy
16. Cable guy, at times
19. *The Office* receptionist
22. Rev
24. Bones to pick
25. Discovery
26. Alloy components
29. Put under the table
30. Lighting instrument
32. Fix
34. Finish, with "up"
36. Bridge
39. Bergalls
44. American symbol
46. Serbian beer brand
48. Perth native
50. Purchase
53. Satirical device
54. Kettle
56. Asiatic palm tree
57. Feed bag contents
59. Feminist org.
61. Blue books
62. Bio. info.
63. Party pro.
65. Yoga pad

ACROSS

1. Data unit
5. Taps
9. Advice
14. Benefit
15. Chill
16. Lagos money
17. Part of Q.E.D.
18. Eat
19. Oscar winner for *Tootsie* Jessica
20. ___ out
22. Los Angeles ballplayer
23. Ba in Chemistry
25. Aviary sound
27. Treat with contempt
28. Crown vetch
32. Lying
33. Audio equipment maker
35. Berth place
37. Balsam
38. Put to the test
39. Hair piece
40. ___ & Span
41. Canton cookware
42. Big name in pasta sauce
43. Lustrous fabric
45. Strikes down
47. Casbah headgear
48. Floods
49. Refuse
53. Exceedingly
55. Bank
56. Breezy
57. Creep
61. Catkin
62. Frenchman
63. Don Juan, e.g.
64. As such
65. Shaded with certain trees
66. Arts prize since 1949

DOWN

1. Kind of ribs
2. "___ can do it!"
3. Also
4. Assembly-line output, perhaps
5. *Pterocarpus*
6. AARP concern
7. Air
8. Arils
9. Acquired relatives
10. Indian bread
11. Engine knock
12. Advocate
13. Old Chinese measure
21. Popular drink in juice boxes
23. Dances to jazz music, maybe
24. Aviator Earhart
26. Canned
27. Cave-dwellers
29. Writing desk
30. Dissolved matter
31. Funeral hymns
33. Sumer's era
34. Lout (UK)
36. "Not only that…"
38. Too cute
44. Delicate
45. In a nimble manner
46. "More," in Barcelona
48. Emergency fluid
49. Applaud
50. Blood pigment
51. Affirm
52. Sloughs
54. Container for nitroglycerin
58. ___ de guerre
59. Summa ___ laude
60. "Hiya!"

ACROSS

1. Honey
5. ___ *Afraid of Virginia Woolf?* by Edward Albee
9. Pitmaster's specialty: Abbr.
12. Land on Lake Victoria
15. Farm call
16. Not I
17. European subways
18. Visored cap
19. "___ hot to handle"
20. Loincloth
21. Add
23. Putdowns
25. Office holder, for short
26. Joint problem
28. African antelopes
32. Go-getter
36. Reorganize
37. Egg on
38. Burden
40. Ballet frock
41. Entirely exposed
44. Facade
47. Alaska Native
48. Kind of palm
49. Holiday drink
50. Not mine
53. Graphics machine
56. Bartender on TV's *Pacific Princess*
58. "___ we're talking!"
59. Hightail it
62. Chip off the old block
64. Blackguard
65. Sanction for bad behaviour: Abbr.
66. Noble Italian family name
67. "___ Ya!": Outkast hit
68. Colorful salamander
69. Catch

DOWN

1. Depress, with "out"
2. Ancient
3. Soaks
4. Become a member (var.)
5. Kitchen implement
6. Get a move on
7. Theoretically
8. Bit of slalom gear
9. Information unit
10. Benefit
11. *Ad ___ damnum*
13. Excessive fondness
14. Devised the Three Laws of Robotics
22. Missouri feeder
24. Cooking fat
27. Snares
29. It may be proper
30. Precise points
31. Pivot (var.)
32. Chill
33. Bamboozles
34. Commit a computer crime
35. In neutral
39. ___-___ vision: Superman power
42. Resembling parasitic protozoa
43. Flower once used to treat rabies
45. "I" problem
46. Dishevel
51. Busts
52. Creeping juniper
53. Creep
54. Grimace
55. Not straight
57. Blind guts
60. Way in which a batsman can be dismissed in cricket: Abbr.
61. Lil one
63. Fix, as an election

ACROSS

1. Lowlife
5. One of TV's Simpsons
9. Ruler fraction
13. Arm bone
14. Icky and sticky
15. Blemish
16. Blocks
17. Exterior
18. Atomic particle
19. ___ King Cole
20. Rock experts
22. Kill, as a bill
24. Jazz horn
25. Unsaturated alcohol
27. Dirt
29. Cooking vessel
32. Like a challenging cross-country course
33. Absurd
34. ___ and order
35. Deeply
36. ___ tectonics
37. Hawaiian high chief during the reign of King Kamehameha III
38. Geese formation
39. Afrikaners
40. Coffee break snack
41. Blue
42. Elegant
43. Carved poles
44. Afghan coin
45. Put an edge on
46. Lingering flavor
52. Apprehend
54. Data transfer unit
55. Sicker
56. Imagine, old style
58. Advocate
59. Thump
60. Easter flower
61. Chuck
62. Checked out
63. *Lux et veritas* school

DOWN

1. Grinder
2. The Kardashians, e.g.
3. Untangled
4. Skillful
5. Bummed out
6. Chevy, for one
7. Angler's equipment
8. Amino acid
9. Commingle
10. Entre ___
11. Blood ___
12. Cluckers
14. *Dead Souls* author
21. Battering wind
23. Cracker Jack bonus
25. Handmade weapons
26. Skin problem
27. Animal catcher
28. Feed bag contents
29. Hayden and Adler
30. Caulking fiber
31. Dweebs
33. Holly
36. Plaster
37. Strongly
39. Cloud
40. Exclamation popularized by Homer Simpson
43. Hip-and-booty centered dance
44. Feet, according to Ovid
46. Adjoin
47. Betting game
48. Yanks
49. Compatriot
50. Pivot (var.)
51. Be inclined
53. ___ weevil
57. 25th letter

ACROSS

1. *Buddenbrooks* novelist
5. Like kelp
10. Messy dresser
14. Margarine
15. Police officer in Ireland
16. Food sticker
17. Areas on weather maps
18. One of the five basic tastes
19. Adjoin
20. Alcohol, e.g.
22. Slang for "gossip"
23. Change, as a clock
24. Census datum
25. Josh
26. Call, as a game
28. Be a go-between
31. Mad cow acronym
34. Adds
38. *China Beach* setting: Abbr.
39. ___ Mound in Florida
40. Lining up perfectly
41. Shareholder meeting: Abbr.
42. Tater ___
43. Mountain climbers' tools
44. Post hole tool
45. Forever, poetically
47. Dispose (of)
49. Attach
50. Boil stuff
53. Three-dimensional graph line
57. Two-masted ship
59. Birth of a child, e.g.
61. Sworn pledge
62. Arise
63. Data
64. Dart
65. Swelling
66. Bolted
67. Come clean, with "up"
68. "See ya"
69. ___ election

DOWN

1. Grinder
2. Solo
3. Pond creatures
4. More intrusive
5. Chill
6. Reading lights
7. Shred cheese
8. Blend
9. Flock member
10. Sporting venues
11. Lusty
12. Obligation
13. Actress Behrs
21. Editorial action
25. Extra large
27. Madcap comedy
28. Introvert
29. 2006 mine disaster site
30. Television award
31. Information unit
32. Ashy residue
33. Intestinal inflammation
35. Billiard stick
36. Mauna ___
37. Half a dozen
46. ACLU concern
48. Boat hoists
50. Bamboo-eating bear
51. Discomfit
52. Foam
54. Arc lamp gas
55. Prefix with red
56. South African porch
57. Belly laugh
58. Breathing noise
59. Command to a dog
60. Calendar span

ACROSS

1. Do laps
5. ___ about (roams)
9. Atmosphere
13. Flax: Latin
15. Not much
16. "Tabula Rasa" composer Pärt
17. *Non plus* ___
18. Bottom
19. Breakfast, lunch, or dinner
20. Flew
22. Fleshy mushroom
23. Spouse
24. Restaurant reading
25. Big-time
27. Blatant deception
30. Drudgery
31. Ranked
32. Bearing false witness
34. DC Comics supervillain, the Polka-___ Man
37. Affirm
38. Borscht need
39. Antelope of Africa
40. Lent's start, e.g.: Abbr.
41. Stick-on
42. Like a rainbow
43. Em, to Dorothy
44. Designate
46. EGOT winner Whoopi
50. Early pulpit
51. Chopped
52. Enemy
53. Maracas materials
56. Close, as an envelope
57. Creep
59. Creeper
60. Combustible heap
61. Small child (var.)
62. Aquarium fish
63. Transmit
64. Boat with an open hold
65. Appear

DOWN

1. Wallop
2. *Elf* star Ferrell
3. Insinuated
4. Whodunit revelation
5. Blah-blah-blah
6. Counters
7. Bring down
8. "My boys, by marriage"
9. Bat, cat, or rat
10. Companion of Artemis
11. Egg-shaped
12. Handouts
14. Attendant on Dionysus
21. Clunker
26. Napoleon in *Animal Farm*, e.g.
27. Stick in one's ___
28. Possess
29. The "E" in EDM
33. Assent
34. Advanced degree
35. European auto
36. All alternative
38. Vacation and insurance, e.g.
39. Public defenders
41. Add sound to video
42. Maximally
43. Confused
45. Bother
46. Short pants
47. Daisy variety
48. Discover
49. Small lizard
54. Acute
55. Close forcefully
58. Conform

ACROSS

1. Japanese soup
5. Ices
9. Cornered, 2 wds.
14. Creep
15. Game on horseback
16. Blush
17. Lowlife
18. Coll. figure
19. Breathtaking part of a sentence
20. Suddenly, on a score
22. ___Smurf
24. Bigotry
26. Chilled
30. Inch or mile, e.g.
34. Grin
38. Aquarium
39. Commanded
40. Accept
41. Dispel
42. Quark-plus-antiquark particle
43. Board member, for short
44. Jaywalking, e.g.
45. Driver's lic., e.g.
46. Dimmable light, once
49. Cook, as clams
50. Informant
54. Energy
57. Casual top
59. Cyclist's wear
63. Inclined
65. Margarine
66. Babel, e.g.
67. Chill
68. Bandmate of Keith
69. Deep-sixes
70. Beethoven's birthplace
71. Deduct

DOWN

1. Sandra Bullock film ___ *Congeniality*
2. Bring upon oneself
3. Deep-sea diver's gear
4. ___ resistance
5. Counter
6. In favor of
7. Bomb
8. Couch
9. Esoteric
10. Also
11. Depress, with "out"
12. Shareholders' summit
13. Assent
21. Countdown device
23. Fried-rice additive
25. ___ of honor
27. Fix firmly
28. ___ and desist
29. ___ a high note
31. Peter, Paul, or Mary
32. Annuls
33. Camping gear
34. Abandon
35. Flammable wormwood derivative
36. Dead to the world
37. *LOST* castaway John ___
42. Diminished by
44. Dog tag information
47. Lepers
48. No-good
51. Diamond, e.g.
52. Eyelashes
53. At attention
55. Q-tip, e.g.
56. Like some orders
58. Drag
59. Inc., abroad
60. "___ are my sunshine"
61. Semicircular basin in a mountain
62. Congressional title: Abbr.
64. Mother Teresa, for one

ACROSS

1. Red ink amount
5. Genuine
9. The "C" in U.P.C.
13. Sea eagle
14. Send to the canvas
15. Having round projections
16. During
17. Cause to continue indefinitely
19. Easy out
21. Secretary of State Blinken
22. Fragrant resin
23. Antiquated
24. Short-order order, for short
27. Celtics legend Bill ___
29. Chemical compound
30. Emerging again
35. *Challenger* and *Atlantis*, e.g.
38. Building at O'Hare
39. ___ gin fizz
40. Sour milk
45. Detachable container
46. A place for China
50. Debonair
51. Capital on the Sava River
52. Himalayan region
53. Vitamin E form
57. *The ___ Ranger*
58. Certain exams
59. *Apteryx australis*
60. Bed or bunk (UK)
61. Sicilian volcano
62. Ad headline
63. Runny nose output

DOWN

1. Ballerina, at times
2. Ersatz gold leaf
3. *Blade* star Wesley ___
4. Stonecrops
5. Barely get, with "out"
6. Poultice
7. Howler
8. Law school class
9. Homey
10. Martial arts belt
11. Actor Levy or Aykroyd
12. Fraction of a joule
15. Ancestry
18. Discouraging words
20. Go through
24. Cheese on crackers
25. Camera's "eye"
26. What "it" plays
28. Bad look
29. www.youtube.com, e.g.
31. ___ Beta Kappa
32. Festive centerpiece
33. And others, for short
34. "Finally!"
35. Fodder holder
36. Egg on
37. Absorbed, as a cost
38. Egyptian snake
41. Erects
42. African primate
43. "Be that as it may…"
44. Take back to the lab
46. Chance occurrences
47. "Blech!"
48. Exhausting trips
49. Glass-polishing compound
51. French novelist Émile
53. Digit
54. Crumb
55. "___ you hear me now?"
56. Deception

ACROSS

1. Boring
5. Coll. degrees
8. Barrel downhill
14. Abounding
15. Crooked
16. Move in a leisurely way (UK)
17. Blends
19. Rocky Balboa's wife
20. Schwarzenegger title character
22. Tried to get home
23. Burdened
24. Believes (archaic)
25. Apostle to the Slavs
29. Ammonia derivatives
31. Forested
33. At the first opportunity
36. Quiet
37. Sumatran ape, for short
39. Black, as *la nuit*
41. Commonwealth's capital
43. Without difficulty
45. Airport area
47. "Good" mob member
48. Hoisted, nautically
51. Socrates disciple
53. Can of worms
54. John Wayne Gacy, e.g.
59. Harden
61. Lock up
62. Consider again
63. *The Grapes of Wrath* protagonist Joad
64. Complain
65. "Valse ___": Sibelius work
66. Grinder
67. Sort

DOWN

1. No angel
2. Citrus fruit
3. Way out
4. Bridge site
5. Swahili for "boss"
6. Fighting force
7. Efficiency experts
8. Bandy words
9. Atlantic catch
10. Savvy
11. Handy
12. Assassinated
13. Mails
18. Fish features
21. French ___ soup
24. Cyst
25. Semicircular basin in a mountain
26. "No More I Love ___": Annie Lennox song
27. Roster (UK)
28. A spy might have many
30. Chief official of Venice or Genoa
32. Part of BYO
34. Dirt
35. Cash register
38. Level connectors
40. Scandinavian rug
42. Offensive word in multiple contexts
44. Happening
46. Lozenge
48. Cancel
49. Electric dart shooter
50. Hindu poet
52. Opposable digit
54. Combustible heap
55. Agreement
56. "Go ___!"
57. Ballfield covering
58. Hoopla
60. Word with Tuesday or cat

ACROSS

1. Cole ___
5. Give rise to
10. "Cut it out!"
14. "That hurt!"
15. Asian capital
16. Insect stage
17. Fancy cheese
18. Church vestibule
20. Guard duty
22. Early job for Caesar
23. Satellite ___
24. Burned up
26. Deck (out)
28. Assent
29. Bad grades
33. Short for "chromolithograph"
36. G.Q., e.g.
37. ___ Deo Gloria
38. University of Hawaii ___ Warriors
40. Beef thief
42. Advocate
43. ___-com bubble
45. Ammonia derivatives
46. Dec. holiday
47. "___ you know"
48. Full Metal Jacket setting: Abbr.
49. Obscure
51. Easy dupes
54. Better half
58. Petroleum distillates
61. Gap
63. Farm call
64. Smeltery refuse
65. Canadian Nobel laureate Alice
66. Miles per hour, e.g.
67. Apprentice
68. Encourage
69. High-five, e.g.

DOWN

1. Breaks down
2. Drawn
3. Blackberry drupelets
4. Sharpening tools
5. Open carriage
6. Broad-bladed knife
7. Opposite word
8. Anguish
9. Rubén Darío, e.g.
10. Mining nail
11. ___-Guarani languages
12. ___ Corsa
13. Blanched
19. ___ Arnold! animated TV show
21. Diamond, e.g.
25. Reverse, e.g.
27. "Heavens!"
29. Assessors
30. Close up
31. Beat it
32. Gentlemen
33. Central point
34. Do damage to
35. Baltic capital
39. Golf club
41. "All Star" band ___ Mouth
44. Lacing
49. Sticker
50. Computer shortcut
52. Elixir container
53. December 24 visitor
54. Atomizer output
55. Deeply
56. Celebrity
57. Utah ghost town
59. Drudge
60. Beehive
62. Tow a vessel

ACROSS

1. Afternoon tea (UK)
6. Curtain materials
12. Away from the ocean
14. Loss of voice
15. Small anchor
17. Without a hitch
18. Wavy
19. Little Italy dessert specialty
20. Medal of Honor's recognition
22. Beaujolais, e.g.
23. Leftovers
24. Country singer's sound
26. Colo. neighbor
27. Famed conquistador
28. Obsequious one
32. Bar worker
33. Fibulae neighbors
34. Flipper
35. About
36. Australian lizards
40. ___ Day
41. Delusions
43. ___ king crab
46. Clogged
48. Finch family birds
49. X-shaped cross
50. Coop flier
51. Twerp
52. Enter
53. Daphnaie, e.g.

DOWN

1. Butts
2. Disassemble
3. Flat
4. Skin blemish
5. Chronicles
6. Expand
7. Olympic figure skating gold medalist Nathan
8. Reddish horse
9. Be creative
10. Bonnet crafter
11. Idioms
13. Captive
14. African capital
16. Borrower's need
21. Butter holder
24. Haul
25. Crooked
27. Vatican dogma
28. Playoff survivor
29. State of limbo
30. Get the W
31. Singer ___ King Cole
32. Blooms in Whitman's dooryard
33. Hot stuff
34. In favor of
36. Big house
37. Chilled
38. DH part
39. Lustrous
41. Eucharist plate
42. Glass-polishing compound
44. Become unhinged
45. Visored cap
47. Act

ACROSS

1. Donkey (UK slang)
5. Australian runner
8. *Habeas corpus*, e.g.
12. Get ready, for short
13. Schumer, e.g.: Abbr.
14. ___ hoop
15. Inexperienced
17. Explosive
18. ___ says…
19. *Fantasy Island* prop
20. Propeller
21. Software program, briefly
22. Listless
25. Did laps
29. Fare reductions
30. Catch
34. Multicellular animals, collectively
36. Malevolent
38. ___ *dictum*
39. Bimetallic Canadian coin
40. Lego® ___ toy line
42. "Black dragon" teas
43. "-zoic" things
44. Civil rights org.
46. Fraction of a newton
47. Cast out
49. Nave bench
51. ___-crab soup
52. Amateur video subject
55. "Love, all alike, no season knows, nor ___": Donne
57. Final: Abbr.
58. Antipasto morsel
61. Arizona tribe
62. Back stabber
63. Assortment
64. Mimic
65. "___ we having fun yet?"
66. Blue hue

DOWN

1. Automobile sticker fig.
2. Hockey legend Bobby
3. Fall (over)
4. Blunted blade
5. Baltic nation
6. Household
7. Falsehood
8. Beat to a froth
9. Beef cut
10. UN workers' org.
11. Lay out
16. *Nada*
18. Blue
23. Like fans
24. Heavy hydrogen, e.g.
25. Walloped, old-style
26. Sociologist Max
27. Ancient city NW of Carthage
28. Arithmetic, to a Brit
30. Endured
31. Fool
32. Adjust
33. "Silly" birds
35. ___ *and the Art of Motorcycle Maintenance*
37. *Costa del* ___
41. Break in poetry
42. Group of eight (var.)
45. Building stone
47. Wooly female
48. Bert and Ernie, e.g.
49. Snowman prop
50. Ruler
53. Fluffy mass
54. Greasy
55. When doubled, a dance
56. Chop (off)
59. By way of
60. Long, long time

ACROSS

1. Flatten, as a fly
5. Attired
9. Disney shuttle
13. Famed tower locale
14. Maxims
16. Rend
17. African antelope
18. Lumberjacks
19. Not many
20. Blue jean fabrics
22. Testifiers
24. Inched
26. "A likely story!"
27. ___ Hall in Buddhist temples
29. Czech diacritical
32. Blue
35. Delivered
36. Mechanical solar system model
37. Blackguard
38. Crazily
39. Native New Zealander
40. Pay (up)
41. Swampy marsh
42. Cinematic
43. Bard's instrument, maybe
44. Cracker Jack bonus
45. Book of maps
46. Debaucher
47. Destroy the interior
48. Legislate
50. Scorning
55. Eastern bishop
58. Arm bone
59. Who "ever loved you more than I," in song
61. Lecher
62. Lays down the lawn
63. Outfit
64. Spoil, with "on"
65. ___ motion animation
66. Drunkards
67. Didn't dillydally

DOWN

1. Geek (UK slang)
2. Bank transfer
3. When things occur at unrelated times
4. Cabstand, at Heathrow
5. Catch
6. Bagel topping
7. Ancient
8. Acute
9. Garbage
10. Abounding
11. Affirm
12. Cat calls
15. Varying slightly from a perfectly spherical shape
21. Big Apple attraction, with "the"
23. Like certain trees
25. State of submission
27. To the rear
28. Beau
30. Bouquet
31. Red shade
32. Group with merit badges
33. Familial nickname
34. Clothesline alternative
36. Leaving out
40. Displayers of protest slogans
42. Caprine deity
46. "Bleeding Gums" Murphy's instrument in *The Simpsons*
47. Clutch
49. Turnips (with haggis)
50. Figure (out)
51. Connive
52. Annul
53. Denials
54. Attend
56. Adorable
57. Attention
60. Cashew, e.g.

ACROSS

1. Divine Hindu spirit
5. Diving duck
10. Almanac tidbit
14. Affirm
15. "Hungry, hungry" critter of a kid's game
16. Not straight
17. Green, in heraldry
18. "Halt!" to a salt
19. Acquire
20. Cemetery ceremony
22. Artful move
23. Unit of volume (usually for wood)
24. Anklebones
26. Apron tops
28. Catches on
29. Boxer
32. Little one
34. Audio accessory
36. Certain pitch
38. *Hamilton*'s Lin-Manuel ___
39. Groups of eight (var.)
41. Openness
42. Anguish
43. Em, to Dorothy
44. All alternative
45. Bad looks
47. "Beat it!"
50. Ground cover
54. Tummy settler
56. Baltic capital
57. *The Godfather* subject
58. Not much
59. Not many
60. Proficient
61. Beat it
62. Govt. officials
63. Affirmatives
64. Be inclined

DOWN

1. "Birth of the Cool" trumpeter
2. Javelin, e.g.
3. Like a sunfish but not a starfish
4. Blood vessel connected to a capillary
5. Bogus
6. Cat of Africa
7. Grant of resources (var.)
8. Against the current
9. Stovetop vessel
10. Betting game
11. Blown away
12. Mountain goat's perch
13. Sort
21. Contradictions, in court
22. Disparagement
25. Stringent
27. Alfresco art
29. Cogitable
30. Annul
31. Reverse, e.g.
32. Boat with an open hold
33. Somewhat, in music
35. Knitting or whittling, e.g.
37. Apostate or traitor
40. Bitter conflicts
46. Marsh bird
48. Roswell crash victim, supposedly
49. Allotted, with "out"
50. Five-time U.S. Open champ
51. Abounding
52. Ancient
53. Adages
55. Heaters
57. ___ Day

ACROSS

1. Feathery accessories
5. Sleep in a tent
9. Roger Daltrey, Pete Townshend, John Entwistle, and Keith Moon, collectively, with "The"
12. Scoreboard stat
15. Aroma
16. Afflict
17. Flat, narrow molding
18. Fictionalize (var.)
20. Largest crustaceans
22. Countable
23. Easy to sketch
24. Cuban actress de Armas
27. Skye or Wight
30. Intestinal parts
31. *Blazing Saddles* director Brooks
32. Market town
34. "___ moment"
35. 13th-century Anglo-Scottish raider
37. Fraction of a joule
38. Like a summertime tea or coffee, maybe
40. Artless one
41. Fraternity letters
42. Tax enforcers
46. Precedence
49. Meticulously
52. Minded the mansion
53. Bitter disagreement
54. Doc bloc
55. Locale
56. Tapeworm
57. Beige shade
58. Caribbean and others
59. Animal shelters

DOWN

1. Road shoulder
2. Mountain nymph
3. ___-bargle
4. Protective book-shaped box
5. Makes a treatment inadvisable
6. Darling
7. Not fixed
8. Give prior approval
9. Farm cart
10. Sibilant
11. Nashville's Grand ___ Opry
13. Come again
14. Leaf opening
19. Deposit, as an egg
21. Clinch, with "up"
24. "What ___ ___, ___ mind reader?"
25. Birthmarks
26. Hebrew leader (var.)
27. Surefooted goat
28. Fern clusters
29. Big galoots
33. 50-foot woman
34. Excessive accumulation of serous fluid in tissue (UK)
36. Caught
39. Excessively cute (var.)
43. Lunar new year
44. Horace, for one
45. Cyma ___ : molding type
46. Donkey
47. "Crazy" singer Patsy
48. Fey
49. Cell body
50. Chinese currency unit
51. Affirmative votes
52. Fedora, e.g.

ACROSS

1. Wallop
5. Two-thirds of a mile, in Russia
10. *Are You There ___? It's Me, Margaret.*
13. Continental bills
15. Mountain crest
16. Use an oar
17. *Buffy the Vampire Slayer* spin-off
18. Identify
20. Gets ready to drive
22. Nutty
23. European auto
24. Copy of a sketch
26. Actress Mae
27. Jerk (var.)
30. Distributed
32. Aerial maneuver
33. Putting the squeeze on
38. Cool
40. *Andrea Doria*'s home port
41. Rousing
47. *Laugh-In* segment
48. Tapeworm
49. Phoenician trading center
50. In doubt
54. Nerve (var.)
56. Balsam
57. DIY-er's purchase
58. Line from a sail
62. Climbed awkwardly
65. Kidney enzyme
66. Popular fruit drink
67. Development areas
68. Old Asian capital
69. Talk, talk, talk
70. Big name in chicken
71. Ed Sullivan's "really big" one

DOWN

1. Ticket unit
2. Crescent
3. Advocate
4. Deteriorates
5. Alt. spelling
6. Recluse
7. Takes back
8. Fuddy-duddies
9. One-year-old sheep
10. Beef
11. Exudes
12. Lived
14. Aspersion
19. Not later
21. Touch
25. ___ *anglais*: English horn
27. Concrete section
28. Burrow
29. CNN journalist Jeanne ___
31. Grooved on
34. Public facilities next to a highway, 2 wds.
35. Black
36. Film genre
37. Box office take
39. Hale
42. Uncontrollably noisy
43. Brings back on board
44. 1993 Nirvana album
45. Coll. hoops competition
46. See stars
50. Feeling a need to scratch
51. Leaflike layers
52. Intense adverse criticism
53. "Mmmm"
55. Buddy
59. Creep
60. "Good going!"
61. Vex, with "at"
63. Except
64. Noise

ACROSS

1. "___ in the face"
5. Some needles
10. As a result
14. Daughter of Zeus
15. Acoustic
16. Easily maneuverable, as a vessel
17. Common small-town street name
18. Fumes from a fire
19. Anger
20. ___ out
22. Added seasoning to
24. Sought help from
27. Low-alcohol beverage
30. More terrible
35. Arm bone
36. Sorts
39. Grandma's nickname
40. Catcher's gear
41. White heron
42. "___ in a Manger": Christmas carol
43. Drag
44. Macbeth, for one
45. Dole out
46. Hiding place
48. Bleeped
50. Slaughterhouse
53. Feeding tubes
57. Ball carriers
61. Lou Gehrig number
62. Acre divisions
65. Plane, e.g.
66. Detonator (var.)
67. Boredom
68. Car
69. Feed the pigs
70. Fix
71. What 'X' marks

DOWN

1. Jerk (var.)
2. Ballet move
3. Not much
4. Passes through
5. Consumes
6. "Delicious!"
7. Two-thirds or three-quarters, e.g., 2 wds.
8. Matured in barrels, as chardonnay
9. Caught some Zs
10. One of four, on a lorry
11. Sea fret
12. Advocate
13. Lentil, e.g.
21. Raise to knighthood
23. Detachable container
25. Change, as a clock
26. Whinny
27. Deadens
28. *Four Quartets* poet
29. Bone cavities
31. Lady loves
32. Less cooked
33. Related maternally
34. Emitted sunbeams
37. Article of faith
38. Court figure
47. "A likely story!"
49. Sis or bro
51. Exposed
52. Past, quaintly
53. Bad grades
54. Essence
55. Anise-flavored liqueur
56. Get ready, for short
58. Masterstroke
59. Instrument with thirteen strings
60. Coin opening
63. Directly
64. Half a dozen

ACROSS

1. Rhus plants (var.)
8. Holds
14. Bothering
16. Atoll center
17. Worldwide crime-fighter
18. Curved high-back bench
19. Drops from the sky
20. British dandy
22. "Shoot!"
23. ___ place
26. "Here We Go 'Round the Mulberry ___"
28. Support person
30. Anxiety
35. Cecum, 2 wds.
39. Morphine or codeine, e.g.
40. Houston university
41. Catnip and basil, e.g.
43. Attention ___
44. Badly mannered Australians
46. Malcolm Gladwell's 2008 book
48. Zoom alternative
49. Long, narrow groove
50. Joint problem
52. Puts down
57. Sprint
61. Not much
63. Contributed
64. "Begone!"
66. Winked
69. Mosquito-borne fever
70. Some stable work
71. Dialects
72. Stretch

DOWN

1. Sudden discharge of liquid (var.)
2. They stretch from the elbow to the smallest finger
3. Canonical hour
4. Bond, for one
5. Blackguard
6. Cool
7. ___ rocket
8. Staff leaders
9. Calif. airport
10. Ancient
11. Fizzy drink
12. Blue books
13. Catch
15. Traveling
21. It's a wrap
24. "We've been ___!"
25. "Ah!" and "Whew!"
27. Fictional duo ___ and Leonard
29. Expected
31. Not yet final, in law
32. Be slack-jawed
33. Antares, for one
34. Addition column
35. Movie studio Warner ___
36. Beat
37. Gross
38. Turnip, in Edinburgh
39. Port of ancient Rome
42. Sticker
45. Not decaf.
47. Popular family dog, for short
49. Grinder
51. Prolific author Joyce Carol ___
53. Blue-headed lizard
54. Fancy fabric
55. Balances
56. Bulrush, e.g.
57. Arp's art
58. Affirm
59. Caroled
60. Justice Black
62. Radial, e.g.
65. Cashew, e.g.
67. *Succession* actor Brian ___
68. Blouse, e.g.

ACROSS

1. Offerings on *The Great British Baking Show*: Abbr.
5. Steps to the Ganges
9. Kiss
13. Basket material
15. Gray wolf
16. Deeply
17. Blind mice head-count
18. Knitter's need
19. *Charlie's Angels* actress Cameron
20. Rewards
21. Rugged cliff
22. Jealousy
23. Inverse function in trigonometry
25. Hoover or Three Gorges
27. One-year-old sheep
28. ___ pick (quibble)
29. Breviloquent
31. Mimicry
33. "___ you know"
35. Know (Archaic)
36. Latin for "heart"
37. Hot drink
39. Bulgarian currency
41. Ending for ab- or ad-
43. Deity
44. Holiday drink
46. Hairy coat
47. Grave marker
49. Type of solution (as in a lab)
51. *Foxy Brown* actor ___ Grier
53. Pro's opposite
54. Ewe homonym
56. Adriatic Sea republic
58. Blown away
60. Havana's home
62. Amalgam
63. "___ good and ill…": Tennyson
64. "Follow me!"
65. Any Platters platter
66. Blue-green hue
67. Prefix with -crat or -graph
68. Like a shoe
69. Cry
70. Disorder
71. Apprentice

DOWN

1. British pub worker
2. Showing
3. World Health Organization leader, e.g.
4. Top competitors
5. Antifreeze compound
6. Frost
7. Rub
8. Polynesian island nation
9. Dwell
10. Continuously
11. Drivel
12. Celestial alignment
14. Change chairs
24. ___ *Jack City*: 1991 Wesley Snipes film
26. Certain computers
30. Court figure
32. Sound that indicates a sudden disappearance
34. Sweater material
38. Aussie greeting
40. Fissures in the earth's crust
42. More bright
45. Long-jawed fish
47. Lacking discretion (UK)
48. Long-tailed bird
49. Loose, brightly colored dress
50. Los ___: band known for "La Bamba" cover
52. Got by
55. Philosopher William of ___
57. Apportion
59. Plaything
61. Twitter scourge

ACROSS

1. Obi, e.g.
5. Duke Ellington's "Take ___ ___ Train"
9. To the left, at sea
14. Ford product
15. Affectation
16. UK Prime Minister Tony
17. Apothecary's weight
18. Atlantic fish
19. Deep-voiced singer
20. Nonstop
22. Glued
24. European tax
25. Cafeteria carrier
26. Queen (Latin): Abbr.
28. Aggravation
33. Backs out
39. Not posh (UK)
40. Hurting
41. Haul
42. GPs
43. Beehive
44. Kitchen towels, 2 wds.
47. Maidenheads
50. Nanki-___: The Mikado
51. Goals
54. Aisle escorts
59. Teary
63. Kind of network
64. In conflict with, with "of"
65. Hit the road
67. Big name in pasta sauce
68. Taste, e.g.
69. Binge
70. Bygone talent show ___ Search
71. More dainty (UK)
72. Active
73. Chuck

DOWN

1. Slang for a socially inept person (UK)
2. Containing gold
3. Begin
4. Marge's husband
5. More delicious
6. Popular kids' drink
7. Belch
8. According to, 2 wds.
9. Nuns' milieus
10. Agenda
11. Kiln for drying hops
12. Get up
13. Trample
21. Fireplace supply
23. "Welcome" object
27. Intl. commerce pact
29. Annul
30. Carrot, e.g.
31. Creep
32. Figure (out)
33. B.C. neighbor
34. Gross
35. Not us
36. Promote
37. Anguish
38. Cashless deal
45. Tim McGraw's music
46. Ditch
48. Worker who attaches something
49. ___ card
52. Dairy treats
53. Snooze
55. Imitation of Life novelist Fannie ___
56. A muse
57. Indian melodies
58. Epithets
59. Bringing up the rear
60. Not many
61. Ice cream vessel
62. Con
66. ___ cry

ACROSS

1. Limp Bizkit's Fred ___
6. Bad grades
10. Appear
14. Muse of love poetry
15. All-Star pitcher Pappas
16. Forearm bone
17. *Doctor Dolittle* actress Samantha ___
18. Cloud
19. Baa
20. Destined
21. After-bath wear
22. Lo-cal
23. Pasta shape
25. Addict, e.g.
27. Wisdom
31. Of city govt.
32. British dessert, for short
33. Group of eight
35. Ayatollah's decree
39. Ever, 2 wds.
41. Police, with "the"
42. Frock wearer
43. Kind of pain
44. Chip away at
46. "The Rum ___ Tugger": *Cats* song
47. *Fast and Furious* actor Diesel
49. Ill-tempered (UK)
51. *Top Gun* top-billed
54. Ax-like tool
55. ___ Christian Andersen
56. Caution
59. Available
63. Creep
64. Blown away
65. Tennis star Osaka
66. Whimper
67. Box office take
68. ___ ___ a high note
69. Didn't dillydally
70. Checked out
71. Feed, as a fire

DOWN

1. Adjudge
2. Advocate
3. Eastern music
4. Ballad part
5. Wryneck
6. Make delicate
7. Flaky dough: Var.
8. Bungle
9. Watch Netflix or Hulu, e.g.
10. Situated between the earth and the moon
11. ___ Island National Monument
12. Related maternally
13. *Alma* ___
24. ___-tac-toe
26. Neutral regions between warring parties
27. Bandy words
28. Mercedes, for one
29. Aussie greeting
30. A long time
34. Ambidextrous
36. South American monkey
37. Cry (UK)
38. ___ brat
40. Showered, as gifts
45. "___ not!"
48. Enya genre
50. Renter
51. Side with fish
52. Incurred
53. "I give up!"
57. Not a home game
58. Anatomical nerve network
60. ___ list
61. Crazily
62. Durable wood

ACROSS

1. Beach feature
5. American boxer ___ Willard
9. Globular
14. History muse
15. Run ___: go wild
16. Frigid
17. Annul
18. Calf-length skirt
19. Metal-bending tool
20. ___, present, future
21. Curses
23. Bottom
25. Introverts
26. Bay of Naples isle
29. "Cut it out!"
31. Spanish for "spin"
32. "___ with you!"
33. Brand suffix with Star or Sun
37. Distilled Levantine spirits
38. Republican, for short
39. Like a forest of firs
40. Fraction of a newton
41. ___ mortals
42. Bavarian river
43. Scottish pirate Captain ___
44. Glasgow's river
45. Back problem
49. Sit in the sun
51. Teen idol
54. Absorbed
58. Atlas enlargement
59. Not hard
60. Get-up-and-go
61. Nickel, e.g.
62. Chimney channel
63. Prize since 1949
64. Flat
65. Addition column
66. Fledgling bird

DOWN

1. Atlantic porgy
2. Arm bone
3. Clears
4. It'll slow you down, 2 wds.
5. Door beams
6. *South Pacific* hero
7. Mountain Dew, e.g.
8. Goes downhill
9. Australian thrift store, 2 wds.
10. Aftermath
11. Hold responsible
12. Avid
13. Shift, e.g.
22. Clever tactic
24. Affectation
26. Neighbor of Libya
27. Breezy
28. Agenda
29. *The ___ in the Stone*: 1963 Disney film
30. Bind
32. Ancient
33. Aggressive stinger
34. Deeply
35. Lentil, e.g.
36. Phoenician trading center
39. Basketball maneuver
41. In perfect condition
43. Ticklish (Scot.)
45. Adjusts with a wedge
46. Article of faith
47. Bob Marley fan
48. "He's ___ ___ nowhere man" (Beatles lyric), 2 wds.
49. Bill Bobstay on the H.M.S. *Pinafore*
50. Makes up for (archaic)
52. Bulk
53. Breathing noise
55. ___ of one
56. Cotton fabric
57. Marine Corps charity ___ for Tots

ACROSS

1. "Grand" feat at Wrigley or Fenway
5. A head
9. Blotto
14. ___ ___ list
15. Charge
16. Kind of cycle
17. Anise-flavored liqueur
18. Cleaving tool
19. Build on, 2 wds.
20. Small songbird
21. Desolate
22. Tiny openings
23. Bakery treat
25. Hearing specialist
26. Engine part
29. Big shot
30. Brinks vehicle, 2 wds.
33. Easy dupes
37. "Crazy" bird
38. *Only Murders in the Building* actor Martin
39. Uncontaminated
40. Kid
41. Publishing employee
43. Use an axe
44. Election decider
45. Lost one's lunch
49. Black ___
51. Bicker
52. Central points
53. Follower of Mary
57. Practice
58. A little lamb
59. Deuce topper
60. Crack
61. Forearm bone
62. Affirm
63. Escalator feature
64. Get-out-of-jail money
65. Creep (along)

DOWN

1. House
2. Frown
3. Cutting tool
4. Feldspar variety
5. Bloomed
6. Composer ___ Copland
7. Ten million rupees
8. Axed
9. Excellent meal (UK), 2 wds.
10. Elizabeth I was the last one
11. Large lemur
12. Clotho and friends
13. Garden threat
24. N.T. book
25. Concourse, 2 wds.
26. Season
27. *Iliad* city
28. Crazily
29. Be different
31. Arab sailboat
32. Police officer
33. Band in a 1984 film parody, 2 wds.
34. Ford, for one
35. Coll. figure
36. Peasant
42. Add sound effects
43. Followed commands
45. Verb with thou
46. Drop the ball, e.g.
47. Catlike
48. Part of the female anatomy
49. Slang for "money"
50. Blackberry drupelets
52. Bungle
54. Composer Pärt
55. Docile
56. Cow barn (UK)

ACROSS

1. Give away
5. Hurting
9. Breathing noise
13. Bumpkin
14. Chimney channel
15. Scout's mission
16. Deeply
17. Eastern music
18. Olympic decathlete Ashton
19. Adventures
21. Heavy accent in Sydney, jocularly
22. Cool, once
23. Rupture
24. Grammy-winning *Late Show* bandleader Jon
27. Ancient
28. Huge
29. Bond
30. Discouraging words
31. Two-year-old sheep
32. Thomas Jefferson, religiously
33. Destroy the interior of
34. "A likely story!"
35. Campus military org.
36. NYC art institution
37. Rake
38. Ready for more
40. Asian wild sheep
42. Blue
43. Arranged in layers
44. Certain young fish, pl.
49. Reggae musician faith, often
50. "Hold it right there!"
51. The "C" in T.L.C.
52. Absolute
53. "Take it ___"
54. Experienced
55. Call for
56. Foundational garments
57. Open wide

DOWN

1. Get-up-and-go
2. Bergman in *Casablanca*
3. Well
4. Ottoman governors
5. A figure in Arabic mythology
6. Shooter's target, 2 wds.
7. Holds close
8. Assent
9. Rejiggered
10. Tyke's attention-seeking, 2 wds.
11. Most out-to-lunch
12. Group of nine
15. Anatomical nerve network
20. Catch, as flies
21. Sleep on it
24. Generous
25. Buttonholes, e.g.
26. City on the Black Warrior River
28. Classic Gary Cooper film, 2 wds.
31. Saturate
32. Ancient Celtic priest
36. Cry like a baby
37. Busy side road (UK), 2 wds.
39. ___ horoscope
41. *Laughable Lyrics* writer Edward ___
44. Blacken
45. Gross
46. Mama's mama
47. Got bigger
48. Stitched
50. Fly catcher

ACROSS

1. They may provide relief
5. Aloe, e.g.
10. Excellent (Scot.)
14. Adjoin
15. Primmer (UK)
16. Cleanse
17. Prisoner?, 2 wds.
19. Ancient
20. Big name in hand tools
21. Leftovers
23. Male sheep
24. ___ mortals
26. Pergola
29. Of city govt.
30. Hamlet's father, e.g.
35. Blacken
36. Father of Leah and Rachel
38. Black
39. Spanish for "I gave in"
40. Something to remember, in Texas
41. Two aces, e.g.
42. Baltic capital
43. Ballpoint pens (UK)
44. Durable wood
45. About
47. Needlefish
48. Cities with piers
49. Farm call
51. IG post
52. America or sandwich, e.g.
56. Gas station purchase
60. Chimney channel
61. Everlastings, as flowers
64. Discomfit
65. Disappearing phone features
66. Strengthen, with "up"
67. Nose substance
68. Provide, as with a quality
69. Bandy words

DOWN

1. Foot pads
2. Not much
3. Fast feline
4. Loud
5. Prepare, as tea
6. Not straight
7. Money in Sofia
8. Certain intersection
9. Blunder
10. Boring
11. Anger
12. Affirm
13. Joins
18. Aspersion
22. Certain sheep
24. Egyptian president for 30 years
25. Bewitch
26. African capital
27. Bonn's river, auf Deutsch
28. Symbol of authority
29. Libel
31. Wallet holders, 2 wds.
32. Broadcasting, 2 wds.
33. Strapped for cash (UK)
34. British wheels
36. ___ coat
37. Discouraging words
46. Cracker Jack bonus
48. Pub order
50. Ammonia derivative
51. Analyze
52. Bad grades
53. Agenda
54. Anise-flavored liqueur
55. Depilatory brand, once
56. Balsam
57. Bomb
58. Long bone in the forearm
59. Bad look
62. Equal to 60 sec.
63. Ticked off

ACROSS

1. High-hatter
5. Power glitch
10. Hogwash
14. Apple leftover
15. Self-replicating protein
16. Cart
17. Not designated
19. Puerto ___: U.S. territory
20. Its name means "black mountain"
21. Hurting
22. Colored like a certain hound
23. Cyst
25. Floor it
27. Cartography
33. Stick in one's ___
34. Corsages
35. Comedian and writer Elaine
36. Holed up
37. Great view at the opera
38. Lulu
39. Anguish
40. Exhaustive
41. British slang for time off school
42. Destructive felons
44. Bloated
45. Actor-director Stiller
46. Bainter and Wray
47. An inflorescence
50. Tocology
56. Frost
57. Highly pleasing
58. Anise-flavored aperitif
59. Accustom
60. Cat's scratcher
61. Small songbird
62. Arises
63. Custodian's collection

DOWN

1. Lowlife
2. Pitcher's goal
3. Fruity drinks
4. Scatter
5. Like a cactus
6. Advocate
7. Cabal
8. Attendee
9. Gift
10. Contracted
11. Flock member
12. "That hurt!"
13. Clever tactic
18. Lentil, e.g.
24. "Take it ___"
25. Pronunciation symbol
26. Former
27. Gals of guys with gats
28. Neck scarf
29. Devout
30. *Mission: ___* (film and TV franchise)
31. Manicurist's concern
32. Musical that introduced the standard "Everything's Coming Up Roses"
34. Recanting odes
37. *Bête noire*
41. Frame attached to a wagon to increase its load
43. Moon of Uranus
44. Intl. commerce pact
46. Stool
47. Dog with a blue-black tongue
48. Part of BYO
49. Labyrinth
51. Bowed
52. Pivot (var.)
53. Semester
54. Kind of court
55. Puts in stitches

162

ACROSS

1. Attempt
5. Early pulpit
9. Attired
13. In person
14. Latin American instrument made of a gourd
16. Blood pigment
17. Utopian
19. Good vantage point
20. Not giving up
21. Black
22. Travelled
23. Comedian's supply
25. Young salmon
27. Impish girl
31. Affectations
32. Draw (off) (var.)
36. British parent, familiarly
37. Quarterback Prescott
38. Driving away
39. Not a PC
40. Directly
41. Goes off
42. Exhausted, with "in"
43. Senescence, 2 wds.
45. Eucharist container
46. To no degree (UK)
48. "Exactly"
49. Jerk (var.)
52. Jabberers
57. Withdraw gradually
58. Reptilia type
59. Like certain trees
60. "Holy cow!"
61. Plod along
62. Big dance
63. Phoenician trading center
64. Allocate, with "out"

DOWN

1. Berth place
2. Conceal
3. Exploited
4. Old World prickly plants
5. Disparager of seniors
6. Essential
7. Angler's hope
8. Gasket
9. Consecrated oil
10. Boxer Spinks
11. Frenzied, with "run"
12. Buck
15. Eight-sided figures
18. Fluff
24. Jets or Sharks, e.g.
25. Uncool person (UK)
26. Meow
28. Everlasting flower
29. Delhi sides
30. Host
32. Astutely
33. Marvin Gaye's 1967 single
34. Appear, with "up"
35. Bestseller
38. ___ lily
42. Taoist principle
44. Alias
45. Chevy EV model
47. Blue eyes or baldness, e.g.
48. Breviloquent
49. Barter (UK)
50. Take in
51. Ocean menace
53. Gross
54. Swerve
55. Brawl
56. Thanksgiving herb

ACROSS

1. Wall hanging
6. Punish
12. Monkey bread tree
14. Bannister, Ryun, and Coe
15. Blended
17. "The way things are…"
18. Igneous rock
19. Talk, talk, talk
21. Focal point
22. Less cordial
24. Endure
26. Black
27. Balder's wife
28. *B.C.* comic-strip creator Johnny
29. Ad headline
30. Joys
31. Mucus
32. Reward
33. "A likely story!"
35. *True Lies* actor ___ Arnold
37. Tried to get home, maybe
41. "No problem!"
43. Metrical accent
48. Traffic marker
49. Catch
50. Like Eric the Red
51. Campus military org.
52. Ax-like tool
53. Inexperienced
54. Outline
56. A's opposite (UK)
58. Physics units
59. Type of gland
60. Desert wind
62. Supplement
63. Door-to-door salesman (var.)
64. Gets rid of
65. Drunken

DOWN

1. Degrading
2. Extreme
3. Salad ingredient
4. "Official Storybook Capital of America"
5. Lisa Simpson's instrument
6. Almond liqueur
7. ___-en-scène
8. Snobbery
9. 21-across, times two
10. Corrugation
11. Tried
13. Ottoman governor
16. Wiener dog
20. Meditation question
23. Foolhardy
25. Female mentees
34. Attacks
36. Like some vases
37. Fatal sheep disease
38. Coiling
39. Vivid
40. Edicts
42. Tease
44. Damage
45. Goo
46. It may be a lemon, 2 wds.
47. Kind of overload
55. Grocery bearer
57. Pickpocket, in slang
61. NBA stat

ACROSS

1. No angel
5. Cole ___
9. Jars
14. Ancestry
15. The "C" in UPC
16. Caribbean spiritualism
17. It is longer than the radius
18. Confusion
19. Car dealer's offering
20. Flourished
22. Breakfast meat units
23. Blue hue
24. Slope wear
26. Fancy clothes, 2 wds.
30. Emphatic
34. Coll. hoops competition
35. "Dang!"
36. Go-getter
37. Not much
39. In a line
41. Band member
42. Critic's write-up
45. Cleaner
48. Acorn, e.g.
49. "The ravell'd ___ of care": Shakespeare
50. "Lamb of God," 2 wds.
52. Force over matter
54. Sea mist (Scot.)
55. Electrical unit
58. Prepares potatoes
63. Prior to, old-style
64. Whispers sweet nothings
65. A frantic way to run
66. Enter, as a car, 2 wds.
67. Em, to Dorothy
68. Carp and minnows
69. Sign of exertion
70. At liberty
71. Halt

DOWN

1. Underwater exhalation sound
2. Brook
3. Instructional
4. Kidded around
5. Librarygoer
6. Sand, silt, and clay soil
7. Ax
8. Tends a garden
9. Joviality
10. Deferential
11. Economical
12. Charge
13. The Rolling Stones' "___ a Rainbow"
21. Reddish-brown gem
25. Josh
26. Growls
27. Actionable words
28. Needlefish
29. Leaf opening
31. Place to wash up
32. Permeate
33. Cousin of a raccoon
38. Coffee-flavored liqueur, 2 wds.
40. Shake
43. Clear
44. Cyst
46. Hurriedly, 2 wds.
47. Kind of household income
51. Lunchtime meals, maybe
53. Coffee order
55. Scottish radio comedy ___, *Mags and Bags*
56. Not many
57. Automatic
59. Bar order
60. Christmas decoration
61. Somewhat, in music
62. Large round wicker basket

ACROSS

1. Cashless deal
5. Anticipate
10. Easy dupes
14. Cleanse
15. Democratic Republic of the Congo, 1971-1997
16. Ball of thread or yarn
17. Canned
18. Austrian province
19. Arm bone
20. Fool's gold
22. Rebuffing
24. Vomit
26. Chameleon cousins
27. Follower of the Bushido code
30. Blackguard
31. Eternal flower
33. Yellow parts
38. Fashion designer Kenneth
39. Bestseller
41. Colorado resort
42. Brakes and slides
44. Some Vivaldi compositions
47. Holed up
50. Committed a hockey infraction
51. Champion of the people
55. Barks
56. Bawdy doings
58. Earthquakes
62. Ancient
63. Savory, rich flavor
65. Bond
66. Amount of work
67. Christmas song
68. Fuselage of an aircraft
69. ___ base
70. Mournful poem
71. Be a snitch

DOWN

1. High-five, e.g.
2. Like candles
3. Affirm
4. Groomed, as in feet
5. From the halls of Montezuma
6. "No ___!"
7. Affectation
8. Like some humor
9. Dravidian language
10. Deep-sea diver's gear
11. Final bet, 2 wds.
12. Feather
13. Decorative hangings above a window
21. *Gone With the Wind* plantation
23. Hide well
25. Friends and neighbors
27. Anatomical pouches
28. Run ___
29. Post-colonial French Sudan
32. Popular juice-box drink
34. Lapse
35. Enrich
36. Claimed as the invention of 5th-century Chinese philosophers Mozi and Lu Ban
37. Tried to get home
40. Country singer Keith
43. Jewish house of prayer
45. How one might drive to the muffler shop
46. Super garb
48. Make happen
49. Skin-related
51. Start of a refrain
52. Asperity
53. Construction girder
54. Villain
57. Ready, once
59. Pivot (var.)
60. Think (over)
61. Unload
64. *Spaceballs* species that's its "own best friend"

ACROSS

1. "To thine own ___ be true"
5. Highland toppers
9. Ice mass
13. Cry like a feline
14. Habeas corpus, e.g.
15. Checked out
16. Goshawk or sparrowhawk, e.g.
18. Cup of joe
19. Hypothyroidism treatment
20. Chaotic
21. Little ones
22. Figurehead's place
24. "Don't move!"
27. Charms
31. Large cask
32. Chest protector
34. Rainboot (UK)
35. Crazily
37. Child of your unc
39. Pie perch
40. Fashionable
43. British "bub"
45. *China Beach* setting
46. Fast
47. Volcanic crater
50. They're all in the family: Abbr.
52. Fill to excess
53. ___'s razor
56. They have morals
61. Love handles, essentially
62. Toxicodendron, 2 wds.
63. "___ 'er up!"
64. "Setting the ___"
65. Blood's partner
66. Bind
67. Slaloms, perhaps
68. Become unhinged

DOWN

1. Belt
2. ___ one, teach one
3. She always tricks Charlie
4. Coquettish
5. Laundry necessity, once, 2 wds.
6. Creatively skilled
7. Appearance
8. ___ throat
9. Adorns with precious stones
10. Fledgling bird
11. Guns, as an engine
12. Aussie greeting
17. Feces
20. Slang for cell phone, to a few
23. Mary-Kate and Ashley Olsen's fashion label, with "the"
24. Postage item
25. Abnormal growth
26. One end of a battery
28. Skirt type
29. Pulmonary ___
30. 1965 MLK arrest site
33. Impede, with "down"
36. Attractive
38. Ratatouille ingredient
41. Autoinjector carrying drugs for emergency use
42. Fireplace part
44. Luggage
48. Bananas
49. Demises
51. Ninth mos.
53. "Offenhauser Racing Engine"
54. Renault supermini car
55. Seal (var.)
57. Captured
58. Sometime today
59. Actress Reid
60. Domed twisted straw hive

ACROSS

1. Not now
5. Brouhahas
10. H.S. subject
14. ___ *floresiensis*
15. Female demon
16. Deeply
17. Boss on a shield
18. Flower cluster
19. Chris Hemsworth Marvel role
20. Appearance
21. It knows the score, 2 wds.
23. Moisten
25. "Monster Mash" setting
26. Hems partners
30. Certain sailboat rope
33. Paint container
37. One who suspends an action, legally
38. Astute
39. Knotting
41. Drop
42. As a precaution, 2 wds.
44. Damned
46. Verbally attacked
47. "Trick" joint
48. Pup's foot
49. Mediterranean vessel
54. Outcast
61. American filmmaker ___ Baumbach
62. Some deer
63. Kind of pain
64. Ford, for one
65. May, to Peter Parker
66. Banana plant fiber
67. Hoof sound
68. Catches on
69. In need of a cleaning
70. Perfect scores

DOWN

1. Finger raised on the shoulder
2. Friend, slangily
3. Fix firmly
4. Nobody, 2 wds.
5. Bugs
6. Light
7. Early pulpit
8. Dock
9. Seasoning
10. Countdown of top tunes, 2 wds.
11. Populated
12. Plod along
13. Also known as Sur
22. Concrete section
24. Agatha Christie's ___ *Didn't They Ask Evans?*
27. Didn't dawdle
28. "___ to go!"
29. Minor cut
30. Bore
31. Cromwell's nickname
32. Colored like a speedy hound
33. Park City gear
34. ___ Station
35. One who receives
36. Metrical units (var.)
40. Mother Teresa, e.g.
43. Like a seam
45. Census datum
50. Legislate
51. Ancient Greece's legislative assembly
52. Use as a dining table, 2 wds.
53. Whacks
54. Attack a fellow soldier
55. Womanizer
56. Eighth of an ounce
57. Brain area
58. Fledgling bird
59. Bags
60. Cut down

ACROSS

1. Temps
5. Lurk
10. Loretta Lynn's "Fly ___"
14. Jersey, e.g.
15. Provide, as with a quality
16. Jerk (var.)
17. Gross
18. Reefy
19. Good, long bath
20. Moody film genre
21. Charge
22. Arctic diving bird
23. Gristly tissue
25. Basketball official
28. One-dimensional
31. Assimilates
33. Animate
35. Spoil, with "on"
36. Chat
39. Blue-headed lizard
40. Eighty-six
41. Alternative to acrylics
43. Bondages
46. Prognosticator
48. In a chair
51. Cities in Spain and Ohio
53. Acknowledges the crowd
55. Fill anew, 2 wds.
56. One of the Ws in "www."
59. "Rambling Wreck From Georgia ___"
60. "Aquarius" musical
61. Spanish for "beach"
63. Black
64. Cabal
65. Exudes
66. Unload, as stock
67. Advocate
68. Heavy water, for one
69. *South Park* creator ___ Parker

DOWN

1. Hides
2. Straighten out
3. Barely-there beachwear
4. Component of synthetic rubber
5. ___ -esteem
6. Wounded ___, South Dakota
7. Milk dispenser
8. Big galoot
9. E or G, e.g.
10. Confident
11. Love child (archaic)
12. Italian almond biscuits
13. Bind
22. Computer storage unit, informally
24. Cyst
26. Moisture overload results, in plants
27. Coda
29. Having wings
30. "I getcha, mate!"
32. Census datum
34. Alt. spelling
36. "Red" letters
37. Missile type, 3 wds.
38. Hitting a fly-ball just past the infield
42. Blow one's budget
44. Actor Jude
45. Believer in a strong centralized government
47. Cool, once
49. Plane, e.g.
50. Paper's rough edge
52. Bantu language also known as Siswati
54. Coyly
55. By way of, briefly
57. Checked out
58. Bottom
61. Cutesy suffix
62. Nova, e.g.

ACROSS

1. ___ back
5. British bread roll
8. Box office take
12. Dash gauge
13. Canadian novelist ___ Maud Montgomery
14. "That's a ___!"
15. Prefix with -correct or -immune
16. Check signer
17. Bind
18. Having a decorative edging
20. More leonine in color
22. *Six Feet Under* setting, 2 wds.
24. Holiday drink
25. Daughter of Tethys
26. Big cask
27. Doubly dangerous
29. Nibble
30. Baby buggy (UK)
31. Animal shelters
32. Trampled (on)
33. Holding fast
38. That man
39. Street-gang member?
40. Fly catcher
41. Byzantinism
46. Decorated
48. Eulogies
49. Film
50. Contents of some urns
52. Long, for short
53. Castle part
54. Enlarge, as a hole
55. Old
56. Figure (out)
57. Blue
58. Bed or bunk (UK)

DOWN

1. Workers
2. Modern-day Pleasant Island
3. Be part of the cast of, 2 wds.
4. Call
5. Accept
6. Common solvent
7. Giza attraction
8. Lover of Charles II
9. Scaring off: modified Shakespearean exclamation
10. To-go meals
11. Centerpiece
13. Dipped out, as punch
16. Christmas wish
19. Best man's best friend
21. Lent's start, e.g.: Abbr.
23. Beldam
27. "Seventy Six ___"
28. Large amount of money
29. Actor Affleck
30. Devotional bench
31. Co-winner of 1933 Nobel Prize in Physics
32. Smacks
33. Debts
34. Great salt lake, 2 wds.
35. Consumes
36. Favor
37. Horse controls
39. Grant or Lee, e.g.
42. Bedouin
43. Adult insect
44. Upside-down nines
45. Brides' attendants
47. Gym set
51. "We've been ___!"

ACROSS

1. Dull finish
6. Czars, e.g.
13. Dislike, and then some
14. Decade
15. Sky sight
16. Emptying
17. Swindled
18. Comes before
19. Awarded since 1949
21. Cribbage piece
22. "Close to You" singer Carpenter
24. Faithfulness, in a wedding vow
27. Follows surreptitiously
29. "High" time
31. Braves' slugger Henry
32. Bird not to be confused with a Mediterranean bread
33. Couturier Christian
34. Most dear
36. Has a strong craving
39. Directs
40. Small rug
41. Bat's home
42. Dirges
46. Brothers who sang "The Glow-Worm"
51. Tinea
52. Freeze, 2 wds.
53. Art appreciator
54. Fish that lays a "mermaid's purse"
55. Act as chairperson
56. Used a keyboard

DOWN

1. Safari runners
2. Not much
3. By way of, briefly
4. Conflicted
5. ___ divergens
6. Cabinet div.
7. Named (archaic)
8. Have-not
9. Enmity
10. Agitated state
11. Food sticker
12. Declines
14. Contradict
16. Curses
20. Copy cats
22. South Africa's ___ lark
23. Decorations
25. Carries
26. Have the ___ for
27. Blue
28. Acclaim
30. Singer ___ King Cole
32. Writer who argues in opposition to others
34. Gorge
35. Third bk. of the Bible
37. The "Father of India"
38. Put away
41. Neb
42. Mouth, in slang
43. Field worker
44. Con
45. Spoil, with "on"
47. Gross
48. Ballet move
49. Medieval instrument
50. Went too fast

ACROSS

1. Take a break
5. Congregation leader
10. *Brandenburg Concertos* composer
14. A piece
15. "Here we go ___"
16. Hurting
17. Cheese on crackers
18. *Around the World in Eighty Days* writer
19. Felt bad about
20. Did a sheepdog's job
22. Cad
24. Infatuated with, once, 2 wds.
25. Willy Loman, for one
27. Bay
28. List on Etsy, say
29. Half a dozen
30. Bellyached
31. Compensates
32. Mattel offering
33. Salsa or guacamole
34. Know, archaically
37. "D"
39. Ancient debarkation point
45. "What's that?"
46. Crescent
47. Shipworm
48. Echoes
50. Admonished
51. Hair piece
52. Heavy drapery fabric
53. Cymric hamlet
54. More fitting
57. Barter (UK)
59. Bringing up the rear
60. Hon
61. Break
62. Fledgling bird
63. Ant, in dialect
64. Smeltery refuse

DOWN

1. Confederate soldier, for short
2. Football helmet feature
3. Kind of fair
4. From that cause
5. Devoured
6. Ancient
7. Keep out
8. Coal container
9. In a sluggish way
10. *Chimera* author John ___
11. Maximally intense
12. "Ta-ta!"
13. ___ acids, a.k.a. fruit acids
21. Hawk's opposite
23. Alternative to acrylics
24. Chatter
25. Has dreams
26. ___ tide
33. Finished
34. Ref's need
35. Clerk's need, once (UK), 2 wds.
36. Former Prime Minister ___ May
37. Agenda
38. Make obsolete
39. If everything fails, 2 wds.
40. Back
41. Picks up
42. Library extension
43. Benign tumor
44. Strauss's "___ und Verklärung"
49. Travels on whitewater
52. ___ out
55. Little dog, for short
56. "Free Fallin'" musician Petty
58. Cribbage piece

ACROSS

1. Possesses
4. Beanie Babies, e.g.
7. Honey
11. Peke squeak
12. Blue
13. Less-traveled road
14. Get
16. Be generous
17. Artsy one (var.)
18. Raided
19. Molecular synthesis process
21. Beginnings
24. Italian bacon
28. Uniform group
29. Not low
30. Barbecue offering
31. San Francisco's ___ Hill
32. "___ for glory": Keats
35. Assent
36. Directly
37. Amount of work
38. Bronze age arm band
39. Conifer cones
41. Birthplace of Solidarity
43. Vex
45. Long-legged bug
48. Scams
52. Henry Clay, e.g.
53. Lacking serviceability
54. Olden magistrates
55. Was introduced to
56. Census datum
57. ___-crossed
58. Memorial Day month
59. "Get your hands off me!"

DOWN

1. Slang for "promotion"
2. Affectation
3. Advance, slangily
4. Masterful
5. Main arteries
6. Dork
7. How roll is called, 2 wds.
8. "Get ___ from me!"
9. Diminish
10. Checked out
13. Bygone belt
15. Cautious
16. Affairs
18. Pizzazz
20. Snakes
21. ___ of time
22. Rainbow ___
23. Color of honey
25. Check for fit, 2 wds.
26. Layers
27. One way to be taken
32. Planetary reflections
33. Drudge
34. More healthy
38. Divination deck
40. ___ dictum
41. ___ pig
42. Number two
44. Fairy tale brother
45. Lays down a lawn
46. Bring (out)
47. Eastern song
49. ___ sticks
50. Beat it
51. Alluring

ACROSS

1. Shredded cabbage
5. Gossip
9. Synagogue
13. Come down hard
14. Two-time Nobel Prize-winner Marie
15. Ice cream vessel
16. Olympic sled
17. About 1% of the atmosphere
18. Bad humor
19. Goals
20. Devote, as time
21. *Habeas corpus*, e.g.
22. ___ fly
24. Looks for
26. Deeply
27. Indo-Aryan language
30. Takes out
31. Swindler, 2 wds.
36. Dead to the world
37. Director's cry
38. 1/100th of a Finnish markka
39. Ecclesiastic's dwelling
41. Heirloom location
42. Worse, as excuses go
43. Not kosher
44. Band worn above the elbow
48. Berth places
50. Lad in Limerick
51. Its license plates say "Famous Potatoes"
55. Breathing noise
56. Boss on a shield
57. Abalone
58. Cut short
59. Milk source
60. Chivalrous
61. Clue
62. Lays grass
63. British geek
64. Declines

DOWN

1. Comics sound
2. N.O.'s state
3. Booster
4. Hulk Hogan and Triple H, e.g.
5. Pat on the back
6. Advocate
7. Heaven
8. *Euphoria* actress
9. Pronunciation symbol
10. Beautiful maiden
11. Ill-suited
12. Boxing blows
14. Beer buy
23. Part of a heartbeat
25. Hostile course, 2 wds.
27. Programming language developed by David May
28. Blush
29. Prefix with -national or -net
30. Sauce
32. Roman governors
33. Among other things
34. Blubbering
35. Regular twitch
40. Countries
44. Borders
45. Beau
46. "I messed up!"
47. Despoils
48. Had on
49. Ninth mos.
52. Discontinue
53. Early pulpit
54. Detained

ACROSS

1. Big trucks
6. Charge
9. Exfoliation
14. Acoustic
15. Calif. airport
16. Every sixty minutes (UK)
17. Antheral
19. Fireplace
20. Spouse who manages the household
21. Injured
22. ___ place
24. The "one" in a one-two
27. Bronx Bomber
32. Like the great unwashed, to a Brit
33. *The Playboy of the Western World* author
37. Breezy
38. Black
39. Elizabeth or Victoria, e.g.
40. Had on
41. Blanched
42. Dark area
43. Blown away
44. Guide
46. Slang for "good"
47. Collar stuff
52. Like a ham
56. TV screen test display, 2 wds.
62. Hip region
63. Eating of raw food: Dionysiac myth
64. Gorilla-like
65. Actor Richard E. Grant, to fans
66. Fragrant resin
67. "Likewise"
68. Discouraging words
69. Assisted

DOWN

1. Beat to a pulp
2. ___-correct
3. Jam
4. Glacial deposit
5. ___ chance
6. Goofball
7. Consumed
8. Apply, as pressure
9. Non-Jewish woman
10. Mass. neighbor
11. Advocate
12. Breathing noise
13. Ran off
18. D.C. major leaguer
23. Howler
24. Bringer of bad luck
25. Bracelet site
26. One who should beware
28. Governor in Mughal India
29. Great Plains people
30. Blew it
31. Checked out
32. Barely beats
33. Crouch
34. "___, that's delicious"
35. Colo. neighbor
36. Switz. neighbor
45. Hitchcock's biggest hit
48. Squash type
49. Beau
50. Clunky shoes
51. Bounce
52. French WWI plane
53. Amazonian language
54. A trifle
55. Essence
57. *Better Call Saul* actress Seehorn
58. Indonesian province
59. Ancient
60. "The ___ of the Ancient Mariner": Coleridge
61. Aforementioned

ACROSS

1. Bakes eggs
7. Uncontrolled
11. Gland that secretes melatonin
12. Stationer's supply, 2 wds.
16. Hire
17. Appraisal of a substance using a test organism
18. Beloved
19. Tortoise
20. Frontiersman Carson
21. Belabor, with "on"
23. ___-fetched
24. Heaven
25. *Cosmo* and *GQ*, e.g.
26. Uranus, e.g.
28. Bring out
30. Checking out
31. Battery units
32. ABC's ___ *Anatomy*
33. Audio setup
35. Kennel sound
36. Insignificant
37. "Get ___!"
38. Dullards
40. Sticker
43. Adjustment
46. Cephalopod creatures
49. Abandon
50. Bang and zoom
51. Equity
52. Impish girl
53. Bed board
54. Mounts

DOWN

1. Command to a dog
2. Yogi's language
3. Bullion unit
4. Back
5. Anger
6. Goings
7. Mud dauber, e.g.
8. By its very nature, 2 wds.
9. Drips
10. Laundromat array
12. Out
13. Brook
14. Plane, e.g.
15. Handle clumsily
22. Anguish
24. Eccentric
25. Stubborn beast
26. Burning desire
27. Willingly
28. Late-day prayers
29. Fishing vessel
30. Product of superego assimilation, 2 wds.
33. Quills
34. Male sheep
35. Berth places
38. Eat
39. Enormous birds of myth
40. Bösendorfer piano, familiarly
41. Defeat
42. Gets promoted
44. After-dinner drink
45. Large sea snail
47. Checked item
48. Weekly reader, since 1923

ACROSS

1. Golden Triangle country
5. Become unhinged
9. Bawl out
14. Not much
15. Hyperbolic function
16. Asian capital
17. Burrowing animal
18. Spanish Inquisition's ___-da-fé
19. Kind of jack
20. Salve
21. Undergarments
22. Pleats
23. Small amount
24. Clergyman's white linen garment
26. Commercial makers, once, 2 wds.
28. Lump
29. Instigated
32. Red, in the 1940s
35. Device in some courtroom or political strategies, 2 wds.
37. Common sense
39. Challenges
42. Binary compound
45. Fast food list
46. "I thought ___ never leave!"
48. Flat-bottomed basket
49. Astronomer Sagan
50. Crush
51. Gross
52. Crazily
53. Santa's helpers
54. Ado
55. Bumpkin
56. Catkin
57. Ending for Oktober
58. Raced

DOWN

1. Sorority letter
2. On the train
3. Wick holder, 2 wds.
4. Spriggers
5. Runs through
6. Its flag depicts a twelve-pointed star
7. Southern hemisphere feature, 2 wds.
8. Luminous result of eye pressure
9. Confined, 2 wds.
10. Canadian superhero Captain ___
11. Chilled, 2 wds.
12. "Check it out!"
13. Rackets
25. Playful
27. "___ a chance"
30. American writer ___ Piercy
31. Litigant
33. Blue
34. Public transit units, 2 wds.
36. Concoct, 2 wds.
37. Dutch cheese
38. Senior
40. Attire
41. Pouted
42. Wait on
43. "The Sorcerer's Apprentice" composer Paul
44. Pharaoh's land
46. Nervous *Hedda Gabler* character
47. *Alien* actor Ian ___

ACROSS

1. Chew
5. Blackens
9. Gigantic
13. Quick to the helm
14. Spinachlike plant
16. Gross
17. Bank of Paris
18. Like vintage fashion
19. China problem
20. Stretching out
22. Promo
23. Science of matter's deformation and flow
25. After-bath wear
28. Pivot (var.)
29. Purse
32. Uses a voucher
35. Salt of element no. 35
37. Big Brother's state
38. Deodorant type
39. Democritus, for one
40. Gets back
41. Noise
42. "Jane, you ignorant ___": sexist *SNL* catchphrase
44. Deeply
45. Personal magnetism
48. Jerk (var.)
51. Swimwear option, 2 wds.
56. Milne character, for short
57. Character
58. Eastern music
59. Boss on a shield
60. Bad looks
61. Not many
62. Symbolic gift on *The Bachelor*
63. Nest of a squirrel
64. Revenuers

DOWN

1. Circular course
2. Hammer target
3. Composer Pärt
4. Aaron Freeman and Mickey Melchiondo, collectively
5. Ark contents
6. Mountain crest
7. Odds, basically
8. Browser window part, 2 wds.
9. Capital of occupied France
10. Hurting
11. Bypass
12. Sort
15. Recipient of recognition (UK)
21. Pond scum-colored
24. Pre-Victorian period
25. Prefix with linear
26. Ancient Greek theater
27. Laser light
29. Royal herb
30. Lack of muscle firmness
31. Hair goops
32. Street
33. Identify incorrectly
34. Soaked through
36. "Oh, my aching head!" e.g.
43. Church supporter
45. Silver salmon (var.)
46. Beach
47. "Work It" rapper Elliott
48. Cowboy boot attachment
49. Genus for humans
50. Black Friday participants
52. German seven-time Wimbledon champ
53. Van Gogh's ___ *Terrace at Night*
54. Ancient
55. Dog's "dogs"

ACROSS

1. Yogi's accessory
4. Hindu Mr.
8. Dandy
11. Adjoin
13. Buff
14. Chimney channel
15. Snowman prop
16. Companion of Artemis
17. Kiln
18. "Upper": Abbr.
19. Rebels
21. Nervous
23. Photocopying process, once
26. Rubber
30. Senior
31. One of 100 in a baht
33. Inclination
34. Curly diacritic
35. Food on sticks
37. Alaska Native language
38. Least accessible
42. Procurers
43. False teeth
45. NASA's *Voyager 1* and *Voyager 2*, e.g., 2 wds.
49. "___ as pie"
53. Bean curd
54. Hands out
55. Be a monarch
56. Ancient
57. Cancel
58. Like a bug in a rug
59. Skid ___
60. Animal shelters
61. Certain sheep

DOWN

1. They may provide relief
2. Not much
3. Paraguayan people
4. Bailey's partner
5. Ancient writings of Persia
6. Humdingers
7. Disrobe
8. Custard concoction
9. Boot
10. Strokes
12. Medication marketed as Restoril
13. Churn
14. "Them"
20. Chimp or gorilla, 2 wds.
22. Augur
23. Office furnishing
24. More sick
25. Building block
27. People who exploit (UK)
28. Talking cat in *Sabrina, the Teenage Witch*
29. Eventually become, 2 wds.
32. Acquires
36. New family member
39. Attire
40. Runner
41. Potatoes and yams, e.g.
44. Arm ___
45. Hollywood Walk of Fame symbol
46. ___ stick (bouncing toy)
47. Not many
48. Something to chew
50. Becky, to DJ, on *Full House*
51. Pivot (var.)
52. Burglar

ACROSS

1. The ___ Pack
5. Teary
8. Admiral who explored the Antarctic
12. Critic
14. In the capacity of
15. Hellraiser
16. Cavern, in poetry
17. Steady
19. Cluster beans
20. Brevity
21. Foretold
23. Harsher
24. Stopper
28. Piano piece
31. Goiter
33. Fertile soil
34. Packed with parsley flavor
35. Not alert
37. Blink-and-you'll-miss-it roles
38. Explanations
39. Explicit insult
43. Pop song rankings, 2 wds.
46. Galvanizers
50. General ___ cereal
52. Pertaining to swimming
53. Freeze, 2 wds.
54. Comprehend
55. Charge
56. Carved pin
57. Open wide
58. In favor of
59. Any set of items

DOWN

1. Act the blowhard
2. Incurred, 2 wds.
3. Essential oil perfume
4. Threatens (UK)
5. Sound of stepping in mud
6. Mame, for one
7. Speed demons
8. Breakfast fiber
9. Bind
10. Regrets
11. Animal shelters
13. Answer
18. Holed up
20. Disney's ___ Leg Pete
22. Embrace
24. Before doctoral
25. Artificial bait
26. Boss on a shield
27. Part of PFLAG
28. Barbecue side
29. "2.0" comic of Comedy Central
30. Depend (on)
32. Pertaining to the brain's third ventricle
36. Separate into couples, 2 wds.
37. ___-anglais: English horn
40. Sound system
41. More active
42. Possesses
43. Bestseller
44. Fragrant resin
45. Swings around (var.)
46. Black
47. *Peter Pan* character
48. House
49. Stooge
51. ___ check

ACROSS

1. Jest
5. Commoner
9. Agitated state
13. African antelope
15. Zero, on a court
16. Jaywalking, e.g.
17. Asian appetizer
18. Ancient
19. Like certain trees
20. Pranksters
22. Explanations
23. Able to travel, biologically
24. Clothing
26. *Sister Act* disguise
27. Upright
31. Bacteria-dwelling viruses
34. Ancient Roman coins
35. Canaanite deity
36. Crustacean's feeler
37. Shrink
41. Honor
44. Send another way
45. Chevy or Porsche
46. "Chop-chop!"
47. Met productions
51. Arp's art
54. Natural sweetener, 2 wds.
57. Brawl
58. Well
59. Crossbeam
60. Advocate
61. Coagulate
62. "Nights in White ___" by the Moody Blues
63. Parting words
64. Hoopla
65. Advance

DOWN

1. "Surely you ___!"
2. Auto option
3. Place for a barbecue
4. Legislate
5. Typewriter parts
6. Balcony section
7. Inside out
8. Concern for one who's laid up, 2 wds.
9. Wintry scene
10. *Stranger Things* actor Schnapp
11. Black
12. Plays with
14. Creating a watercourse (UK)
21. Pivot (var.)
25. Lee, e.g.: Abbr.
28. Mouth, in slang
29. Bounce
30. Peke squeak
31. French door part
32. Mist with a chill wind (UK)
33. Assigns
35. Keep out
38. Co. that owns KFC, Pizza Hut, and Taco Bell
39. Tolerate
40. In a defensible manner
41. Altar aide
42. Outerwear
43. Tops
48. Bucolic
49. Banded stone
50. Creeping juniper
51. Clobber
52. Breezy
53. Chief official of Venice or Genoa
55. Alka-Seltzer sound
56. Cleave

ACROSS

1. Banquets
5. Fail to see
9. Zoomed
13. Objects on sets
15. Creep
16. Fleshy fruit
17. Acquiesce
18. Bad word
19. Archaeological site
20. Extend
21. Mostly
23. Wet, as morning grass
25. Certain print
26. Shoot for, with "to"
29. Easy dupes
31. "This is fun!"
32. Madam
34. British dandies
39. Some deer
40. Solder
42. Reduce, as expenses
43. Busybody
45. Appearance
46. Fore
47. ___ ap Nudd: Welsh mythology
49. Roaring motor sounds
51. More clever
54. Parting words
55. Improvable
58. Blows
62. Reward
63. Be sour
64. Development areas
65. In need of resupply, maybe
66. Annul
67. Arrive, as darkness
68. Antelope species
69. Toiler
70. Dressing ingredient

DOWN

1. Bandy words
2. Advocate
3. Blue books
4. Fastest
5. Ballerina Copeland
6. Deeply
7. Atlantic fish
8. "You're telling me a ___ fried this rice?"
9. Herring
10. Young fowl
11. Inventor ___ Berliner
12. Contradict
14. Ratty place
22. Actors
24. James ___ Space Telescope
26. Not straight
27. Loafer, e.g.
28. Hammer part
29. Beau
30. Tool used to cut and shape wood
33. Soldiers, collectively
35. Black and white, e.g.
36. Betting game
37. Gift tag word
38. Puts in stitches
41. The green-eyed monster
44. Like fine wines
48. Conclude, 2 wds.
50. Concentration puzzle
51. Attack ad
52. Apprehensive
53. The Dow, e.g.
54. Chance, 2 wds.
55. Early pulpit
56. Cram, with "up"
57. Classic board game
59. Greek cheese
60. Love goddess in Anglo-Saxon paganism
61. Trig function

182

ACROSS

1. "A ___ in the face"
5. Well
9. Bring
14. Imitated bird call
15. Rake
16. Convex molding
17. Black
18. Biological classes
19. Kindled anew
20. Old Chinese money
21. Increases in volume
23. Hard-to-read writing
25. Exactly
26. "And ___ thou slain the Jabberwock?"
29. Combined meal
33. Part of a larger group of devices
38. Native New Zealander
39. Jersey, e.g.
40. Early time, 2 wds.
42. Captured
43. Hung around
45. Turpitude
47. Back biters
49. By way of, briefly
50. Grimace
52. Like living organisms
57. Like income or diapers
62. Easily maneuverable, as a vessel
63. Up to
64. Aggravate
65. Stuck-up sort
66. Inclination
67. Kid
68. Kiln
69. Wrote two-handed
70. Worked the soil
71. "Hogwash!"

DOWN

1. Barbecue rods
2. Radiation device, for short
3. Information booth visitor
4. Biology sections
5. Place for posers, 2 wds.
6. Big pig
7. Elegance
8. Bakery supply
9. A radius is part of it
10. Come about
11. "I ___ you so!"
12. History muse
13. Mini cinnamon candies: red ___
22. Corn holder
24. "___ me?"
27. Fastener
28. Article of faith
30. Twelve o'clock
31. Gator's cousin
32. Go backpacking
33. Whole alternative
34. Annul
35. Tab
36. Heating conduit, 2 wds.
37. A whole lot
41. Divided
44. Dribbled
46. Directly
48. Spanish for "your"
51. Gaia
53. Disinfectant brand
54. Enclosed porch
55. Notched
56. Arrears
57. Do some cleaning
58. Deeply
59. Halt
60. Lad in Limerick
61. YouTube vote

ACROSS

1. Pare
6. Slang for "cadavers"
12. Add on
13. Short piece
14. Infant's woe
15. Nicknames
16. Class
17. Arrange systematically
18. Farmer's marketables
20. Fed. rule
23. Colorless solvents
26. Durable fabric
28. Neighbor of Ger.
29. Cheap magazine
30. 26th president, to pals
31. Less obvious
33. Ear problem
35. Dark area
36. Cram, with "up"
38. Bulgarian monetary unit
39. ___ preview
40. First three digits, 2 wds.
42. Blue
43. Corrode, 2 wds.
45. Greek god of the sun
46. Deprive of weapons
51. One of Saturn's moons
54. Juliet's beau
55. Long-lasting
56. Big brasses
57. Part of ships' bows
58. Stifle a laugh

DOWN

1. Pouches
2. Bow
3. Deeply
4. Cover
5. Apart from
6. Video-game hedgehog
7. Betting option
8. Gross
9. Charge
10. ___-flung
11. Wild boar, e.g.
13. Type of argument, literally "method of affirming"
15. Example
17. Continuous network of urban communities
19. Catch
20. Like corduroy
21. Bitter salad green
22. *La Maja Desnuda* painter
23. Barnard College grad, e.g.
24. Delivered
25. More
27. Hit song title for Adele and Lionel Richie
31. Figure out
32. War of 1812 locale, 2 wds.
34. Milk source
37. Betelgeuse's constellation
41. Trial sites
44. Assumed name
45. Cluckers
47. It may be proper
48. Early pulpit
49. Back
50. Lion's share
51. Sarcastic laughter
52. Assent
53. "Wham!"

ACROSS

1. Prismatic
5. Halftime lead, e.g.
9. R-rated, maybe
13. Abated
15. Argentine timber tree
16. Currency in Cologne
17. Foreword, for short
18. Adjoin
19. Bone-dry
20. Cut corners
21. William Tweed's territories, say
23. Colorado resort
26. "Catch!"
27. "Not to mention…"
31. Units of corn
32. "-zoic" things
33. Rural poems
35. Triage sites, briefly
36. Pariah
37. Superficial vein of the leg
41. "Interesting…"
42. Car wash employee
43. Dreary (Scot.)
45. Unadulterated
46. Commoner
47. Goal on a staycation
48. Auto option
50. Affecting the body generally
52. Disparager of seniors
57. Equal
58. Certain compass points
60. Separate the strands of, as rope
61. Length x width
62. *Damages* actor Donovan
63. Administrative district in some South Asian countries
64. Sounds of disapproval
65. Looped handle
66. *ER* star Noah

DOWN

1. Certainly, old style
2. Captain, e.g.
3. Former Peruvian currency
4. Skin dr.
5. In-flight info, for short
6. Patters
7. Theoretical neutral, massless particle
8. Diner sign
9. Editorial's audience
10. Dawn goddess
11. Burglary and battery
12. Hebrew letters
14. An amino acid
22. Guide
24. Earthquake
25. Agreement
27. "Give it ___ ___!"
28. One hundred bani in Romania
29. Boozehound
30. Groups of people who know the score
34. Reproductive cell
35. Fast finisher
37. *Buona ___*
38. A bend in a pipe
39. Born, in bios
40. Short trader
42. Mimosas (archaic)
43. Washer partners
44. Look for again
45. Pal
49. Malt, in Edinburgh
50. Clash
51. Intro to physics
53. Vex, with "at"
54. In a bad way
55. Nobel-winning writer Bellow
56. Kid
59. Caribbean, e.g.

ACROSS

1. Grandson of Cain
5. German physicist Georg ___
8. Certain palm
12. Any Greek commune
13. Outdoor outfitter
14. Bane
16. Lyrical
17. Wiping
19. Word with "cycle" or "calendar"
21. Swelling
22. Spanish for "law"
23. Confuse
25. Brings down the house, in Liverpool
27. Bony protective coverings
29. Scottish bard
33. Sun, e.g.
36. Blue
37. Like some reminders
38. Water buffalo
41. Driver's need
42. Kind of recording
43. Newspaper div.
44. Morse distress signal
45. Brace
46. Cries for attention, in Australia
49. Humidor item
51. Fairway boundary
54. Lawyers' org.
57. Easy to stick a needle in
59. "Nothing," in legal phrases
61. Roast veal
64. "Forget it!"
65. Assistants
66. Ampersand
67. Rams
68. Seal's "Kiss from a ___"
69. "I" problem
70. Place for a coin

DOWN

1. Icon
2. Copy again, as a tape
3. Nitrogen compound
4. After-dinner coffee choices
5. Singer-actress Rita
6. Greek goddess of youth
7. Sketched badly
8. Firearms supplier ___ Sauer
9. Blue dye
10. Characteristic carrier
11. Bacchanal
14. Radiation dosages
15. Describing blood toxic with waste products (var.)
18. After-dinner selections
20. *Arabian Nights* menace
24. Solzhenitsyn's The ___ Archipelago
26. "___ here"
28. "___ bad!"
30. Some male dolls
31. In addition
32. Bakery selections
33. Wood sorrels
34. Bluster
35. Highlands hillside
37. Mason, at times
39. Actor Guinness
40. South American independence leader
41. WC
43. Eye coverings (var.)
46. Local administrator in Algeria, e.g.
47. Long, long time
48. Wool greases
50. Grant and Lee: Abbr.
52. Demon
53. "Hungry, hungry" critter of a kid's game
54. Way, way off
55. Get-up-and-go
56. Helps
58. Yin's opposite
60. For fear that
62. Average
63. Japanese vegetable

ACROSS

1. Not halal
6. Well
10. Bad-mouth
14. Accused's need
15. Flock member
16. Creep
17. Crimean seaport
19. Loafer, e.g.
20. Floor exercise (UK), 2 wds.
21. Huey, Dewey, and Louie, to Donald
23. Ran
25. Hardly rich
26. *The Women* playwright Clare Boothe ___
27. Invigorating drinks
30. Boring
34. Connect
36. Kind of position
37. Breathing noise
38. Type of tot
40. Chesterfield, e.g.
41. Admittance
43. Part of the Hindu trinity
44. Deuce topper
45. Cleared a frosty windshield
47. Unpleasant smell (UK)
49. Stubborn beast
50. Buried
55. Finish
58. Type of sculpture
59. Bread spread
60. Rejected
62. *Cheers* actress Perlman
63. Abbr. on folk music
64. ___ friends
65. Ball material
66. Believed
67. Dentist's direction

DOWN

1. Door fasteners
2. Argus-eyed
3. Snake or Hudson, e.g.
4. Belittle
5. Prayer book
6. Losses of hair
7. Bi bim ___
8. Animal with a mane
9. A maiden ___ Marian (archaic)
10. Not straight
11. Son or daughter
12. Boat with an open hold
13. ___ *the Man*: 2006 Amanda Bynes film
18. Fracas
22. Cosmo and Wanda's son in *The Fairly OddParents*
24. Tooth component
28. ___ *au lait*
29. Cut down
30. Born's partner
31. Channel
32. Cockpit gauge
33. Extremely difficult
35. The 26th prime minister of Australia
39. Took on the Colorado
42. Cry
46. Scarcity
48. Of leaves
51. Algonquian tribe member
52. Chance, 2 wds.
53. Balances
54. Artful move
55. Active
56. Laugh
57. Bill
61. Amigo

ACROSS

1. Perform on the street
5. Bandy words
9. Provide for free
13. Church part
15. Every
16. Sea mist, to a Scot
17. A cubic meter, informally
18. Italian appetizer
20. Like Liam Neeson
21. Performed again
22. Cambridge student
24. Dough (archaic)
25. Deaden
28. *Hogan's Heroes* setting
32. Broken chords
37. Surrender
38. Phobos, to Mars
39. Haul
40. Confusion
41. "My word is my ___"
42. Dessert cakes (UK), 2 wds.
45. Classic theaters
48. Antares, for one
49. Masked critter
51. Mug
56. Miniature universe
61. Saltpetre
62. Unappealing
63. Work, as dough
64. Scrape, as the knee
65. Bond
66. Taste, e.g.
67. Ballyhoo
68. Checked out
69. Hangnails, e.g.

DOWN

1. Alkaline
2. The "U" in UHF
3. Draft holder
4. Limestone terrain
5. Brand
6. French door part
7. Didn't dawdle
8. Horned herbivores
9. Dance syllables
10. Brewer's equipment
11. Buddy
12. Egg on
14. Move, as a picture
19. After
23. Creepy-crawler
26. Catcher's need
27. Yokels
29. Pipe problem
30. Ax-like tool
31. Orders to plow horses
32. Early pulpit
33. Cross
34. Corn ___
35. Hormonal
36. Belt
43. Talk, talk, talk
44. Edges
46. Breakfast area
47. Land tenure
50. In a high-minded way
52. Strength
53. Court figure
54. Delete
55. Advises (archaic)
56. Command in the Iditarod
57. Black
58. Cut short
59. Pivot (var.)
60. Reward

ACROSS

1. Secret language
6. Parsonage
11. Hostile course, 2 wds.
14. First
16. Asmara is its capital
17. Fuchsia
18. Conveyed an estate
19. Take by theft
20. 60 sec. equiv.
21. Held back
22. Gull-like bird
25. Ice-melting aid
26. Cyst
27. Breakfast, lunch, or dinner
29. Body
33. Fervors
35. Sweet, dark wine
36. Aerospace measure
37. *Christmas in ___*: 1940 film
38. Photo
39. Appetizer on a take-out menu
41. "What ___ God wrought?"
42. Household units
45. Certain intersection
47. Come (from)
48. Act of reparation
52. Behind bars
53. Cicero's forte
54. Big cat
55. Archaeological site in north-eastern Peloponnese, Greece
56. ___ of time
57. Current

DOWN

1. Blown away
2. Uncommon
3. Bleak, as an outlook
4. Ideals
5. Anklebones
6. Animals that move seasonally
7. Artist studios
8. Curtain fabric
9. French composer Erik
10. ___ Mountains of Antarctica
12. Freshman, probably
13. "We've been ___!"
14. Drive
15. Like some knots
21. Arabic letter
22. Booty
23. Cut made by a saw
24. Annul
25. Possesses
27. Glues
28. Hermits
30. Mama's partner
31. Buttonhole, e.g.
32. "To ___ his own"
34. Candidate for priesthood
35. Ornamental flower, for short
37. *Au ___*: how a French dip is served
40. Top competitors
41. Auto device
42. Has an opinion
43. Embryo sacs
44. Georgia birthplace of Jason Aldean
45. Quite
46. Legislate
48. A cheerleader's need, when doubled
49. ___ of the above
50. -berry lead-in
51. Checked out

ACROSS

1. Bogus
5. Foot pads
9. Break by striking
13. Latin for "hip"
14. Adjoin
15. Literary work made out of parts of other works
16. Archaeological site
17. Dietary, in ads
18. In conflict with, with "of"
19. As often as necessary (Latin), 2 wds.
21. "Build it somewhere else" acronym
22. Asian dish
23. Gentle slope
25. Perform
26. Overly concerned with masculinity
28. Fizzles out
29. Cover
30. Workarounds
31. More ancient
32. Clobber
36. Barbary Coast pirate
37. Honeydew, e.g.
38. *The Fiddler on the Roof* setting
39. All excited
40. Indian condiment
41. Panama and Suez, e.g.
45. Commercial makers, 2 wds.
46. Loafer, e.g.
47. Lofgren of The E Street Band
48. Kind of board
49. Porous rock
50. Big name in pineapple
51. Domed tent
52. Stammer
53. Agitated state

DOWN

1. Abraded
2. Born Erik Weisz, in 1874 Budapest
3. Armpits
4. Nuts
5. Bamako is its capital
6. Not much
7. Nobel Peace Prize-winner Desmond
8. Preserved zingiber root, 2 wds.
9. Shortage
10. Socially disoriented
11. Hard pencils to sharpen
12. Sacred
15. Hors d'oeuvres
20. Except
24. L.A. hooper
26. Power-sharers
27. Pie cuts, essentially
29. Great time
30. Inchon natives
31. Having the highest high
32. Cancels financing
33. Jack-o'-lantern feature
34. Baroque composer Arcangelo ___
35. Israeli parliament
36. Bell-ringer
37. British parent, familiarly
38. Hindu holy man
40. R-rated, maybe
42. Close
43. Bean curd
44. Bulk

ACROSS

1. Film rolls
6. Jerks
12. Like much plant life
15. Flowering shrub
16. Grape variety
17. Departure
18. Someone who displays exaggerated religious zeal
19. Swaddles
20. Foretold
22. "I walk into someone's place of work, they ___ ___": Explicit *Repo Man* quote
28. Charming
33. Blue-headed lizard
34. Beside one another
35. Stolidly
37. ___ artery
38. Quintet on a calendar
39. Part of the system that produces white blood cells, 2 wds.
42. Stars
47. Diner surface
52. In greater want
54. Most viscous
55. Prepare for inurnment
56. Dragonflies and damselflies
57. Former Edmonton football team
58. Fire stirrers
59. Restrict

DOWN

1. Coarse file
2. Outfit
3. Noted blind mathematician
4. Starbucks order
5. Composed
6. Devotes
7. Singer known as The Little Sparrow
8. Composer Pärt
9. Sheet to the wind
10. Darn, as socks
11. Declines
13. Demands
14. Get a scolding, 2 wds.
15. Cold shower

21. Unconscious movement
23. Horseshoe projection
24. Like some cheeses
25. Eastern music
26. Actor Rossum
27. Quite a while
28. Daily delivery
29. Well
30. Bleak
31. ___ tide
32. A head
35. Act of reparation
36. Insecure bettors
38. Grow, in a way
40. Some trick-or-treaters
41. Greek penny
43. Stinks
44. Let in
45. *Dexter* series setting
46. ___ Hall University Pirates
47. Bomb
48. Adriatic resort
49. Wildly
50. Food sticker
51. Binge
53. Remnant

ACROSS

1. Reciprocal trig. function
6. ___ & Span
10. Egg on
14. Also known as Odia people
15. Hyperbolic function
16. Counterclockwise
17. "Let the ___ begin!"
18. Advocate
19. Not many
20. Scornful
21. ___ War (1899-1902)
22. Fix
23. Fish
24. Windbag
26. More bigheaded
28. Palestinian leader
29. Brushes aside
30. Unfriendliness
31. Grooved on
32. British dessert
33. Adjust (UK)
36. ___ split
39. Birchbark
40. Intrepidity
42. Immunity provider
44. Blockhead
45. Cutting tools
46. Litter member
47. Bat an eye
49. Blockhead
50. Annul
51. Network, e.g.
52. Channel
53. Chick's sound
54. Court figure
55. Checked out
56. Anchovy containers
57. Cast

DOWN

1. Gear teeth
2. Some apes, casually
3. Apes
4. Ocular relief medicine
5. Journal articles, maybe, 2 wds.
6. Cause of foot pain
7. Lets out
8. Engaged, 2 wds.
9. Fine-grained silica
10. Clinical-trial need
11. Renovations
12. Binge
13. Widows' inheritances
25. Inviolable, as rules, 3 wds.
27. Shallow gardening basket (UK)
30. Back financially
32. Tropical tree canopies, 2 wds.
33. Bolted, 2 wds.
34. Fold
35. Beamed
36. Obligated (archaic)
37. Stone Age implement
38. Ambitious one
39. Royal home
40. Country on Borneo
41. Calm
43. Blow
48. Believe (archaic)

192

ACROSS

1. Literally, "for this"
6. Line of cliffs
11. *Alla* ___ (2/2 time)
12. Hate
13. Actress Sophia
14. Armada component
15. In pieces
16. Bright
17. Curly diacritic
18. Microsoft product
19. *Super Mario* ___ : Nintendo video game
20. Feel-good brain hormone
22. ___ stick: incense
23. Feed
24. Brawl
25. Egyptian Christian
26. *Peanuts* sound effect
27. Sail constellation
28. Become tiresome
29. "I ___ you so!"
30. Salt made of palm oil
35. Old German duchy name
36. Chipper
37. Buckwheat cereal
38. Gossipers
40. Atlas enlargement
41. Line segment from the center of a regular polygon to the midpoint of one of its sides
42. Dorm annoyance
43. Conical dwellings
44. Personnel director
45. Actress Spacek
46. Anxious

DOWN

1. Remove by cutting
2. Visit, 2 wds.
3. Announce
4. Cook too long
5. Magazine middle, maybe
6. Princes, e.g.
7. Money ledger, 2 wds.
8. Eager
9. Horned herbivores
10. Diarist Samuel ___
12. Swedish birthplace of Max von Sydow
14. Chuck (UK)
16. Dirt
18. Put an edge on
21. Insect stage
22. Rickshaw
24. Be itinerant
25. Certain keyboard instruments
26. Boxing prize
27. Short for "popular opinions," 2 wds.
28. Armed conflicts
29. City southwest of Keelung
30. Make waves
31. Astringent in red wine
32. Catalog
33. "___ no place like home": Dorothy's refrain in *The Wizard of Oz*
34. Diner
35. Sports figures
36. Passes water
39. He and she

ACROSS

1. Art able to
6. In doubt
10. Minnesota state bird
14. Cremona artisan
15. Novice
16. Composer Pärt
17. Energize
18. Ball of thread or yarn
19. Appearance
20. Breaks small pieces off
21. Command to a dog
22. Large mass of ice
23. NYC Chinatown's neighbor
24. Robin or jay
25. Bowed
26. Vegetable that brings tears
28. Peritoneum
31. Grooved on
32. CoverGirl purchase
33. Tackle box item
37. Lacy mat (UK)
38. Cork locale
40. Not dry
41. Mountainous region of Israel
42. Out of practice
45. A load
46. China problem
48. Saws with the grain
51. Bop
52. Subatomic particle
53. Old Toyota
54. Advocate
55. Crazily
56. Jellied garnish
57. Bavarian brew
58. *The BFG* author Roald
59. Animal in a roundup
60. Lays down the lawn
61. Cut down
62. Hercules victim

DOWN

1. Horseshoe parts
2. Kind of group, in chemistry
3. Apache language (var.)
4. Walk over, 2 wds.
5. Anchovy containers
6. Result of some joke-shop powders
7. Secretary, at times
8. Liberty
9. Long, dismal cry
10. Gleam
11. *Monopoly* avenue name
12. Musical opening
13. Foolish person (Australia)
24. Spy of Ludlum novels played by Matt Damon
25. Gets loaded
27. High marks
29. Concocted
30. Permissive word
33. Famous
34. Handel bars
35. Fit in
36. Turn signals
39. Point
40. In need of an iron
43. Reliable
44. Barked sharply
47. Ado
49. Nosey
50. Pelvic bones
51. Chicago team
52. Football equipment
53. Belt

194

ACROSS

1. Dinner bird
6. Squirmer
14. Hide, 2 wds.
16. Sanskrit for "abode of snow"
17. Hebrew prophet
18. Gave the OK
19. Historian
21. Joins
22. Commercial suffix with Star- or Sun-
23. Nancy Sinatra's "___ Boots Are Made for Walkin'"
24. Believers
25. Engine part, for short
29. Plague
33. Erupting volcano, e.g.
35. A single rubber shoe
36. Halogen salt
37. Exceedingly, 2 wds.
38. Sauntered
39. Wet, as morning grass
40. Ant's place
43. Ancient reference marks
44. Container weight
48. Bell ___
52. Air on Twitch, say
54. Invalidate
56. Calamitous
57. Brain membrane
58. Like tears
59. Some tea tools
60. Billiards technique that produces a curving shot

DOWN

1. Magician's wrist movement
2. Hindu poet
3. A long time
4. *The Waste Land* poet
5. Bookbinding leather
6. Creators of big splashes
7. Least green
8. Monet or Cassatt, e.g.
9. Former Civil War veterans organization: Abbr.
10. Radiate
11. Cleanse
12. Checked out
13. Physics units
15. Peppermint bark layer, maybe, 2 wds.
20. Gambler's marker
24. Bad-mouth
25. Formally surrender
26. Out of town
27. Anatomical nerve network
28. Born's partner
29. Got old
30. Short for "best-liked"
31. Sped
32. Swimming companion of Alice
34. Floral arrangement
38. Beauty mark
41. ___ *dictum*
42. Crowbars, essentially
44. Start of a refrain
45. Auspices
46. Torrents
47. Host
48. Pool exercise
49. Not much
50. Highlands hillside
51. Those who like it hot
53. Way around London
55. Breach

ACROSS

1. Applies sloppily
6. Bowls
12. Loosen, in a way
14. Forestalling, with "off"
15. Competitor
17. Pakistani port
18. Reptile hunter
19. Clytemnestra's slayer
20. Hindu prince
22. Links rental
23. Container for nitroglycerin
24. Adorable
25. Neutralize, as a cobra
28. Compound used in fire extinguishers
29. Chunks of fairway
30. Capital of Tasmania, Australia
31. ___ orange
32. Gentlemen: Abbr.
33. Department store department
34. Harmed
35. Be a rat
36. Brunch order
41. Consumes
44. Holy ones are hard to handle
46. Distribute, 2 wds.
47. Method for acquiring knowledge
48. Armies
49. Roman coins introduced by Constantine
50. Builds
51. Not playing, in music

DOWN

1. The Everly Brothers, e.g.
2. Per ___ (yearly)
3. Ne plus ___
4. Calvinist Karl
5. La ___ opera house in Milan, Italy
6. Lead actor
7. Container weight
8. Without blood vessels
9. Pinochet, Castro, e.g.
10. Essential
11. Disparager of seniors
13. In a weakened state
14. "Cheers!"
16. Gets in shape
21. Bender
24. Street fleet
25. Release
26. Pertaining to the gospel
27. Obscures
28. Stableboys
29. Rule
30. Regarding this point
32. Ornamental flower, for short
34. Legions
35. Edge
37. *Claviceps purpurea*
38. Start of a refrain
39. Bartender's supply
40. Chip away at
42. Dirty coat
43. Cask barrels
45. Agitated state

ACROSS

1. Steam engine sound
6. Welsh "Siobhan"
10. Not straight
14. ___-guided
15. Annul
16. Small salmon
17. Occupied, 2 wds.
18. Farm equipment
19. Ball of thread or yarn
20. 1962 and 1990 Tony winner Robert ___
21. Like the Louvre's landmark entrance
23. Two-footed
25. Checked out
26. Eq. to 60 sec.
28. Bad smell
32. Food for sea urchins
36. Bit of sweat
38. Anoint with sacred oil, old-style
39. Hammer's target
40. Globular
42. It wags
43. Happen
45. Chesterfield, e.g.
46. British geek
47. Like an amusement park
49. Aircraft compartment
50. Handle roughly
52. Depleting, 2 wds.
58. Aquatic bird
62. Anatomical horn
63. Adjoin
64. Decree
65. Follow
66. Baptism, for one
67. Advocate
68. Arctic boat
69. Fastener
70. Equal
71. Oceanic tunicate

DOWN

1. Scale
2. Asian capital
3. Appropriate
4. Heraldic band
5. Let go
6. Providers
7. Deeply
8. Dig, so to speak
9. In no manner, 2 wds.
10. Mishaps
11. Tract of open rolling country
12. Actress Seehorn of *Better Call Saul*
13. Bellow
22. Prefix with -physical or -bolism
24. Early pulpit
27. Bigwig
29. ___ tide
30. Annual advertising award
31. Believed
32. Bow
33. A head
34. Vermin
35. Dropped sharply
37. Nonpayer
41. Quite a while
44. Back
48. Beat severely (UK), 2 wds.
51. French tank ___ MK
53. Metrical accent
54. Marilyn Monroe's first name
55. Holy ___
56. Open, as a bottle
57. First class
58. ___ of the Roses
59. Not much
60. Ballet dress
61. "Minimum" amount

ACROSS

1. Beat to a pulp
5. Jam
9. A-lister
13. Cars
15. Like mud
16. Havana's home
17. ___ test dummy
18. Good vantage point
19. Deeply
20. Backpacker
21. They keep practicing
23. Currency in Ghana
24. Catcall
25. Fishing net
29. Lightweights (var.)
33. Banana kin
37. "The sweetest gift of heaven," according to Virgil
38. Three stripes, to Adidas
39. Big name in cheese
42. *All in the Family* creator Norman
43. Cast out
45. How one thing can lead to another
47. Moistens
49. Sort
50. Bridle parts
52. A head
56. State of being within
61. German Renaissance painter
63. Midday
64. Lady Macbeth, e.g.
65. Chip away at
66. Bean ___
67. Knot of wool
68. Animal droppings
69. Cluckers
70. Put an end to
71. Convene

DOWN

1. Airspeed ratio
2. Containing gold
3. Investment
4. Bamboozled
5. Protagonist in Colson Whitehead's *The Underground Railroad*
6. Carrot, e.g.
7. Mercury, in alchemy
8. "Yeah, right!"
9. Little bit
10. Melody
11. Well
12. Beams
14. Priest's absolution
22. Column crossers
26. Tartary ox
27. White wine aperitif
28. Legislate
30. Casting need
31. Loud ringing
32. Active
33. Commoner
34. Balcony section
35. Ancient
36. Headstall parts
40. *King Kong* actress Wray
41. Sign in cuneiform writing
44. Double
46. Ranked, pre-tournament
48. Rears
51. Fido's nose
53. Caesar's gold
54. Witchy woman
55. Beat around the bush
56. Creep
57. Grimace
58. Neil Diamond's "September ___"
59. Ad award
60. Canine cry
62. Take a break

ACROSS

1. Attack a fellow soldier
5. Charades, essentially
9. Early pulpit
13. Rescuing
16. ___ ___ song
17. *QE2*, e.g., 2 wds.
18. ___ jacket
19. Scripted together
20. Returns land to an undeveloped state
22. Puerto Rican rapper ___ Bunny
23. Turned right
24. Geek (UK)
28. Mercury ore
32. The "C" in TLC
33. Bait
35. Bad habit, so to speak
36. Annul
37. ___ tube
38. Creep
39. 20-20, e.g.
40. Part of a simple bouquet
41. Figure skater Lipinski
42. NOW and NATO, e.g.
44. Concrete section
45. Miles per hour, e.g.
46. *Mork & Mindy* actor ___ Dawber
49. Ancient skin-scraping instrument
52. Some, 2 wds.
57. F. Scott Fitzgerald's ___ *Side of Paradise*
58. Site for dining, 2 wds.
60. Advocate
61. Small cozy rooms (UK)
62. Big pig
63. ___ Canaria island
64. Active

DOWN

1. Fluffy mass
2. Mob-busting law: Abbr.
3. Not many
4. Reverse, e.g.
5. Gozo Island is part of it
6. Like some walls
7. Egyptian god of reproduction
8. Stimulates (UK)
9. Written declarations under oath
10. Gangster's gal
11. *The Incredibles* director Bird
12. Trees that drop acorns
14. Country club type
15. Foliage
21. Cyst
24. Latin for "shields"
25. Pre-exam feeling, maybe
26. Command
27. Agent that destroys offensive odors (UK)
28. ___ Major
29. Double
30. African capital
31. Detox locale
33. *Layia platyglossa*
34. Plating
43. Bother
46. Broad-bladed African knife
47. Adjust, in a way
48. Cheese nibblers
49. Ballgame souvenir
50. Daniel Defoe's *A Tour ___ the Whole Island of Great Britain*
51. Baltic capital
53. Blackens
54. Excursion
55. Bad look
56. Not difficult
59. Blackguard

ACROSS

1. High-hatter
5. ___ and desist
10. Not many
14. Didn't go straight
15. Stems used for thatching and bedding
16. Unacceptable
17. Like a fine wine
18. AIDS activist group of the 1980s
19. Composer Pärt
20. Comedian Sahl
21. It's a snap
22. Big name in chips
23. *Pachinko* author ___ Jin Lee
25. "___ don't we…"
27. *Golden Girls* setting
29. Epidemiologist's study
34. Attack
35. Promises too much
37. Boeing 747, e.g.
38. Uses
39. Guacamole, e.g.
40. Like some sandwiches
43. Rumer Godden's *In This House of* ___
45. Completely bare
46. Broadcast
47. Soaked
48. Bio info
49. Bogus
52. Moscow currency
57. Milk source
60. ___ ___ list
61. Dental filling
62. White Stripes' hit "Seven Nation ___"
63. Anise-flavored liqueur
64. Bring out
65. Clip
66. Small songbird
67. Clad in a caftan
68. Kid

DOWN

1. Did laps, say
2. Canceled, as a mission, 2 wds.
3. Dominate
4. Midnight, maybe
5. Crack
6. A head
7. Ford, for one
8. Slattern
9. Authorizes
10. Break down (UK)
11. "It's ___ ___ good cause"
12. Green sin
13. Coaxes
24. Coll. hoops competition
26. Possesses
27. Magic charm
28. All thumbs
29. Federico Fellini's *La* ___ *Vita*
30. Harvard, Yale, Brown, etc.
31. Top competitors, often
32. Black-blue fruit
33. Item with a ladder
36. Raced
38. Measlier
41. Lunar calendar start, 2 wds.
42. Charge
43. Entertainment company ___ Robot Productions
44. It may be read before a grounding, 2 wds.
49. House
50. 2:00 or 3:00
51. Ax-like implement
53. Cancel out
54. Underwater exhalation sound
55. Shoestring
56. Checked out
58. Crazily
59. Sort

ACROSS

1. Item passed in a relay
6. Backsides
11. Tail's motion
14. Kind of group, in chemistry
15. Indigenous Canadian
16. *Heaven and Hell*, to Black Sabbath fans
17. Caught, in a way
18. ___ sling: cocktail order
20. Scrape, as the knee
21. Corp. phone line
22. Sage
23. Key material
25. "As if that ___ enough…"
26. More Broadway-bound
29. Medical advice, often
30. Stock market figures
31. Blown away
33. Starting place
37. Mountain crest
38. Assent
39. Meow (var.)
40. Some Beatles-era Brits
41. Some male dolls
42. Braided linen tape
43. Bound
45. Exasperated
47. Capital of New York
50. Grunts
51. Buildings with lofts
52. Email action, e.g.
53. Yanks
57. No-frills
59. Asian capital
60. Make a sharp turn
61. Bequeath
62. Assisted
63. Not go straight
64. Encouraged, with "on"
65. Dorm annoyance

DOWN

1. Blocks
2. Crazily
3. Dakota's dwelling (var.)
4. Single performance, 3 wds.
5. Affirmative action
6. Disordered
7. Accord
8. Enjoyable activities
9. Newton fruit
10. Balanced states
11. Like some milk
12. Composer ___ Copland
13. Netherlands treaty city
19. Birthmark, 3 wds.
21. Anguish
24. Workbench attachment
25. Married
26. Bogus
27. Novice
28. Ancient
29. Went up again
32. Cyst
34. Sitcom *Black-ish* setting Sherman ___
35. Stubborn beast
36. Ran, as colors
39. Appearance
41. E or G, e.g.
44. Boot part
46. Coal carrier
47. Full of activity
48. Hawaiian island
49. North Carolina garrison Fort ___
50. Annoy
52. Catch
54. Annul
55. Attendee
56. Fries, maybe
58. Elton John's birthname, for short
59. Holds onto

ANSWERS

1

```
C L A S S _ C O C A _ A R U M
L I P P Y _ E B O N _ P A P A
U N S A D D L I N G _ E D E N
E T E R N A L _ V E E R I N G
_ _ _ T E N _ W E L L T O D O
E S S A Y _ M A X _ F U S S _
R O E _ _ T O Y _ A I R _ _ _
E L E C T R O M A G N E T I C
_ H A Y _ A C E _ _ _ A L P _
_ F L O C _ A R T _ B U R K A
P E A C E N I K _ G A S _ _ _
A M R I T A S _ D Y N A M I C
T O R C _ I L L U M I N A T E
T R U E _ V E A L _ S C U L P
Y A P S _ E S P Y _ H E L L S
```

2

```
P I L A F _ G A R D A _ G O T
A M I G O _ A T E A M _ R A W
S P E A R _ R E P L I C A T E
_ _ I T S _ _ E A R A C H E _
S T O N E W A L L S _ T E S T
C R U _ P O L E _ I N N _ _ _
R O T _ I R K E D _ E A V E S
A L R E A D Y _ I C E P I C K
G L E N N _ D I R E R _ S L Y
_ _ T O P _ R A N D _ T A P _
D E C O _ E L E C T O R A T E
E R E M I T E _ _ O W E _ _ _
B A R B A R O U S _ E N U R E
U T E _ M E N S A _ L A S E R
G O D _ B L E E P _ L L A M A
```

3

```
P L O W S H A R E _ S T A C K
H O T H E A D E D _ O R L O N
A T T A I N I N G _ M O O R E
T H O R N _ T E E _ A T O N E
_ _ _ F I R _ W R A T H F U L
S T Y _ N U B _ S K I _ _ _ _
Y O U N G M A N _ A C I D L Y
N I L E _ D U O _ _ V I O L
C L E W E D _ T R I C Y C L E
_ _ M A R _ E M U _ E L M
V A S C U L A R _ P E W _ _ _
O C T A L _ D E N _ B A S R A
L A R V A _ A L A B A S T E R
T R A I T _ R E S U L T A N T
S I D L E _ S T A B L E B O Y
```

4

```
A D A G E _ D E B T _ S N O B
C O L O R _ E A R N _ T O D O
R E E V E _ B R A T _ A V O W
E R S E _ O U T S _ S N A R L
_ _ _ R O U G H S H O D _ _ _
S H I N E R S _ H A M I T U P
H O N O R _ P A G A N I N I
A G A R _ B E A T S _ G A I T
R A N G I E S T _ A O R T A
K N E E C A P _ C A N V A S S
_ _ N E U R A L G I A _ _ _
S T E E D _ E P E E _ T U P I
C H A R _ A S I F _ R I G O R
U R S A _ I S N T _ H O L L O
D U E L _ L O G S _ O N I O N
```

5

```
B A B A _ O R B I T _ A M E N
A G O G _ S E I N E _ R I P E
R H E A _ C A N S T _ T R E E
M A R I T A L _ T H R I V E D
_ _ _ N O N E _ R E E F _ _ _
A B U S E _ S C U R F I E S T
T E N T S _ T I M E S C A L E
O B I T _ F A T E D _ I R A N
M O T H E A T E N _ S A L V O
S P E E D I E S T _ P L Y E R
_ _ _ G A L A _ A M A H _ _ _
B E E R M U G _ L A Y E T T E
A G R A _ R E F I T _ A R E A
R A N I _ E N A T E _ R U E S
E D E N _ S T A Y S _ T E N T
```

6

```
P Y R O P E _ T R I C H I N A
L O A V E S _ R A R A A V I S
A R D E N T _ A N A G R A M S
G U I N E A P I G _ Y E N _ _
A B O _ S T O N E D _ S T A B
L A T H _ E D I S O N _ H I E
_ _ E A T S I N _ S E C E D E
C I L I A _ A G E _ T O T E R
O C E L L I _ C L O T H E _ _
C A P _ A D J O I N _ O R F F
O O H S _ S A L T E R _ R I O
_ _ O U R _ P L E N A R I L Y
G I N G I V A E _ E N A B L E
A V I A T I N G _ S U T L E R
D E C R E A S E _ S P E E D S
```

7

O	S	L	O		S	E	A	R	S		I	C	B	M
S	C	O	W		U	Z	B	E	K		S	H	O	E
A	R	I	L		B	R	A	D	Y		R	A	N	T
K	I	R		C	H	A	S	E		S	A	R	A	H
A	M	E	B	A	E		E	S	C	H	E	W		
		O	M	A	N			O	O	L	O	G	Y	
A	R	C	H		D	O	P	A	N	T		M	O	O
G	E	A	R		I	D	O	L	S		P	E	R	U
E	A	R		I	N	S	I	T	U		O	N	E	S
S	P	R	A	N	G		O	L	I	O				
	O	F	F	S	E	T		S	C	R	I	M	S	
I	N	T	R	O		M	U	S	H	Y		R	O	C
C	O	T	E		D	E	L	H	I		P	A	T	H
E	G	O	S		A	E	S	O	P		I	T	E	M
S	O	P	H		D	R	A	W	S		P	E	S	O

8

S	I	L	V	A		F	L	E	E	T		E	W	E
W	O	O	E	D		R	E	F	E	R		A	I	D
A	W	N	E	D		E	X	T	R	A		S	K	A
B	A	G	P	I	P	E		G	O	Y	I	M		
	S	C	A	M	P		J	I	B					
S	A	W		T	R	A	F	F	I	C	J	A	M	S
C	Z	A	R	S		S	E	R	B		E	M	I	T
R	I	V	E		D	O	N	E	E		C	O	L	A
I	D	E	A		A	N	N	E		S	T	U	N	T
P	E	R	M	I	S	S	I	B	L	E		R	E	S
	E	T	H		G	A	I	L	Y					
M	Y	R	R	H		S	E	V	E	R	E	D		
Y	E	A		A	C	I	N	I		A	S	I	D	E
N	A	G		C	O	L	O	N		G	E	O	D	E
A	H	A		A	L	O	N	G		E	S	T	O	P

9

D	R	A	W		C	E	L	E	B		A	F	R	O
E	A	C	H		I	M	A	G	O		C	L	A	M
A	N	T	I	C	L	I	M	A	X		C	O	T	E
D	I	S	G	U	I	S	E	D		P	E	C	A	N
		M	A	S		R	I	P						
B	L	I	N	I		A	B	D	U	C	T	O	R	S
L	I	K	E	N		R	U	R	I	T	A	N	I	A
A	V	O	W		S	I	R	E	N		B	I	L	L
S	E	N	S	E	L	E	S	S		A	L	O	E	S
E	S	S	A	Y	I	S	T	S		M	E	N	S	A
	G	A	M		S	O	U							
C	E	R	E	S		M	A	H	L	S	T	I	C	K
A	V	O	N		M	O	B	I	L	E	H	O	M	E
R	I	S	C		O	P	E	R	A		A	W	O	L
S	L	A	Y		B	E	L	T	S		W	A	N	T

10

R	U	T		A	B	B	E	S		I	N	S	T	
E	N	E		P	I	L	O	T		B	L	E	A	R
A	W	L		N	E	O	N	A	T	O	L	O	G	Y
P	R	E	S	E	N	T		S	O	U		C	O	S
P	I	P	K	I	N		S	I	G	N	P	O	S	T
E	T	H	I	C	I	S	T	S		C	A	N		
A	T	O	M		A	K	A		E	R	S	E		
R	E	N	O		L	I	N	O	S		F	E	T	A
	N	E	V	E		D	I	E		A	R	C	S	
	N	E	O		A	B	L	A	T	I	V	E	S	
C	H	U	R	C	H	L	Y		P	O	T	A	T	O
R	E	M		E	R	E		M	O	I	S	T	E	N
U	R	B	A	N	S	P	R	A	W	L		I	R	A
S	T	E	L	E		P	A	Y	E	E		V	A	N
E	Z	R	A		O	P	A	R	T		E	S	T	

11

T	O	S	S		S	M	E	L	T		T	Y	P	E
E	P	I	C		P	O	L	A	R		H	E	I	R
M	E	T	A		E	L	E	M	I		O	T	T	O
P	R	I	N	T	E	D	C	I	R	C	U	I	T	S
S	A	N	D	E	D		T	A	E	L				
	A	M	O	U	R		M	A	T	T	E	R		
S	C	A	L	P		S	O	M	E	W	H	E	R	E
H	A	L	O		M	E	M	O	S		E	A	S	E
I	N	A	U	G	U	R	A	L		I	R	K	E	D
V	E	R	S	U	S		G	L	I	D	E			
	S	C	A	N		R	E	A	V	E	S			
C	R	E	A	T	U	R	E	C	O	M	F	O	R	T
R	E	A	P		L	E	T	O	N		T	I	N	E
E	A	R	S		A	N	I	M	E		E	L	S	E
E	R	N	E		R	A	C	E	D		R	E	T	D

12

A	N	I	M	A	S		B	A	A	S		A	B	C
G	E	N	E	V	A		A	N	N	E		B	R	A
A	B	A	T	E	D		R	I	G	A	D	O	O	N
	M	E	N		M	O	R	A	V	I	A			
S	P	O	R	T	S	W	E	A	R		C	E	L	L
M	A	R	S	U	P	I	A		A	S	H			
O	V	A		R	A	G	S		P	A	C	T	S	
C	A	T		I	N	S	T	A	T	E		O	R	T
K	N	O	W	N		E	L	B	E		C	O	O	
	H	E	M		R	O	A	D	S	H	O	W		
S	A	F	E		O	W	N	E	R	S	H	I	P	S
L	U	L	L	A	B	Y		K	I	N				
A	R	U	M	L	I	L	Y		S	A	R	E	E	S
C	A	N		I	L	I	A		O	T	T	A	W	A
K	E	G		T	E	E	M		W	E	S	L	E	Y

13

```
T R A M P   S P I T   L A R D
B I J O U   W I N O   A V E R
S P A R S   A L S O   V I N O
P E R T   C R A P   P A S E O
    G O L D F I S H B O W L
C A N A D A   F R O Y O
A M I G O S   S E W S   W H O
R A C E R S       B I S H O P
T H E   L I F T   E Q U I N E
    D E C R Y   L U N G E D
P R E A S S E M B L E D
S O N G S   S P A Y   R O U E
H U N G   C H A T   F E N N Y
A G U E   W E N T   A S I D E
W H I R   T R A Y   A S T O R
```

14

```
C R A M B O   I N D U R A T E
R E L A I D   N A R R A T E S
U N T R O D   S P I N N E R S
S T E E P S   E E L   L E A
T A R S I   C R Y   T I N Y
A L E   C A T T Y   P I E C E
L S D   C A R   W A R R E D
    V A R I E G A T E
S P L I C E   P I G   A R K
C E A S E   H E G E L   G E E
R A C E   S O L   A M I C E
I C E   I L L   C R E T I N
M O R P H E M E   L Y R A T E
P A T H O G E N   U N I T E S
S T A I D E S T   E X T O R T
```

15

```
B A R F   A S A P   S C R A M
A G U E   M E G A   T R A C E
B A B A   A P O S T R O P H E
U R E T H R A   T W I S T E D
    H E A R   A I D S
P A T E R N A L   T O R P O R
A M A R E T T O S   R E E V E
W A C O   H E G E L   F L A M
E Z I N E   D O N I Z E T T I
D E T E S T   S O M E R S E T
    S T O P   R O T E
E N S N A R E   I N A N I T Y
D I L E T T A N T I   C O H O
I N U S E   C O A T   E W E R
T A R T S   E R S E   S A N E
```

16

```
C H A C H A S   N O H O P E R
R A M P A G E   O V E R A W E
A V I A T O R   T I M B R E S
B O G   G A G E D   E S T
S C O T T   P U P   M A G
    R A C H M A N I N O F F
    P R O L E S   D E N A R I I
D E E P E N   W I P I N G
E A T I N T O   R E B E C S
B R O N T O S A U R U S
    R E S   M I N   S T O M A
M E T   N O M A D   N O N
A R I O S O S   W O R K I N G
L I N E A G E   A M N I O T E
I N G R E S S   Y E A R N E R
```

17

```
R O D   S T O L E S   W A S P
I R E   U R B A N E   A S I A
S E E   L E I D E N   D I G S
C O M P L E T E   D R E A M T
    L E T   N A S A   N A Y
U S T I N O V   B U Z Z
T E R N   P O O H P O O H E D
A M I T Y   I L O   R O O T Y
H I G H A N D D R Y   L O C K
    S L O E   S T R O P H E
L E O   T O R E   T E G
I N R O A D   S T R A Y I N G
B E R G   L I T H I C   N O R
E M I R   E K E O U T   T A I
L A S E   S E R U M S   O H M
```

18

```
P E R I   R A J A   M A S T S
A X O N   O N U S   A L P H A
L A B U R N U M S   S P O O L
E M E R Y   S P E W   H U L A
    R E E F   I T E R A T E D
E S T   O W N   N A B
Y E S   T R A G E D I E N N E
E R O S E   N O V   S T E E R
R A N K A N D F I L E   G A S
    I L O   F L U   O T T
S O F T S O A P   G R I T
H U R T   K E L P   A V I S O
A T O L L   G A L A T I A N S
P E W E E   I C O N   E T A L
E R N S T   S E P T   S E G O
```

19

PITTA OWNS SCUM
ONAIR SHIP THRU
STOCKSTILL RIBS
III KIT IPECAC
EMS CYAN TSWANA
SATAY ESPY NET
ESSAY YIELDERS
ANOA PALE
COMPOUND SINKS
OVA GNAW UTICA
PEGLEG EDAM BAH
PREENS LOP BRO
ETNA TALETELLER
ROTS EGOS SEERS
SPAT RENT PASSE

20

SONGS JAG WHIFF
CLOAK OWE RENAL
ALIBI HEN ESSAY
BAR TAN DAT
TEN ABC PAT
GROCERY REHEATS
REBURY GMT MYTH
AVERS DUE OBELI
SERB GOT JEERER
PROSAIC HANDSET
SEN FLU IDO
IDS GEL BEG
AGATE OOH OPERA
NASAL AWL GRAIN
APHID PLY YOUNG

21

FIB CAPS STAPLE
IMITABLE CORRAL
SPRAYCAN ALCOVE
TIER YIELD TAP
ISM PROBE WITH
CHEMISORB ASIA
OLEOS TRITON
STADIUM COOLANT
THREAD CARVE
ARMS PASSERSBY
BEAT DELHI HOE
LAT TOTEM ERNS
EDUCES NEPOTISM
SERINE DRACHMAE
TREADS SENT PIN

22

TUNE ASSAM SMUG
ASIA PANGA HERO
CENTERFOLD OLIO
TRAIL EWER TICK
NAG TANGO
STAGNANT SOURCE
ARC TOOL UNARM
LAC GENTIAN TOO
EDEMA EARL EAT
SENILE LAMBASTE
TREND SON
SKUA LASH ANGST
MEAD INTEGRALLY
ONTO SCARE LEAP
GOER TERSE SEGO

23

ATM CMON SHANT
BOA OAHU SEINER
BUR ROOMSERVICE
APING BORE SKY
CENTIMO LAND
YEAH EXPO GUTSY
PREY TECHIE
COVERINGLETTERS
PIAGET MALI
ALTAR DYNE HOES
DEWY EXTRUDE
ADS CAKE OSTIA
GETTOGETHER BBC
EMEERS CAST ILO
DOMED HYPE DEW

24

CACHE WHOREDOM
AURORA AEROLITE
PROPEL RARAAVIS
SAWS TEMP STASH
SHAH UTE
PREMIERE SESAME
LINEMANAGER MOA
EVEN ERA POOR
BAM PORTRAITURE
ELYTRA ENSNARED
ROT DESK
SOLAR ANTI FLUB
ABIDANCE SPOUSE
RIVETERS TANNER
ITERATES STERN

25

T	E	N	T	H		S	T	E	P		C	A	S	K
A	D	I	E	U		C	O	T	E		O	G	L	E
T	I	G	E	R		A	G	H	A		V	E	I	N
	T	H	U	R	S	D	A	Y	S		E	D	D	O
		P	A	N			L	E	E	R				
F	D	A		H	A	J	J		S	Y	S	T	E	M
O	P	T	S		F	I	A	T		E	L	I	D	E
S	H	O	T	G	U	N	W	E	D	D	I	N	G	S
S	I	N	A	I		N	E	A	R		P	E	E	S
E	L	Y	T	R	A		D	R	A	T		D	R	Y
		E	D	D	Y				F	A	D			
A	A	A	A		R	O	A	S	T	B	E	E	F	
N	U	M	B		O	U	C	H		L	U	T	E	S
A	R	I	L		I	T	E	M		E	C	A	S	H
L	A	D	E		T	H	R	O		T	E	S	T	Y

26

C	H	I		L	I	M	A		O	L	D	B	A	G
H	A	N		I	B	I	D		B	U	R	E	A	U
I	N	S		K	I	D	S		S	L	I	G	H	T
E	G	I	S	E	S		D	E	L	V	E			
F	I	T	I	N		A	W	E	S		E	T	C	H
S	N	U	G		I	N	A	B	S	E	N	T	I	A
			H	A	N	D	R	A	I	L		E	A	R
V	I	M		R	H	O		S	O	B		R	O	M
A	N	A		C	A	R	E	E	N	E	D			
S	C	H	N	O	R	R	E	R	S		O	L	L	A
T	H	R	O		M	A	N	S		T	R	O	O	P
		A	R	S	O	N			G	O	K	A	R	T
L	A	T	T	E	N		F	I	A	T		T	I	E
I	S	T	H	M	I		C	O	L	A		H	E	S
P	H	A	S	I	C		C	U	L	L		E	S	T

27

G	A	G	A		B	U	L	B			L	O	S	E
A	G	O	G		E	V	I	L		T	A	T	E	R
F	R	U	G		R	E	N	O	V	A	T	I	N	G
F	E	R	R	O	M	A	G	N	E	T	I	C		
S	E	D	A	N			D	R	A	T				
		S	N	I	P	E	D		B	R	U	T	A	L
		D	O	O	F	U	S			D	E	W	Y	
D	E	F	I	N	I	T	E	A	R	T	I	C	L	E
O	Y	E	Z		S	T	R	A	I	N				
N	E	W	E	L	S		S	I	G	N	A	L		
		M	E	E	T			G	R	O	S	S		
	F	E	A	T	H	E	R	W	E	I	G	H	T	
F	R	A	N	C	H	I	S	E	E		A	J	A	R
E	A	R	T	H		R	A	V	E		N	A	P	A
E	Y	E	S		D	U	S	K		S	M	E	W	

28

L	O	B			P	A	S		A	L	M	O	S	T
A	N	O	A		I	R	E		D	O	O	D	O	O
G	E	R	M	A	N	I	C		D	A	N	D	L	E
		D	I	S	C	L	O	S	I	N	G			
S	E	N	S	E		N	E	T		O	R	S	O	
S	P	R	I	E	R		D	R	I	B	L	E	T	S
T	A	L	C	S		S	I	E	V	E		P	E	A
E	T	A		S	T	U	N	N	E	R		L	E	G
R	U	N		O	U	N	C	E		B	L	A	R	E
E	L	D	O	R	A	D	O		P	E	A	C	E	S
S	A	S	S		T	O	M		A	R	S	E	D	
		P	R	A	G	M	A	T	I	S	M			
S	T	A	R	E	R		A	N	I	S	E	E	D	S
P	E	S	E	T	A		N	O	N		S	N	A	P
A	L	K	Y	D	S		D	N	A			T	H	Y

29

P	R	A	U		Q	O	P	H		R	E	M	A	P
E	A	R	N		U	V	E	A		E	X	I	N	E
A	M	I	D		I	A	T	R	O	G	E	N	I	C
R	E	S	E	W	N		S	T	R	A	M	A	S	H
S	T	E	R	E	O	S		S	A	L	P			
			P	R	A	T	S		C	E	L	I	A	C
E	N	D	U	E		E	A	C	H		I	L	K	A
C	A	R	B		A	L	G	A	E		F	L	E	D
H	A	U	L		L	E	A	F		V	I	S	E	S
E	N	G	I	L	D		S	E	P	I	C			
			C	A	R	D		S	A	G	A	M	A	N
A	N	T	I	B	I	A	S		S	A	T	A	R	A
D	I	A	Z	O	N	I	U	M	S		I	C	O	N
O	C	K	E	R		S	P	U	E		O	H	I	A
S	E	E	D	S		Y	E	N	S		N	O	D	S

30

I	M	P	O	S	T	S		S	T	R	A	U	S	S
M	O	R	P	H	I	A		H	A	I	R	N	E	T
P	R	E	T	E	E	N		I	N	D	U	C	E	R
A	C	T		P	E	L	F		E	M	O	T	E	
S	E	E		D	I	L	A	T	E	S		M	O	T
T	A	N	G	A	N	Y	I	K	A		M	I	T	
O	U	T	E	D		R	E	S		A	U	T	O	
		I	N	S	E	T		Y	E	A	R	N		
G	R	O	T		T	I	S		D	E	I	C	E	
L	E	U		A	T	H	A	B	A	S	C	A	N	
U	P	S		P	L	A	I	N	E	R		A	N	D
T	U	N	E	R		N	A	I	F			T	I	E
E	L	E	G	I	Z	E		M	E	S	S	I	N	A
A	S	S	I	Z	E	S		A	L	L	O	V	E	R
L	E	S	S	E	E	S		S	L	Y	N	E	S	S

31

A	L	U	L	A			P	S	H	A	W			L	A	H
F	I	N	E	D			A	M	E	B	A			A	N	I
E	M	P	T	Y			G	A	L	O	P			D	I	G
W	Y	A	T	T		E	L	L			I	R	I	S	H	
			T	E	A	M			L	O	A	T	H	E		
P	A	R	R		I	S	M		F	I	E	S	T	A		
O	L	I	O		S	T	I	F	F			S	I	A	L	
S	L	O	P		L	U	N	A	R			U	N	T	O	
T	A	T	E		A	D	D	T	O			S	W	A	N	
S	H	I	N	N	Y		E	E	N		F	A	R	E		
	C	E	A	S	E	D			T	H	A	I				
S	T	A	R	R		A	N	T		O	C	T	A	D		
P	O	L		C	A	V	E	R		S	T	I	L	E		
A	L	L		O	B	E	S	E		T	O	N	G	A		
S	L	Y		S	A	S	S	Y		A	R	G	A	L		

32

A	C	E	R		M	A	T	S		A	B	A	S	H
L	A	Z	E		E	S	A	U		D	E	M	U	R
A	S	I	F		T	H	R	E	N	O	D	I	E	S
M	E	N	U		H	Y	S	T	E	R	I	C		
O	D	E	S	S	A			R	E	M	A	N	D	
	S	E	E	N		M	I	D			B	O	O	
	N	E	O	C	O	N		S	A	L	V	O		
V	A	N	I	L	L	A	I	C	E	C	R	E	A	M
A	R	A	K	S		P	R	A	X	I	S			
I	C	Y		P	O	E		P	O	O	L			
N	O	S	I	E	R		A	N	N	E	A	L		
	A	N	D	E	R	S	O	N		I	N	F	O	
E	R	Y	S	I	P	E	L	A	S		S	T	O	W
S	H	E	E	T		D	O	S	E		T	I	R	E
P	O	R	T	S		O	P	T	S		S	L	E	D

33

P	O	D	S		A	L	O	N	G		O	G	E	E
O	P	E	N		S	A	R	E	E		F	R	A	T
D	A	M	E		C	U	T	T	L	E	F	I	S	H
C	L	U	E	S	I	N		S	T	R	E	T	T	O
A	I	R	R	A	I	D	S			A	N	T	E	S
S	N	E	E	R		R	A	S	P		S	E	R	E
T	E	R	R	A	C	O	T	T	A		E	R	N	S
		H	O	M	I	E	S	T						
S	A	L	T		P	A	R	A	S	I	T	I	S	M
U	R	E	A		S	T	E	M		B	A	N	T	U
L	E	A	R	N		S	I	L	E	N	C	E	R	
C	O	N	T	O	U	R		R	A	T	T	L	E	D
A	L	T	E	R	N	A	T	O	R		R	O	P	E
T	A	O	S		I	C	I	N	G		U	S	E	R
E	R	S	T		T	E	N	S	E		M	E	N	S

34

D	I	N	E		K	H	M	E	R		A	L	A	S
E	L	U	L		N	A	I	V	E		N	A	M	E
L	I	C	E		O	L	L	A	S		E	M	I	R
T	A	L	C		W	O	O	D	E	N	W	A	R	E
A	C	E	T	A	L		S	E	T	I				
	O	R	B	E	D			B	I	D	E	T		
M	A	N	I	C	D	E	P	R	E	S	S	I	V	E
E	P	I	C		G	E	E	U	P		E	V	E	R
E	S	C	A	P	E	M	E	C	H	A	N	I	S	M
T	E	S	L	A			K	E	L	T	S			
	L	O	C	H		M	A	R	I	N	A			
T	O	U	R	M	A	L	I	N	E		O	V	A	L
O	R	S	O		S	O	N	A	R		P	E	R	I
R	E	E	L		I	N	D	I	A		I	L	K	S
N	O	D	E		S	K	U	L	L		C	Y	S	T

35

M	A	N	H	U	N	T		S	P	I	D	E	R	S
A	Q	U	A	R	I	A		A	R	S	E	N	A	L
N	U	M	B	I	N	G		L	E	T	T	U	C	E
S	A	B	I	N	E	S		A	D	H	E	R	E	D
		E	T	A			S	L	I	M	N	E	S	S
M	O	R	A	L	I	S	T		G	U	T			
I	R	O	N		M	E	R	G	E	S		S	P	A
S	E	N	T		P	E	A	L	S		A	T	O	P
T	O	E		G	A	R	N	E	T		M	A	L	E
			S	A	T		G	E	S	T	A	T	E	S
S	O	D	A	L	I	T	E			A	R	E		
C	R	U	L	L	E	R		G	O	R	I	L	L	A
A	I	R	L	A	N	E		A	N	T	L	I	O	N
T	E	R	E	N	C	E		S	T	A	L	E	S	T
S	L	A	T	T	E	D		H	O	N	O	R	E	E

36

R	E	F	S		T	A	C	K		J	A	M	B	S
A	X	L	E		O	M	A	N		A	F	O	U	L
S	P	I	T		M	E	R	E		G	E	N	R	E
P	O	R	T	M	A	N	T	E	A	U	W	O	R	D
	S	T	O	A	T		O	L	L	A				
		C	O	H	O		O	R	C	H	I	S		
E	C	A	S	H		I	N	D	O		H	O	L	T
T	I	M	E	O	F	F		A	F	F	A	B	L	Y
C	A	M	E		L	I	S	T		E	R	O	S	E
H	O	O	D	O	O		W	A	T	T				
		R	O	S	A		A	I	T	C	H			
S	E	C	O	N	D	C	H	I	L	D	H	O	O	D
M	A	U	V	E		R	I	C	K		A	C	A	I
E	S	T	E	R		A	L	O	E		N	O	G	S
W	E	E	N	Y		M	I	N	D		K	A	Y	S

37

E	R	S	T		C	I	V	E	T		A	D	A	M
C	A	P	E		A	D	I	E	U		P	O	R	E
A	D	E	N		S	E	N	N	A		P	U	C	E
S	I	C			H	A	Y		R	H	E	B	O	K
H	O	T	B	E	D	S		P	E	A	R	L		
		R	I	F	E		L	I	G	H	T	E	S	T
S	H	O	R	T	S	T	O	P			A	S	T	I
E	A	S	T		K	O	R	E	A		I	T	E	M
R	I	C	H			F	I	R	S	T	N	A	M	E
F	L	O	R	I	S	T	S		P	E	E	N		
		P	I	L	E	S		C	H	E	D	D	A	R
S	P	I	G	O	T		B	R	O			A	G	A
A	R	C	H		T	A	R	E	D		D	R	U	B
G	O	A	T		E	L	O	P	E		I	D	E	A
A	W	L	S		E	A	S	E	L		P	S	S	T

38

O	C	C	U	R		P	H	I	S		A	R	U	M
B	O	R	N	E		S	I	N	E		L	A	R	I
E	X	U	L	T		I	N	U	N	D	A	T	E	D
	S	E	R	F			R	E	E	M	I	T	S	
B	A	T	T	A	L	I	O	N		N	O	N	E	T
A	M	O	T	I	O	N	S		R	A	S	E	R	S
D	I	S	E	N	C	U	M	B	E	R				
S	N	E	D		C	R	U	E	T		D	R	O	P
		R	E	E	N	G	I	N	E	E	R	S		
I	N	U	R	E	D		D	E	M	E	S	N	E	S
M	I	N	E	D		W	A	T	E	R	I	E	S	T
P	E	C	C	A	V	I			S	O	N	G		
A	L	I	E	N	I	S	M	S		L	E	A	F	S
C	L	A	N		S	P	A	E		I	N	D	I	E
T	I	L	T		A	S	C	I		S	T	E	L	A

39

O	D	D	S		C	O	A	S	T		H	O	B	O
D	R	O	P		O	O	M	P	H		E	N	O	W
E	I	D	E		U	S	U	R	Y		T	Y	R	E
A	P	O	C	A	R	P		U	R	T	E	X	T	S
		T	A	T	E		C	O	I	R				
P	E	A	R	L	E	R		E	I	D	O	L	I	C
U	N	B	O	S	O	M	S		D	E	T	A	C	H
R	O	B	S		U	S	A	G	E		H	A	T	E
E	L	E	C	T	S		E	U	C	H	A	R	I	S
E	S	S	O	I	N	S		I	T	A	L	I	C	S
		P	E	E	P		D	O	L	L				
M	A	T	I	S	S	E		A	M	M	I	N	E	S
U	D	O	S		S	E	G	N	I		S	E	E	K
S	H	O	T		E	D	U	C	E		M	O	R	E
T	D	K	S		S	O	N	E	S		S	N	Y	E

40

O	R	B	S		A	F	A	R		M	A	G	U	S
W	A	R	I		D	E	F	I		E	N	U	R	E
E	P	I	T	H	E	L	I	A		T	A	L	A	R
D	E	M	E	A	N	O	R		S	A	T	A	R	A
		G	Y	N	E	C	O	L	O	G	I	C		
C	R	A	S	S	L	Y		Y	L	E	M			
H	O	M	E			A	M	I	D	I	N	E	S	
I	T	E	M		D	R	Y	A	D		S	E	A	T
A	L	N	I	C	O	E	S			E	A	S	Y	
		L	O	O	T		T	R	U	S	T	E	E	
C	O	R	E	P	R	E	S	S	O	R				
A	B	A	T	I	S		H	A	U	S	F	R	A	U
T	O	P	H	E		G	O	D	P	A	R	E	N	T
C	L	E	A	R		A	J	E	E		O	D	E	A
H	E	R	L	S		M	I	S	T		W	O	W	S

41

S	E	E	P		A	B	A	S			B	A	S	T
A	N	G	A		P	L	E	W		G	I	G	H	E
G	A	O	L		N	O	R	I		L	O	G	I	C
I	M	M	U	N	O	C	O	M	P	E	T	E	N	T
T	O	A	D	I	E	S		S	U	B	A	R	E	A
T	U	N	I	C	A		M	U	R	A	S			
A	R	I	S	E		Z	A	I	R	E		C	O	G
T	E	A	M		T	O	R	T	S		G	O	N	E
E	D	S		M	O	O	L	S		N	A	R	C	O
		D	I	N	G	Y		R	A	M	R	O	D	
A	C	C	U	S	A	L		P	I	P	E	A	G	E
G	A	R	R	U	L	O	U	S	N	E	S	S	E	S
I	C	O	N	S		E	G	O	S		M	I	N	I
S	A	R	E	E		A	L	A	E		E	V	E	S
T	O	E	D		E	Y	E	R		N	E	S	T	

42

B	O	T	H		T	O	D	S			P	U	L	P	Y
O	R	R	A		O	P	A	H		O	V	O	L	O	
B	L	O	C		R	E	G	I	S	T	E	R	E	D	
S	E	M	I	S		D	U	N	E	L	A	N	D	S	
		B	E	A	M		E	Y	R	A					
S	P	O	N	G	I	E	R		A	C	C	O	S	T	
H	I	N	D	E	R	E	R	S		H	A	V	E	R	
I	X	I	A		I	L	E	A	C		S	E	N	E	
M	I	S	D	O		Y	O	G	H	O	U	R	T	S	
S	E	T	O	U	T		T	S	U	N	A	M	I	S	
		T	O	D	Y		M	U	R	A					
B	A	R	O	G	R	A	P	H		S	I	N	E	S	
A	B	E	R	R	A	T	I	O	N		N	A	N	A	
G	U	A	C	O		O	S	S	A		A	G	O	N	
S	T	R	A	W		S	T	E	W		S	E	W	S	

43

```
T A R P   R A F T S   R E D S
A V E R   E B O O K   I L I A
M E M O   D O R M Y   C A S T
P R O M   C U K E   B O S S Y
A R R O G A T E   T O T T E R
    E S T O P   D R A S T I C
    D E E R   F L I P P A N T
        G A L I L E O
    A M P E R A G E   R I S C
    B O R O U G H   J U M P Y
R A D I U M   T H E S P I A N
A L E C S   A N E W   A N N A
D O R K   A M I D E   L O A D
A N N E   W I N G S   A S T I
R E S T   E D G E S   S E E R
```

44

```
G A B B R O S   S L A C K S
U N R E A D Y   H I P H O P
S T A T I O N   C O R P O R A
T I G H T R O P E W A L K E R
    A S P E C T   Y E A S
S T A B   S O A R S
T A I L S P I N   I N S A N E
A P R O P O S   R A I L C A R
R A S C A L   B E L T I N G S
    T I B I A   P E S T
S L O E   T E E T H E
H A R D H E A R T E D N E S S
A T L E A S T   A L G E R I A
C H O M P S   C L E A N L Y
K I N A S E   H O S T E L S
```

45

```
B A S S O   S L A W   M E A D
R E C O N   P A R A   A M M O
A R E A L   I M I T A T I O N
T I N N Y   T I D E M A R K S
S E E D   S E N   R I D
    S O L F A   S C O N E S
S A B O T E U R   K A R A T E
A N I   T E L   J I B   T N T
C O L L O P   S A I L B O A T
S A L A M I   A P N E A
    C A N   R A G   L A G S
S T R O N G M A N   B A S R A
M O O N S C A P E   U N T I L
U G L I   A G E S   S C E N T
T A L C   R I S E   H E R D S
```

46

```
S T O W P   A B B A   F E L L
T O P H I   D R U M   E P E E
O L E I N   M E Z E   T I K I
B E N Z O D I A Z E P I N E S
    T E S T   R A S E
B R A S S I S H   S C H U S S
L E C H   L I A R   S I R U P
O L I O   S O B E R   S I C E
B E E R Y   N I N E   M U R A
S T R E E T   L E A D S M E N
    A L A R   I G L U
A N T I H I S T A M I N I C S
R A I N   G U I D   K E T O L
S A N E   O L E O   E N E M A
E N G S   S U S S   R E M E T
```

47

```
S T I R   L O B E S   A P S E
E R N E   E V A D E   B E A T
T A T S   G O R G E   L O C H
S C U T   E L D E R B E R R Y
C H I C A N O   A S I A N
R O T U N D   T A L L T A L E
E M E R Y   P R O E M
W A D E   P O U N D   C U R S
    W O R S E   J O N A H
P A N P I P E S   S A M I T E
O N I O N   T U R M O I L
S K A T E B O A R D   E N O L
T A C T   A N T I S   N I N E
A R I L   S L O P E   C Z A R
L A N E   H Y P E R   E E L S
```

48

```
T A M P A   B U S T E D
O V O I D S   C E N T A V O
R O S E O L A   U N S E X E S
I N S T R U M E N T A L I S T
    I N T E R N O D E
C U P S   N O E N D   I S M
O T I T I S   S R I L A N K A
R E L I N E D   S T E L L A R
D R A C O N I C   E S T A T E
S I R   C O L O N   E W E S
    D U R A M A T E R
T O T A L I T A R I A N I S M
I M I T A T E   D E V A L U E
P I N E T A R   R E T I E S
S T E R E S   S E A T S
```

49

```
W A T S . A L T E R . R O M P
A U R A . D I O D E . A L O E
I R A N . M E R I T . D I R E
S A N C T I F I C A T I O N S
T E S T E R . . T I R O . . .
. . F I N E S T . N O T B A D
S T E M S . C A F E T E R I A
T A R O . C U P I D . L U N G
E L O N G A T E S . J E S U S
M A R I A N . S H E E S H . .
. . . O U T S . D E C A L S
S E C U R I T Y D E P O S I T
A L E S . C R E A M . P I M A
R A I L . L I A N A . E D I T
I N L Y . E A S E S . S E T S
```

50

```
S P A T . A M A H . I C O N
P I P E D . G A L A . N A P E
A P P L I C A T O R . D R E W
T E L E P O R T E D . E N D S
S T E P P E S . H A T E . .
. . H E D . F L A G E L L A
A R B O R . D E U T E R I U M
S I A N . E L K . M A G I
A L I E N A B L E . T I N E D
P E N N A N T S . P E N . .
. M U N G . C A N A S T A
S H A M . U S H E R E T T E S
H E R B . I T E R A T I O N S
E R I E . S O R E . S O N D E
D O E R . H A R D . N E S T
```

51

```
A L G A . C O M A S . O S L O
B O M B . E N A C T . O H I O
E S A U . R A N E E . L I S P
T E N D . M I S R E P O R T S
. . H O E R . P O N E . .
S A V A N T . F L I G H T S
P L E B E . R A R E . O A T
R E G I S T E R E D N U R S E
A R E . R A K E . O N S E T
Y T T R I U M . A S T E R S
. . A U L D . A N E W . .
H O T D O G G I N G . I R O N
I B I D . E A S T S . S A K E
L O V E . R E L E T . T I R E
L E E R . S L E D S . S L A M
```

52

```
G A S H . E M O T E . B A L D
O B O E . L O W E D . O L I O
B E R I B B O N E D . F U M E
S T E R E O . S N A F F L E S
. . . T W O . R O A S T
C O R P . W R I T E . .
O D I U M . L I N E N . B R O
D I S S A T I S F A C T I O N
A N C . K A S H A . H O R S Y
. . E T H I C . O R Y X
S N A F U . T H O . .
M O N O P O L Y . O H M A G E
E R G S . P O O H P O O H E D
L I E S . A C K E E . L O A D
T A L E . L I E N S . T Y R O
```

53

```
C L A S P . G R A B . F A M E
L I F E R . R A G E . O W E D
U N I N O M I N A L . R O A D
B E C O M I N G . D E L T A
. . I R O N . E G G O N .
F R O S T U P . A R C A D I A
L A N . E T E R N E . M I S C
A J A R . E K I N G . E S A U
M A D E . G I D E O N . G A T
S H O T G U N . T R A D U C E
. . S O N G S . I R I S .
R A P I D . A M A R E T T I
O X E N . C O R O N A T I O N
U L N A . B A G S . T E N D S
T E N S . S T E T . E R G O T
```

54

```
S P A N . B E M A . C A P R I
A E R Y . O P E C . A G U E S
M A G N E T I T E . R E N A L
B L O O M . C H R O N I C L E
A S T R I D E . M E S H . .
. . S L I N K . S Y M B O L
S M O K E S T A C K S . O W E
C O B . E Y E . W E E
A V E . S T R O N G H O L D S
G E I S H A . S T E E R .
. S P I N . I T A L I C S
C H A I N G A N G . R E M A P
H E N C E . B I R D T A B L E
U L C E R . E S A U . N U L L
B L E S S . D I M E . S E A L
```

55

```
TED . . SCAB . ECOLI
ALES . HOUR . CHAIN
BALALAIKA . ZETAS
UNICORN . CLEMENT
. RSVP . STAMINA
VII . ELBE . WAS
ACAI . YEMEN . TBAR
SAND . . AID . ROUE
TOTE . ANNAS . YORE
. NOG . AMID . BAD
. PITCHER . TORY
RECITAL . STRETCH
UTICA . EPHEMERAE
MILAN . COIR . LAVA
STYLE . TENS . PAR
```

56

```
LAVE . SKEP . AMPS
ONIT . INFO . DOIT
BABAS . GETS . DANE
APRIL . HESITANCE
REALEST . TUBFUL
. STEEPLED . SLUR
. TORTOISESHELL
. . RETCH
. HAILESELASSIE
. ERGO . TRADEINS
GRANNY . SEPTETS
OBLIGATES . AURAE
LEST . NAZI . LATTE
FREE . KERF . TIED
STAR . SLAY . EASY
```

57

```
MANAS . HOBO . OPTS
AGENT . ORAL . WHEN
SAUTE . GRID . NINA
. ROMP . KEG . LOG
TWIN . URBANIZING
ARTY . TAEL . GIPSY
REIMPOSE . OUT
ENS . SUPREME . BLT
. WET . CAESURAE
ADIEU . MARL . RETE
COMEDIENNE . ITEM
CUP . OAT . TANH
USAF . MIDI . CAROB
SELL . BEAN . TREFA
ESAU . IRKS . SYNTH
```

58

```
HARSH . AGOG . VALE
ENNUI . SLUR . ODIN
SCARF . TOTALIZES
. DISOBEYED
ALB . INURES . DUB
HEAT . NIL . SIMILE
AUTO . GSA . TOASTY
. IRK . HRS . NIB
MASSIF . COO . NASA
INTOTO . LAX . SNOW
LYE . TROUPE . DUN
. BLESSINGS
SEGREGATE . IAMBI
ARIA . UKES . FLOOD
EGGY . TART . TEMPO
```

59

```
MICRO . ASCOT . CAT
ADHOC . FLOUR . ORR
SOAVE . LINTY . MOO
. READAPTS . SMUT
MPG . NOMORE . TOSH
AHEM . REFIT . ONES
REDINK . TVSHOW
SWALE . THE . EGEST
. FLORAE . TREATY
SAFE . ATTAR . SLOP
PRAT . PTOSIS . TWO
IRIS . TINSMITH
TOR . FUNGI . RIDGY
EYE . ARGUS . ERASE
DOS . BESET . SOYAS
```

60

```
NAPS . INDO . HANGS
AGRA . NEAP . AWAIT
DOOMSDAYS . CARRY
INS . PURL . CIRCLE
RECLASSIFIED
. RANI . GEAN . PHD
SPIT . APHRODISIA
LIBEL . ATM . ANENT
ALEXANDRIA . DUDE
YES . MIRO . BIRD
. CELEBRATIONS
ONSIDE . BILE . COP
POILU . RECOMPOSE
TONIC . ERIN . ADEN
SNEAK . DYNE . LEST
```

61

B	U	N	S		C	E	C	A		A	B	A	F	T
A	R	I	A		O	Y	E	R		Z	E	B	R	A
L	I	N	K		N	E	R	O		A	M	E	E	R
M	A	N	I	A	C		E	M	U	L	A	T	E	S
S	H	Y		M	E	S	S	A	G	E				
			B	O	R	E			H	A	S	S	L	E
A	C	C	O	U	T	E	R	S		A	H	O	Y	
H	O	L	Y	R	O	M	A	N	E	M	P	I	R	E
E	N	O	L		S	T	A	T	I	O	N	E	R	
M	E	T	E	O	R		R	E	A	R				
			S	U	B	Z	E	R	O		P	U	S	
C	O	L	O	M	B	I	A		N	U	D	I	S	M
A	M	I	N	O		T	I	P	I		A	Q	U	A
S	E	M	I	S		T	R	O	T		B	U	R	R
E	N	A	T	E		S	E	X	Y		S	E	P	T

62

G	R	A	P	H		S	L	O	B		B	I	L	E
R	O	D	E	O		I	O	W	A		O	K	A	Y
A	V	E	R	T		T	W	E	N	T	Y	O	N	E
M	E	N	I	S	C	U	S		K	R	O	N	E	R
			S	H	O	P		D	R	E	S	S		
M	I	S	C	O	N	S	T	R	U	E				
I	D	I	O	T			H	I	P		A	M	I	D
S	L	A	P		E	R	U	P	T		L	O	C	O
C	Y	M	E		L	E	D			A	I	R	E	S
			O	D	D	S	A	N	D	E	N	D	S	
	A	L	T	O	S		N	A	A	N				
A	L	T	A	I	R		D	O	G	M	A	T	I	C
C	O	R	N	S	A	L	A	D		A	T	O	N	Y
E	N	I	D		D	O	N	A		N	O	N	O	S
R	E	P	S		O	P	A	L		T	R	E	N	T

63

P	E	T	S		P	L	A	Z	A		U	P	T	O
A	Y	A	H		R	I	F	E	R		N	O	I	L
C	A	M	E	L	O	P	A	R	D		R	I	N	D
E	S	P	R	I	T		R	O	O	F	I	N	G	S
			B	L	O	C		R	A	P	S			
F	O	G	E	Y		R	A	M		L	E	E	C	H
A	B	I	T		B	Y	L	A	W	S		T	O	O
R	E	B		S	O	I	G	N	E	E		T	O	P
M	A	S		I	G	N	I	T	E		F	I	N	E
S	H	O	W	N		G	N	U		C	L	A	S	S
		N	I	G	H			A	C	H	Y			
L	I	G	N	E	O	U	S		H	O	T	D	O	G
O	N	I	T		S	P	A	C	E	P	R	O	B	E
T	O	R	R		T	O	G	A	S		A	G	I	N
I	N	L	Y		S	N	O	W	S		P	E	S	T

64

S	K	I	M	A	S	K		V	O	C	A	L	S	
T	E	R	A	T	O	I	D		A	N	O	X	I	C
E	N	O	R	M	I	T	Y		S	A	L	I	V	A
M	O	N	K		L	E	E	R		I	D	L	E	R
		M	E	T	E		D	O	E	R	S			
A	L	A	T	E	D		I	T	D		H	I	S	S
D	E	I	G	N		S	N	A	G		O	M	E	N
D	A	D	A		D	I	T	T	Y		U	P	T	O
E	V	E	R		A	C	H	E		P	L	E	A	T
R	E	N	D		U	K	E		C	A	D	R	E	S
			E	L	B	O	W		A	X	E	S		
O	P	I	N	E		S	O	A	P		R	O	S	A
R	E	B	I	D	S		O	R	I	G	I	N	A	L
F	R	I	N	G	E		L	A	T	I	N	A	T	E
F	I	D	G	E	T		B	A	N	G	L	E	S	

65

O	F	F	S		H	A	K	E	S		B	O	W	S
P	R	O	P		O	B	E	A	H		L	A	I	C
T	A	R	E		S	U	P	R	A		O	K	R	A
S	U	B	E	D	I	T	I	N	G		O	Y	E	R
			D	U	E				G	Y	P			
S	T	E	W	A	R	D		Z	E	E		G	N	U
L	E	G	A	L	S	E	P	A	R	A	T	I	O	N
O	R	G	Y			F	U	R		H	A	N	D	
P	R	E	S	S	C	O	N	F	E	R	E	N	C	E
S	A	D		H	U	G		S	N	O	R	T	E	R
			B	Y	E				T	A	M			
S	H	O	O		S	U	P	E	R	N	O	V	A	S
I	O	W	A		T	R	A	V	E		S	I	L	L
A	V	E	R		A	G	R	E	E		E	A	S	E
L	E	N	D		S	E	E	R	S		S	L	O	W

66

K	A	V	A		A	M	B	I	T		H	O	M	E
O	W	E	N		G	U	A	N	O		O	K	A	Y
H	A	R	D	P	A	L	A	T	E		U	R	G	E
L	I	D		A	R	I	S	E	N		S	A	I	D
	T	I	G	R	I	S		R	A	T	E			
			L	E	C	H		N	I	A	G	A	R	A
S	O	D	A			P	E	L	L	U	C	I	D	
P	H	O	S	P	H	O	R	E	S	C	E	N	C	E
O	I	L	S	H	A	L	E				S	E	E	N
T	O	E	H	O	L	D		J	I	L	T			
			O	N	E	S		U	N	E	S	C	O	
L	I	E	U		N	A	T	I	V	E		R	U	G
U	S	P	S		E	X	A	C	E	R	B	A	T	E
F	L	O	E		S	O	R	E	S		O	V	E	N
F	E	S	S		S	N	O	R	T		W	E	R	E

67

C	H	O	P		S	C	A	R		H	A	L	T	S
H	U	L	A		K	A	L	E		I	D	A	H	O
A	G	I	N		U	N	I	M	P	R	O	V	E	D
N	E	V	A	D	A		B	A	L	E	R			
G	R	E	C	O		N	I	P	A		E	R	G	S
			H	O	S	E			C	A	S	U	A	L
A	F	T	E	R	T	A	S	T	E	S		B	Y	E
B	A	H		D	U	R	I	A	N	S		L	E	D
B	U	R		I	N	S	T	I	T	U	T	E	R	S
A	V	O	C	E	T			N	A	M	E			
S	E	E	R		M	I	N	T		E	R	A	S	E
		E	M	E	R	Y		U	S	E	N	E	T	
U	K	R	A	I	N	I	A	N	S		N	I	G	H
M	E	E	T	S		S	L	U	E		C	O	N	Y
P	Y	X	E	S		H	A	T	S		E	N	O	L

68

M	O	T	T	O					C	O	M	P	T	
A	B	I	O	T	I	C		T	R	A	L	A	L	A
C	E	N	T	I	M	O		R	A	D	D	L	E	D
H	Y	S	S	O	P	S		A	N	E	M	I	A	S
			S	U	M		N	I	N	A				
	F	O	R	E	L	E	G	S		T	I	P	S	Y
S	O	M	E		S	T	A	L	E		D	A	H	L
C	L	A	P		E	O	S	I	N		I	S	L	E
A	I	N	U		S	L	U	T	S		S	E	E	M
M	O	I	R	E		O	P	E	N	S	H	O	P	
			C	L	O	G		R	A	T				
A	F	G	H	A	N	I		A	R	O	U	S	A	L
C	R	E	A	T	E	S		T	E	R	R	A	N	E
T	E	N	S	E	S	T		E	S	K	I	M	O	S
S	T	E	E	D					S	C	E	N	T	

69

S	L	O	B		A	R	H	A	T		G	A	F	F
T	A	K	A		N	A	I	R	A		R	U	L	E
U	N	R	H	Y	T	H	M	I	C		A	X	O	N
N	E	A	T	E	R		D	I	C	T	I	O	N	
			P	U	M	P		T	R	E	N	D	Y	
B	E	S	T		M	U	U	M	U	U				
L	A	K	E	S		S	P	O	R	T	S	C	A	R
O	C	U	L	I	S	T		I	N	C	L	U	D	E
C	H	A	L	L	E	N	G	E		H	A	B	I	T
			E	S	T	A	T	E		M	E	T	E	
E	R	R	A	N	T		B	Y	R	D				
M	O	I	S	T	E	N		R	O	O	S	T	S	
B	U	G	S		R	E	F	R	A	C	T	I	O	N
A	G	U	E		C	R	O	A	T		I	N	F	O
R	E	P	S		E	D	E	M	A		C	H	U	B

70

T	B	S	P		L	E	M	M	A		S	N	A	P
H	E	E	L		I	V	I	E	D		H	E	L	L
O	N	L	Y		N	I	N	O	N		Y	U	L	E
R	E	F		C	O	L	D	W	A	R		R	Y	A
		R	I	L	L				T	A	C	O		
S	H	I	N	I	E	S	T		E	L	A	P	S	E
C	A	S	S	O	U	L	E	T		E	S	S	E	X
O	N	I	T		M	A	X	I	M		H	Y	P	E
T	O	N	I	C		P	A	R	A	M	E	C	I	A
T	I	G	L	O	N		S	O	M	E	W	H	A	T
		F	L	O	E			A	L	S	O			
G	A	L		L	O	W	C	O	S	T		L	A	V
A	X	O	N		C	A	R	I	B		D	O	V	E
S	L	U	E		O	V	O	L	O		A	G	E	D
H	E	R	B		N	E	W	S	Y		L	Y	R	A

71

H	I	F	I		P	S	H	A	W		S	W	A	G
I	N	O	N		R	A	I	S	E		T	H	R	U
G	L	A	S	S	I	N	E	S	S		R	O	B	S
H	Y	M	E	N	S		D	A	T		A	L	O	T
			C	I	T	Y		M	E	T	I	E	R	S
S	C	O	T	T	I	E	S		R	U	T	S		
H	E	R	R		N	A	I	F		P	O	A	C	H
U	R	G	E		E	S	S	E	X		F	L	O	E
L	E	A	P	T		T	A	R	E		M	E	O	W
			N	E	A	P		L	A	N	T	E	R	N	S
S	M	E	L	T	E	R		L	O	W	S			
T	O	L	L		T	U	B		L	A	S	S	E	S
A	X	L	E		A	P	O	L	I	T	I	C	A	L
M	I	E	N		R	E	L	E	T		N	O	S	E
P	E	S	T		D	E	A	T	H		A	W	E	D

72

S	H	U	N		A	R	C	O		K	A	T	A	
H	O	N	O	R		W	O	R	N		E	X	A	M
A	L	I	N	E		O	P	A	H		E	L	M	Y
S	L	A	P	S		L	E	M	O	N	P	E	E	L
T	E	T	R	A	D			P	L	A	Y			
A	R	E	O	L	A	T	E		D	R	O	P	S	Y
				F	E	M	A	L	E		C	U	R	I	A
M	A	G	I		N	U	L	L	S		R	O	C	K
B	U	S	T	S		T	I	B	I	A	S			
A	G	A	M	I	C		S	E	L	F	H	O	O	D
			A	D	E	N			T	R	I	P	L	E
A	L	I	K	E	N	E	S	S		E	R	O	D	E
L	O	C	I		S	H	A	T		S	T	R	I	P
M	O	A	N		U	R	G	E		H	O	T	E	L
S	M	O	G		S	U	E	T		N	O	S	Y	

73

```
S T A L E S █ U L T █ R A G A
H E G I R A █ S A E █ E X A M
E N A M O R █ P Y A █ A L S O
D E M I T A S S E S █ C E P S
S T A T I S T █ R E S T █ █
█ █ █ C O R A █ T E A M U P
A R M S █ T A L C █ A N O L E
F O U N D A T I O N S T O N E
A T T A R █ H A L E █ S N A P
R E T R O D █ S L A B █ █ █
█ █ E P O S █ A R R A S E S
B A W D █ T H E R M O S T A T
A C E R █ T A D █ I N C I S E
T H R U █ E R G █ S T O N E R
S E E M █ D I Y █ S E T T L E
```

74

```
G O N E █ S K E E T █ P L E D
A V I D █ P A R S E █ R E A R
G E E D █ A B A T E █ E A S E
A N T I P R O T O N █ T R E Y
█ █ Z E E █ B O P █ F E N D S
T O S S E R █ █ S E X █ █ █
A N C █ P E R M U T A T I O N
N I H █ S P O O L E R █ R Y A
S T E P H A N O T I S █ R E V
█ █ S O Y █ █ N O T A R Y
I N L A W █ S O D █ M A D █
N O E L █ I M P O V E R I S H
G H A T █ M I A M I █ P A P A
L O V E █ A L L E N █ O T I C
E W E R █ M E S S Y █ N E C K
```

75

```
S H U S H █ █ S P A S M S
C O P P O L A █ C H A L L A H
A L B U M E N █ H E R B A G E
G L O R I E D █ O E R S T E D
█ O W N E R S H I P █ █ █
█ █ █ O A R S W O M A N
H O U N D D O G █ K A B A L A
U N L E A R N █ S I L I C O N
B I N A R Y █ B O N E S E T S
S T A T E L I E R █ █ █
█ █ I N G R E S S E S █
S T A M I N A █ E X H I B I T
T A K E N I N █ L I O N I Z E
E P I G O N E █ S T A C K E D
P E N A N G █ █ L E E D S
```

76

```
A M P S █ S P A N █ C L A M S
B A I L █ H U G O █ R A D I O
I N C U B A T E S █ I C I L Y
T E T R A P O D █ M E T E S
█ █ █ R E F █ A V E R █ █
M I S C █ F I R E W A L L S
A D H O C █ D I L A T I O N
L E O N A R D O D A V I N C I
L A N D R A I L █ E N D U P
S L E E P I E S T █ G Y M S
█ M A N S █ R A M █ █
B L A N C █ J U R A S S I C
L O G I C █ H E S I T A N C E
A C I N I █ A R T S █ N A A N
B I N G O █ S K Y E █ S P O T
```

77

```
C A R L █ G I M M E █ O A T S
A G U E █ A R I A N █ F L A P
R A N T █ S O N D E █ F O R A
O M I C R O N █ M I S T E R
B A C H E L O R P A D █ █ █
█ █ V I R E O █ L U N A R
C L A W █ N E T T L E S O M E
H U M A N E █ A R E T E S
E X P R E S S W A Y █ S E X T
F E S S E █ H A I R Y █ █
█ █ D A Y D R E A M I N G
D A C T Y L █ M A H O N I A
O I L Y █ A P H I D █ R U T S
T R I P █ T O I L E █ P R E P
H Y P E █ E L D E R █ H E R S
```

78

```
C A P E █ D O F F █ P R O S
A F A R █ E X U R B █ H E B E
R O P E █ T E N O R █ A B I T
T O U C H A N D G O █ L U S T
S T A T I C █ █ C H A R █
█ █ G H A T █ A U R I G A
B E R T H █ H E A D B O A R D
A Y A H █ G E N I E █ P L O D
L A T E C O M E R █ P E S K Y
E S T R U S █ T Y P E █ █
█ L A P P █ █ A S T R A L
S H I P █ E S C R I T O I R E
M I N I █ L O R E N █ T O R E
E R G S █ S L A T E █ A J A R
W E S T █ O P E D █ L A Y S
```

79

T	A	N	G		W	R	A	P			S	P	A	R
O	V	E	R		H	E	L	O	T		C	A	V	E
F	O	R	E	F	I	N	G	E	R		A	R	I	D
U	N	D	E	R	S	T	A	T	E		P	A	D	S
			T	O	P				P	L	U	S		
A	L	B		M	E	M	O	R	I	A	L	I	S	T
W	A	R			R	E	P	U	D	I	A	T	O	R
A	D	U	S	T		R	I	D		D	E	I	F	Y
R	E	S	T	R	A	I	N	E	D			S	I	S
E	N	C	O	U	N	T	E	R	E	D		M	A	T
		H	I	E	S				G	A	D			
S	P	E	C		W	A	G	G	A	W	A	G	G	A
L	O	T	I		E	X	H	A	U	S	T	I	O	N
A	R	T	S		R	E	E	L	S		U	R	D	U
T	E	A	M			L	E	E	S		M	O	S	S

80

G	A	S	L	A	M	P		P	E	D	I	C	A	B
A	R	E	O	L	A	R		O	R	I	N	O	C	O
P	A	P	O	O	S	E		P	A	S	S	A	N	T
	B	A	K	U			R	O	S	E	T	T	E	
	R	I	D		S	A	F	E	S					
C	Y	A	N		N	A	I	F		T	H	E	N	S
H	A	T		B	O	N	N		S	E	A	C	O	W
I	C	E	B	E	R	G		A	N	E	M	O	N	E
P	H	L	E	G	M		G	R	I	M		N	O	D
S	T	Y	L	E		C	A	M	P		P	O	S	E
			T	R	U	L	Y		S	U	M			
	T	E	S	T	A	T	E			P	R	I	M	
B	O	X	K	I	T	E		S	C	A	R	C	E	R
O	R	P	I	N	E	S		A	U	R	E	A	T	E
W	R	O	N	G	L	Y		N	E	E	D	L	E	D

81

S	A	N	D		A	N	G	S	T		H	A	U	L
A	G	U	E		B	O	O	N	E		A	R	M	Y
F	I	L	M		R	O	T	O	R		L	I	B	S
E	N	L	I	V	E	N		W	E	L	F	A	R	E
				E	A	S	T		S	E	N	N	A	S
S	C	O	O	T	S		I	R	A	T	E			
H	O	T	P	O	T	A	T	O		S	L	A	G	S
A	D	I	T			J	A	B		S	U	R	E	
T	A	C	I	T		A	N	E	C	D	O	T	A	L
			M	A	O	R	I		R	U	N	O	F	F
O	P	T	I	C	S		C	R	O	P				
A	I	R	S	H	I	P		H	O	E	C	A	K	E
S	N	I	T		R	A	Y	O	N		A	M	E	X
T	U	P	I		I	N	A	N	E		M	O	P	E
S	P	E	C		S	E	W	E	R		S	K	I	S

82

C	L	I	P		S	W	A	N		M	O	C	H	A
H	O	N	E		M	I	R	O		A	V	A	I	L
O	U	T	S		A	G	E	D		N	E	R	V	E
P	R	E	T	O	R		A	S	S	E	R	T	E	R
	N	O	R	M	A	L		P	U	R	E	S	T	
B	U	D		G	Y	P		J	A	V	A			
E	N	E	M	A		P	H	O	N	E	T	I	C	S
A	D	D	I	N		R	A	H		R	E	N	A	L
M	O	S	S	G	R	O	W	N		A	D	A	G	E
			C	R	U	X		N	A	B		N	E	W
C	A	S	H	I	N		B	Y	P	L	A	Y		
U	N	T	A	N	G	L	E		R	E	D	C	A	P
S	T	A	N	D		A	L	S	O		D	A	D	O
P	R	I	C	E		C	L	A	N		U	S	E	S
S	A	N	E	R		K	E	N	S			P	E	N	T

83

S	W	A	T		P	O	L	S		S	T	A	R	R
T	H	R	U		S	P	O	T		P	I	L	A	U
A	I	M	S		Y	A	R	E		U	T	E	R	I
B	L	O	C		C	H	E	N		R	I	S	E	N
S	E	R	A	P	H		L	O	N	G				
			L	I	E	G	E		A	E	R	I	A	L
G	O	G	O	L		H	I	S	S		U	N	D	O
A	R	E	O	L	A	E		W	H	A	T	F	O	R
U	S	E	S		B	E	T	A		W	H	O	S	E
D	O	S	A	G	E		I	M	P	E	L			
			A	D	I	T		A	D	E	P	T	S	
S	P	U	R	N		N	U	T	S		S	O	R	E
C	A	R	E	T		G	L	U	T		S	L	U	R
A	N	G	E	R		L	A	N	E		L	I	N	G
R	E	E	D	Y		E	R	G	S		Y	O	K	E

84

O	R	F	F		C	A	B	S		G	E	T	U	P
F	I	L	O		A	G	U	E		A	M	U	S	E
F	O	U	R		M	I	R	V		L	O	P	E	R
S	T	E	E	P	E	N		E	G	O	T	I	S	T
			B	E	R	G		R	A	R	E			
D	A	K	O	T	A		C	A	F	E		S	O	S
E	P	O	D	E		P	E	L	F		S	C	U	T
I	N	T	E	R	C	O	L	L	E	G	I	A	T	E
S	E	E	D		A	L	L	Y		E	L	U	D	E
M	A	X		B	R	I	O		U	N	I	P	O	D
			S	E	E	S		S	P	I	C			
T	W	E	L	F	T	H		A	C	C	O	S	T	S
H	A	N	O	I		O	K	R	A		S	O	A	K
A	D	O	P	T		F	I	G	S		I	F	F	Y
W	I	L	E	S		F	R	E	T		S	A	T	E

85

```
MENU  FELT   SKEW
AXON  AMAH   SINAI
KERN  MERE   COAST
OSMOSING  ERUPTS
   TINDERBOX
SHRINE   HOD   BEY
TOUCH  GRIN   GALE
RUNE  CRONY   ONUS
ARID  LIMO   SLATE
WIN  WET   OODLES
   IRASCIBLE
CLARET  IDLENESS
HOMOS  PLEA   AYAH
AGENT  HINT   GENE
DOXY  DATE   ERGS
```

86

```
GROAN  ORSO   BAND
LITHO  FUNS   AWAY
ASHEN  FLAT   LEVA
SHEAF  SERENADED
SIRDAR   FOAL
   TACO   PIAGET
HALT  TERRAFIRMA
AVES  ADMIT   KAME
SEVENTIETH  AMYL
PROTEA   REIN
   SETT   CELLAR
UNDERTOWS  GAUZE
ROOF  AYAH   AUXIN
GIRL  TODO   TREND
ELMY  SNIT   EASES
```

87

```
YOUTH  SOFA   INST
AMNIA  PARR   NIKE
WAINSCOTED  SPIN
PHON  ETHIOPIANS
SANITY   GROG
   EOLITH  SNOWS
BAS  POSIT   TIBET
ULNA  NONCE   AIRY
SLING  TEAMS   SEX
TYPAL  HARBOR
   LUGE   OBECHE
PRAYERRUGS  VAIN
LIBS  IMMISCIBLE
ADIT  TABS   ILEUM
NETS  SLOT   GERMY
```

88

```
BARS  BOBS   ADHOC
ADIT  RIOT   PROTO
LEVY  UNDO   IONIC
SPELUNKER  ALECK
ATTIRE   MARL
   DIBS   DYNAMO
SNAFU  RETD   EVIL
LOVE  PITHY   SEND
USES  HEIR   ASSES
BERTHA  NUMB
   OATH   OUTRUN
ALTOS  ALLOTROPE
MUONS  RIEL   AMEX
PANEL  SETA   MENU
SUEDE  HUSH   PODS
```

89

```
MYNA  SPIEL   ABED
POOR  OUNCE   NONO
HUTCHINSON  CMON
   AIL  ELIGIBLE
SPEND  WRITHE
KAME  FIT   YONDER
YEA  MARSH   STELA
CLIMATE  OPTSOUT
ALLIN  DARES   DAT
PASSIM  TSP   FATE
   SOOTHE  FARED
SPITCURL   RAM
HAKA  SEETHROUGH
ALOT  SETAE   ULNA
GENE  EDEMA   STUD
```

90

```
KAYO  GIGS   CHASE
EMMY  IDYL   REMIX
LACE  GAMETOCYTE
PHARAOH  DECKLES
   BLOC   AIL
BAMBOO  WAR   EASY
ONAIR  EMMET   BAA
MOLOTOV  IRIDIUM
BLT  SPEND   PADRE
SEAR  PRE   BOLEYN
   WHO  WOLF
STRAUSS  CUFFING
ORANGETREE  ENOL
WILDE  EYAS   ULNA
SPEAR  PANT   DYED
```

91

B	O	W	S	E	■	A	V	E	R	■	L	E	E	R
A	K	R	O	N	■	M	A	X	I	■	U	L	N	A
T	R	E	N	D	■	I	N	E	A	R	N	E	S	T
H	A	N	S	E	A	T	I	C	L	E	A	G	U	E
■	■	■	A	M	Y	L	■	■	F	R	Y	E	R	■
E	S	C	A	R	P	■	L	U	S	T	■	■	■	■
R	U	H	R	■	H	E	A	R	T	■	P	L	O	D
G	R	O	T	■	O	X	I	D	E	■	A	U	T	O
S	E	W	S	■	R	E	C	U	R	■	W	A	I	T
■	■	■	C	A	S	E	■	E	U	N	U	C	H	■
L	I	S	L	E	■	■	C	H	O	P	■	■	■	■
A	N	T	I	D	E	P	R	E	S	S	A	N	T	S
P	L	A	T	E	A	U	E	D	■	E	B	O	O	K
S	A	L	E	■	C	R	A	G	■	T	I	N	G	E
E	Y	E	R	■	H	E	M	E	■	S	T	O	O	P

92

C	H	O	P	■	B	L	O	C	■	G	A	S	P	S
H	O	U	R	■	L	O	C	O	■	O	B	E	A	H
I	P	S	O	F	A	C	T	O	■	N	I	T	R	O
D	I	E	S	I	R	A	E	■	P	E	T	A	R	D
■	■	■	■	S	E	L	T	Z	E	R	■	■	■	■
C	O	U	P	S	D	E	T	A	T	■	R	A	F	T
E	N	N	U	I	■	S	E	P	A	R	A	B	L	E
L	I	T	T	L	E	■	■	L	E	V	I	E	R	■
L	O	I	T	E	R	E	R	S	■	S	E	D	A	N
O	N	L	Y	■	G	R	E	A	S	I	N	E	S	S
■	■	■	■	D	O	G	S	L	E	D	■	■	■	■
C	L	O	S	E	T	■	P	A	L	E	T	T	E	S
H	A	V	O	C	■	T	I	M	E	S	H	A	R	E
A	N	I	M	A	■	O	T	I	C	■	U	R	G	E
P	E	D	A	L	■	W	E	S	T	■	D	E	S	K

93

U	R	D	U	■	F	I	L	E	D	■	A	R	T	S
L	O	O	T	■	E	C	O	L	I	■	F	E	E	L
N	O	T	E	■	M	I	R	I	N	■	F	A	R	O
A	M	E	N	D	M	E	N	T	■	D	I	D	N	T
■	■	S	U	E	R	■	E	P	O	X	Y	■	■	■
B	E	L	I	E	F	■	■	A	N	E	M	I	C	■
E	V	I	L	■	A	B	Y	S	M	■	D	O	N	A
L	E	V	■	T	I	E	U	P	■	■	N	U	N	■
T	R	E	K	■	A	G	A	M	A	■	P	E	R	I
S	T	R	O	L	L	■	■	S	T	A	Y	E	D	■
■	■	W	O	O	E	R	■	A	G	E	D	■	■	■
S	T	U	D	Y	■	H	O	U	R	G	L	A	S	S
T	I	R	O	■	G	O	U	D	A	■	O	X	E	N
O	R	S	O	■	A	N	T	I	S	■	C	O	R	A
W	E	T	S	■	T	E	S	T	S	■	K	N	A	P

94

S	L	O	B	■	U	M	B	O	■	G	R	O	T	S
H	U	T	U	■	M	A	L	L	■	R	E	V	U	P
A	B	I	T	■	P	L	O	D	■	E	L	I	T	E
D	E	C	A	L	■	A	B	S	T	A	I	N	E	R
■	■	■	D	E	N	Y	■	E	S	T	E	E	M	■
A	N	N	I	E	O	A	K	L	E	Y	■	■	■	■
W	O	O	E	R	S	■	N	O	D	■	R	U	F	F
A	G	O	N	Y	■	L	A	X	■	K	O	R	E	A
Y	O	K	E	■	G	O	V	■	G	A	U	G	E	D
■	■	■	L	I	T	E	R	A	L	N	E	S	S	■
P	R	E	F	A	B	■	■	O	P	E	D	■	■	■
R	E	V	E	R	E	N	D	S	■	S	E	V	E	N
A	M	E	N	D	■	A	R	T	S	■	L	E	V	O
N	A	N	C	E	■	P	E	R	I	■	A	D	I	T
A	P	T	E	R	■	S	W	A	T	■	Y	A	L	E

95

W	O	R	D	■	S	T	U	B	■	B	E	A	U	S
A	V	E	R	■	T	O	N	E	■	A	L	I	N	E
M	E	M	O	R	A	N	D	A	■	P	Y	R	E	X
P	R	O	P	E	R	N	O	U	N	■	S	W	A	P
U	L	U	L	A	T	E	■	■	O	P	I	A	T	E
M	I	N	E	R	■	■	M	A	N	E	U	V	E	R
S	E	T	T	■	A	M	E	R	C	E	M	E	N	T
■	■	■	W	R	I	T	T	E	N	■	■	■	■	■
F	L	A	S	H	I	N	E	S	S	■	D	O	R	P
L	A	C	H	E	S	I	S	■	■	L	E	P	E	R
A	C	H	E	N	E	■	■	U	R	I	N	A	T	E
T	E	A	K	■	N	E	C	R	O	P	O	L	I	S
C	R	E	E	P	■	A	U	G	U	S	T	I	N	E
A	T	A	L	L	■	C	R	E	E	■	E	N	O	L
P	A	N	S	Y	■	H	E	R	S	■	D	E	L	L

96

F	A	S	C	I	S	T	■	R	E	E	L	O	F	F
A	M	M	O	N	I	A	■	A	R	M	O	I	R	E
R	A	I	L	C	A	R	■	D	A	B	B	L	E	S
M	I	L	L	I	N	E	R	■	T	A	S	S	E	S
■	N	E	A	T	■	■	U	P	O	N	■	■	■	■
■	■	■	T	E	R	E	S	A	■	K	I	L	L	S
R	E	F	E	R	E	N	T	S	■	S	N	O	O	P
A	V	E	R	■	F	R	I	T	Z	■	F	O	C	I
F	E	T	A	L	■	A	C	R	O	B	A	T	I	C
T	R	A	L	A	■	P	A	Y	O	U	T	■	■	■
■	■	■	M	U	T	T	■	■	L	U	S	H	■	■
S	W	A	M	I	S	■	E	M	U	L	A	T	O	R
W	E	B	I	N	A	R	■	U	N	I	T	I	V	E
A	V	E	R	A	G	E	■	S	T	E	E	L	E	D
M	E	T	E	R	E	D	■	T	O	S	S	E	R	S

ANSWERS

97

O	C	C	A	M		U	S	E	S		B	A	L	L
L	H	A	S	A		P	H	A	T		I	C	A	O
D	I	N	K	Y		T	O	R	E		S	I	T	E
S	P	E	E	D		O	R	N	A	M	E	N	T	S
		B	R	A	N	D	T		D	O	X	I	E	S
B	A	R		Y	E	A	H		Y	O	U			
R	Y	A		S	E	T	A		N	A	R	C	S	
O	A	K	S		D	E	N	T	S		L	I	O	N
S	H	E	E	P		D	H	O	W		G	N	U	
		D	I	P		T	E	A	R		M	E	G	
W	R	E	A	T	H		Y	A	K	I	M	A		
R	E	A	T	T	E	M	P	T		T	A	R	P	S
E	A	S	E		N	O	I	R		E	C	O	L	I
A	V	E	S		O	U	S	E		I	L	L	E	R
K	E	L	T		L	E	T	S		N	E	E	D	S

98

S	H	A	M		S	T	U	D			T	H	O	R
H	O	B	O		T	U	N	E			H	O	P	E
I	N	S	T		A	B	I	T		G	R	U	E	L
M	E	T	H	Y	L	E	N	E		W	O	R	D	Y
		R	E	A	L		T	R	A	Y				
	P	A	R	K		S	E	M	I	N	A	T	E	D
P	A	C	T	S		T	R	I	M		S	A	V	E
A	U	T	O		D	A	R	N	S		S	L	A	W
P	L	E	B		A	G	U	E		M	A	I	D	S
S	I	D	E	S	T	E	P	S		O	U	S	E	
			P	A	C	T		B	A	L	M			
Q	U	A	S	I		R	E	B	U	T	T	A	L	S
U	N	M	A	N		A	D	I	T		E	N	O	L
I	D	Y	L		F	L	E	E		R	I	C	E	
T	O	L	E		T	Y	R	O		S	C	O	W	

99

C	L	U	B		E	A	S	T			B	O	W	
W	O	R	E		S	A	T	E		H	O	Y	A	
M	A	G	E		T	R	A	P		E	Y	E	R	
	D	E	T	H	R	O	N	E		L	I	S	Z	T
		L	A	U	N	D	E	R	E	R				
O	B	S	E	S	S			O	V	E	R	D	O	
B	U	T		S	Y	M	P	O	S	I	U	M	
E	Y	A	S		G	O	O	E	Y		S	O	R	E
L	I	T	T	E	R	B	U	G			T	U	G	
I	N	S	A	N	E		P	L	A	S	M	A	
		G	O	W	A	L	K	I	E	S				
I	M	P	E	L		B	O	O	S	T	I	N	G	
N	O	I	R		A	I	R	S		T	O	I	L	
C	U	E	S		F	R	E	E		I	N	F	O	
H	E	D		T	E	A	R		S	E	T	T	

100

D	A	B		B	A	S	T			D	A	W	S
O	I	L	Y		I	N	C	H		L	E	V	E	E
C	R	E	E		D	O	L	E		I	C	E	A	X
	S	W	A	D	D	L	E		N	A	R	K	
			E	Y	E	R		C	E	P			
	C	A	S	T		A	N	I	M	I	S	M	
H	O	S	T	E	L	S		O	V	A	T	I	O	N
E	M	P	O	R	I	A		S	I	N	A	T	R	A
P	E	E	L	I	N	G		E	L	A	T	I	N	G
	T	R	I	O	D	E	S		G	E	N	S	
		D	R	Y		M	O	V	E				
	D	O	N	A		A	D	O	R	N	E	D	
T	E	N	E	T		B	R	E	D		O	Y	E	Z
A	M	U	S	E		A	M	O	K		T	A	M	E
M	O	S	S		M	Y	N	A			S	I	N

101

F	L	U	E		S	C	O	F	F		B	A	K	U
R	A	N	D		L	O	B	A	R		A	V	E	R
A	U	D	I	B	I	L	I	T	Y		Y	E	G	G
P	R	E	T	E	N	D	S		P	O	S	S	E	
S	A	R	O	N	G	S		S	K	I	N			
		G	U	N	S		D	U	N	C	E	C	A	P
S	M	I	T	E		C	O	N	E	S	T	O	G	A
K	I	R		M	I	L	N	E		F	U	R	
I	N	D	E	C	E	N	C	Y		G	O	F	E	R
D	I	S	P	L	A	C	E		B	A	D	E	
		S	I	N	H		C	A	L	D	E	R	A	
S	C	R	I	P		B	A	L	A	N	C	E	S	
N	O	I	L		B	L	O	C	K	H	E	A	D	S
I	N	F	O		A	O	R	T	A		S	K	U	A
T	E	E	N		A	G	A	I	N		S	E	X	Y

102

S	L	I	T		W	H	I	N		C	L	A	M	P
T	O	D	O		H	O	B	O		L	O	B	A	R
O	V	E	R	B	I	T	E	S		A	C	U	T	E
M	E	A	S	U	R	E	R		S	M	I	T	H	Y
A	D	L	I	B		L	I	S	T	S			
				S	K	A	T	E		D	U	M	B	
F	A	T	F	R	E	E		A	L	B	A	N	I	A
A	U	R	E	A	T	E		B	L	A	D	D	E	R
S	T	A	N	D	U	P		L	A	G	O	O	N	S
T	O	P	S		P	E	T	E	R				
			F	O	R	U	M		F	I	R	S	T	
S	U	L	L	E	N		P	A	N	O	R	A	M	A
T	R	E	A	T		H	E	T	E	R	O	D	O	X
A	G	A	M	A		I	L	E	X		N	I	K	E
R	E	P	E	L		P	O	S	T		S	O	Y	S

103

B	L	A	H		W	A	R	M		A	B	Y	S	M
L	U	B	E		H	O	Y	A		B	R	A	K	E
A	T	E	M	P	O	R	A	L		R	E	L	I	T
B	E	D	P	O	S	T		A	C	A	D	E	M	E
			K	E	A		Y	A	H					
A	D	O	B	E		C	A	R	A	C	A	L	S	
D	O	U	R		D	O	L	O	M	I	T	I	C	
U	L	N	A		K	E	B	A	B		S	O	L	E
S	O	C	C	E	R	M	O	M		C	L	A	N	
T	R	E	E	N	A	I	L		D	O	L	C	E	
			G	A	T		B	A	Y					
T	R	A	L	A	L	A		R	U	N	O	F	F	S
A	U	G	U	R		S	T	O	R	E	R	O	O	M
B	L	E	N	D		S	A	K	I		F	O	R	E
S	E	D	G	E		E	X	E	C		F	L	A	W

104

J	A	M	B		G	A	S	P		S	H	A	R	P
A	F	A	R		A	G	U	E		T	I	B	I	A
B	E	L	I	E	V	I	N	G		A	G	L	E	T
	W	I	T	N	E	S	S		E	T	H	Y	L	S
			S	U	M		K	R	I	S				
C	A	T	S	U	P		P	L	E	C	T	R	A	
A	R	E	T	E		C	H	I	C		R	U	D	D
R	H	E	A		F	R	O	N	T		U	N	D	O
B	A	T	T		R	A	T	E		K	N	O	L	L
	T	H	E	R	E	T	O		M	A	G	N	E	T
			H	O	S	E		B	O	D				
S	P	L	O	S	H		M	A	N	A	G	E	R	
A	L	E	U	T		F	I	C	T	I	O	N	A	L
G	O	O	S	E		I	N	C	H		L	O	G	O
O	W	N	E	R		T	E	A	S		F	L	U	X

105

D	R	A	M	A		C	I	S		D	R	A	T	
H	A	R	E	S		D	O	N	E		H	O	V	E
O	V	E	N	S		O	V	E	R	L	A	D	E	N
T	E	A	S	E		N	E	R	V	E	L	E	S	S
I	L	L	A	S	S	O	R	T	E	D				
				S	H	R	U	G		F	L	A	W	
S	U	C	K	E	R		P	A	L		L	O	V	E
A	L	U	N	D	U	M		S	O	F	A	B	E	D
I	N	F	O		B	A	R		T	O	P	E	R	S
D	A	F	T			G	E	T	T	O				
		H	A	N	D	H	O	L	D	I	N	G		
P	R	O	V	O	L	O	N	E		S	I	N	A	I
A	I	R	E	D	A	L	E	S		C	R	U	M	B
D	O	Z	E		R	I	C	E		A	G	R	E	E
S	T	O	P		Y	A	K		P	E	E	R	S	

106

P	A	N	S		C	L	A	M		E	V	I	C	T
A	B	I	T		W	A	V	Y		S	I	D	L	E
L	U	C	Y		M	I	E	N		T	E	L	O	S
S	T	A	L	E		C	R	A	S	H	T	E	S	T
		R	E	X					T	E	N	S	E	S
O	P	A	R	T		S	C	L	E	R	A			
N	O	G		O	C	U	L	A	R		M	I	L	S
Y	O	U		L	O	R	I	S	E	S		N	I	H
X	R	A	Y		S	A	N	E	S	T		C	O	O
		A	E	T	H	E	R		O	P	I	N	E	
S	P	A	R	T	A			M	A	D				
P	O	N	D	E	R	O	U	S		P	L	E	A	D
L	U	N	A	R		P	R	O	W		I	N	F	O
A	C	O	R	N		A	G	U	E		S	C	A	G
T	H	Y	M	E		H	E	R	D		H	E	R	S

107

S	T	O	W		A	W	F	U	L		L	U	S	H
T	U	P	I		M	O	O	L	A		U	N	C	O
O	R	A	N	G	U	T	A	N	S		T	R	O	D
V	I	R	G	I	L		M	A	T	T	H	E	W	S
E	N	T	I	R	E	S			R	E	F			
			T	O	T	E	M		H	I	R	I	N	G
T	O	P			R	U	R	I	T	A	N	I	A	
U	N	O	B	T	R	U	S	I	V	E	N	E	S	S
T	U	L	A	R	E	M	I	A			D	I	P	
U	S	E	S	U	P		C	L	E	F	T			
		M	I	L				S	Y	R	I	N	G	A
C	H	I	L	L	O	U	T		R	A	M	I	E	S
L	O	C	I		P	R	E	D	I	G	E	S	T	S
E	Y	A	S		A	G	A	V	E			R	A	T	E
W	A	L	K		H	E	R	D	S		S	N	O	T

108

F	L	A	P		C	W	T		E	A	R	L	A	P
R	I	V	E		R	A	H		C	H	O	U	G	H
E	M	E	N	D	A	T	E		L	O	O	T	E	D
E	N	R	O	U	T	E		P	A	L	M	E	D	
			L	E	E	R		R	I	D				
C	O	C	O		R	I	G	O	R		E	A	C	H
L	A	U	G	H		N	O	S		B	A	T	H	E
A	T	R	I	A		G	O	O		A	S	T	I	R
S	E	I	S	M		H	E	P		S	T	A	N	D
S	N	O	T		B	O	Y	O	S		B	R	O	S
			P	A	L		P	A	L	E				
	D	E	P	U	T	E		O	V	E	R	T	O	P
M	O	N	I	S	T		D	E	A	D	L	I	N	E
A	T	O	N	A	L		V	I	N		I	D	Y	L
X	Y	L	E	N	E		D	A	T		N	E	X	T

109

S	A	C	S			O	F	F	S			W	E	E
C	L	A	P			B	R	A	W			H	A	J
U	L	N	A		C	L	O	N	E		S	I	T	E
L	E	N	T		R	A	S	T	A		O	T	I	C
P	L	O	T		A	T	T	A	R		D	I	N	T
T	I	L	E		Z	E	U	S		B	A	S	T	E
	C	I	R	R	I		P	I	E	R		H	O	D
		S	E	E	P		A	V	E	S				
L	A	B		D	R	A	B		O	W	N	E	R	
E	R	A	T	O		R	O	L	L		A	V	E	R
T	E	C	H		B	A	Y	O	U		F	I	V	E
S	O	L	E		U	N	C	U	T		F	L	I	P
F	L	A	Y		N	O	O	S	E		L	E	V	O
L	A	V		C	I	T	E			E	Y	A	S	
Y	E	A		O	A	T	S			D	E	L	E	

110

M	O	S	T		W	A	G	S		L	I	P	S	
I	N	C	U	R		A	M	O	K		A	L	L	Y
N	E	H	R	U		L	O	G	E		L	E	A	N
O	R	I	N	G		K	N	O	W		L	I	T	E
R	O	S	S		M	A	G		E	L	A	T	E	R
C	U	M		J	A	W	S		R	A	T	I	N	G
A	S	S	O	C	I	A	T	E		C	I	S	S	Y
			E	L	M	Y		M	A	K	O			
S	T	E	N	O		S	U	B	G	E	N	R	E	S
T	O	Y	O	T	A		P	R	E	Y		H	I	C
A	L	E	P	H	S		R	I	D		L	I	D	O
R	U	S	H		K	N	I	T		V	I	Z	O	R
K	E	P	I		F	I	S	T		A	N	O	L	E
E	N	O	L		O	P	E	L		R	U	M	O	R
R	E	T	E		R	A	S	E		M	E	N	S	

111

S	A	P	S		C	Y	N	I	C		O	P	A	H
A	B	U	T		W	O	O	S	H		F	A	R	E
L	A	N	E		M	U	R	R	E		F	R	O	M
A	C	T	E	D		T	A	W		S	L	U	M	
D	I	S	P	A	T	C	H	E	S		C	A	S	E
			M	O	R	E	L		P	R	Y	E	R	
		S	A	N	E	R		S	H	E	E	R		
	C	I	S	G	E	N	D	E	R	E	D			
	H	A	N	K	S		I	O	W	A	N			
B	E	L	T	S		A	R	I	E	S				
R	A	L	E		A	M	E	N	D	A	T	O	R	Y
A	V	E	R		B	E	L		L	E	V	E	E	
C	E	D	I		A	L	A	C	K		N	O	L	L
T	H	I	N		S	I	N	A	I		C	L	I	P
S	O	N	G		H	A	D	N	T		H	O	T	S

112

M	A	M	A		C	O	I	N		S	L	I	D	
A	B	O	R	T		U	M	B	O		C	A	G	E
D	E	L	T	A		S	N	I	T		H	U	N	T
C	L	A	I	M		T	I	S		M	E	D	I	A
A	I	R	S		L	O	D	E		A	M	A	T	I
P	A	S	T	R	A	M	I	S		M	A	T	I	N
			A	V	E	R			T	O	N	E		
S	T	R	U	M		R	E	P		B	A	R	G	E
C	R	A	N			C	E	D	I					
H	A	I	R	S		P	T	E	R	O	S	A	U	R
T	I	N	E	A		A	I	R	Y		T	U	N	A
I	N	D	E	X		P	O	L		D	I	G	I	N
C	O	A	L		P	A	N	E		A	L	I	A	S
K	I	T	E		E	Y	A	S		G	E	T	T	O
S	L	E	D		P	A	L	S		S	E	E	M	

113

S	K	I	M			D	R	Y		B	A	S		
W	A	C	O		C	O	H	O		F	A	V	E	
E	Y	E	R		B	U	R	I	N		I	L	E	X
D	O	U	B	L	E	B	I	N	D		A	I	R	Y
E	S	P	I	E	S		C	O	E	D	S			
			D	A	T	A		C	R	A	C	K	L	E
C	W	M		D	O	N	N	E		B	O	N	E	Y
Y	E	A	S		W	E	I	R	D		S	A	V	E
M	A	T	C	H		S	H	O	E	D		P	O	D
E	N	T	R	U	S	T		S	T	A	R			
		I	T	C	H	Y		A	R	I	S	T	O	
F	R	O	M		R	E	O	R	I	E	N	T	E	D
L	E	A	P		U	S	U	A	L		G	E	L	D
O	A	K	S		F	I	N	D		E	N	O	L	
P	L	Y		F	A	G			R	O	S	Y		

114

T	O	R	C		P	A	L	M		M	A	G	M	A
A	F	A	R		A	G	U	E		A	R	E	A	L
W	A	V	E	F	R	O	N	T		S	M	E	L	L
	Y	E	A	R	E	N	D		M	E	E	K	L	Y
		T	O	N	Y		K	U	R	D				
S	T	U	N	T		H	O	T		T	H	A	W	
S	M	A	R	T		S	E	P	T		O	A	T	H
P	I	P	E		W	A	R	E	S		T	R	O	Y
O	T	I	C		A	M	O	K		T	H	E	N	S
T	H	R	O		S	O	D		P	O	E	S	Y	
		M	Y	N	A		L	O	O	T				
B	U	F	F	E	T		P	E	R	T	E	S	T	
O	L	E	O	S		H	I	T	T	H	E	H	A	Y
S	N	A	R	E		E	N	O	L		T	O	L	E
H	A	R	T	S		D	E	N	Y		H	E	L	P

115

SNAP · BEAN · DITCH
LOTI · UNDO · INURE
OATS · NOIR · ALTER
WHET · SLOT · LYSES
· NIP · SHMO ·
SKULL · EAGER
ANALYTICAL · FEW
META · ADUST · FAIR
· WET · MORTADELLA
· DEVIL · AMITY
· SLIM · WIZ
BASSI · ZOLA · NAZI
AMONG · ILEX · ABED
SOLON · NAVE · CLAY
SKITS · GLAD · YELL

116

CAYS · ADITS · SANG
UREA · UNCUT · OVAL
PROFITABLY · PAPA
POMELO · MILS · TAN
EYESORE · PIEBALD
DONT · ONE · PERM
· OUTGASSES ·
· ENTERTAIN ·
· INTERESTS ·
DODO · TEE · HESS
CONSUME · ALMANAC
ANI · RUMS · LEGATO
LAZE · LEADINGMAN
ITEM · LEGIT · LONE
FESS · AROSE · ERGS

117

SHIPMATE · PANGA
NARRATOR · WINIER
AREACODE · ANGSTS
GESTAPO · CLOSETO
· DISTINCTION
MANIAC · SAUL ·
IDIOM · POTENCES
SALT · EURO
SMEARIER · CARGO
· ANTI · BUTTON
EATINGAPPLE ·
TRUDGES · RASHERS
HOMIES · DOCTORAL
IMPORT · ALKALIZE
CASTS · LESSENED

118

BREAST · THE · ROAD
LOUCHE · HAM · INLY
OILCAN · RIP · SION
BLOODSPORT · HONE
· GUY · ONCOMING ·
TWIT · PLEURA ·
RAZE · LOST · CLEFT
ENERGY · WEAVER
FESSE · CAGE · RETE
· ASHCAN · GRAY
· HAIRCARE · FEY ·
HORN · APOLLONIAN
ENOL · BEN · AVENGE
ROME · BAY · RESCUE
DRAT · YUM · DASHED

119

CALABASH · GABLE
ORATORIO · RULER
GENERATE · CEDING
· ABA · HEISTS
· RETIREMENTS ·
BRACES · NOES
LATHS · EGIS · COP
OREO · PARSE · RIDE
BED · TROT · RIGOR
· LOTS · SAFARI
· IRISHSETTER ·
WASABI · GOT
ADLIBS · PROLAPSE
GEESE · HEGELIAN
ENTER · ITERATED

120

SCRAPS · SWARMS
EYELETS · CARRION
AMALGAM · OLYMPIA
RELY · POPPA · YELP
· ALLIED ·
HAS · VEER · ARAKS
ALIBI · NOS · LEERY
RIMED · SUM · WAGON
SKOAL · KEA · AMINO
HENRY · TROY · SAD
· RATTUS ·
SNOB · EXEAT · JOLT
WOULDBE · SIBERIA
ASSURED · SNEEZER
TETRYL · GYROSE

121

```
S H O D · M A G · M A R S H
C A V A · A X E S · A G A P E
O B I S · M O N K · C E R I A
W I N K A N T E C E D E N T ·
S T E A L · L A W · · · · · ·
· · · P E R C E N T · S H A D
· T R I V I U M · · · C U B A
P H O T O G R A P H A L B U M
V E L A · · N A I V E S T · ·
C A L L · T R A P P E R · · ·
· · · H I T · · · S O N G S ·
G O L D M E D A L S · T O A T
A F I R E · G R I T · O R Z O
G A M U T · E M M Y · M I E N
S Y N G E · S E X · Y A R E ·
```

122

```
A P P A L L S · M A C A B R E
S H A R I A H · B L O W O U T
P I N K E Y E · A L B A N I A
· · · · F O A L · W R E N · ·
· D A T · F R I S B E E · · ·
R E L I E F · S T U B · B I N
O R I E L · A P E S · R U N E
M I N I K I N · A S P E R S E
A D E N · A N A L · S T E E D
N E D · S M U G · P I R A C Y
· · T A B L E A U · O U T · ·
· B O I L · D A R T · · · · ·
M E A T M A N · R E E L O F F
I N S H O R E · G L E A N E R
D E T E N T E · H Y M N O D Y
```

123

```
N O E N D · B L A H · M A R T
H A N O I · L O B E · A G U E
S P A N S · A V E R · C A B S
· · C O O · C E D E · K I L T
D A T · W O K · O P I N E S ·
A G M · N A B S · F U N · · ·
C U E · S T E A L · G A W K S
C E N T · S A L E M · W A I T
A S T E R · R A V E L · T O O
· · N I P · D I N E · C W M ·
S P E E D O · T U N · H A P ·
C U L M · T A K A · S U B · ·
U R G E · T W A T · C L A M P
L E A N · L A V E · A N N U L
P E R T · E Y A S · P A D D Y
```

124

```
S P A S M · B A A · · C A T
T A M P A · C R U X · D O U R
O P I U M · L O G E · U N D O
O U T R A G E O U S · S T I M
D A Y · A R M S · S T O O P ·
· · B U L K · T H E · · · · ·
Z U L U S · W A I T · G A P ·
E N T R E P R E N E U R I A L
D I D · D O I T · · P I T H Y
· · T O G · R A S P · · · · ·
S A L V O · A J A X · G O T ·
C L I O · S T A T E H O U S E
R I E L · L O S E · E N A T E
A B I T · E N O L · B U R I N
M I N · D I N · · E S S A Y
```

125

```
T O S S · A B Y S S · R U D D
H A H A · W O O L Y · O L E O
I S O C H R O N A L · S N A G
S T O R E Y S · S P R E A D S
· · F A R · U H H U H · · · ·
G A L · E F F S · B I D E · ·
W R Y · O R I E N T · P O N G
Y I P · F O R L O R N · U N I
N A I L · W E E P I E · B U M
· S E A L · S E P T · L I P ·
· · B O L T S · H I E · · · ·
E M P O W E R · S P E C T R A
N O I R · N A S T U R T I U M
O U S E · I L I U M · U M B O
L E A R · N A N N A · S E E K
```

126

```
S L A M · C L I F F · A R M S
L E V O · R A D I I · T E A L
A V E R · A S Y E T · R E T E
W A S P · B E L · L I V E D ·
· · · H A S · L D O P A · · ·
· N E E D · P L E A D · L A B
G I S M O · E A G L E · U N I
A S P E R · R Y A · S T A T E
W E E · A Z T E C · T O T E R
P I C · B E E R Y · A B E D ·
· · I D L E R · W R Y · · · ·
S T A R E · B A R · J O K Y
H O L E · W H I L E · U L N A
A L L Y · O A T E S · G E E K
G U Y S · E J E C T · S O W S
```

127

```
P A N G S . R E D O . N U M B
O R A C H . E X E C . O N U S
P A S S E . P A L E S T I N E
O B S E S S . M I L E . . . .
F I E . H A S S L E . T O T .
F A R . Y A W . H I P . H U H
. . C O W E R . . . M U S E .
. S H O U L D E R B L A D E .
W H Y S . . V E L U M . . . .
O A P . L T D . L O G . A G M
W Y E . A R R O Y O . B A A .
. . S O A K . D E T E S T . .
C R Y P T O G A M . F A L S E
W O O L . P O P E . F R I E R
T O N Y . S N I T . S E A R S
```

128

```
B O T C H . B E T . L I M B S
A L U L A . R A H . I N E R T
A E R O S P A C E . P O D I A
S O F A . R E H A B . S I L T
. . . C O O S . . I C I C L E
T H W A R T . R O O T . . . .
Y A H . T E M P O . M O C H A
P H O T O M U L T I P L I E R
E A S E L . C Y C L E . T A M
. . M A R K . . L E P E R S .
E T H E N E . P U R L . . . .
L E A R . V O T E S . A S B O
U N R I P . O W N E R S H I P
T E S T A . Z E N . I M I D E
E T H Y L . Y E A . P A N E L
```

129

```
F A T S . A F A R . S T R A W
E X E C . C U B A . A R U B A
T E A R F U L L Y . M I N U S
A D R O I T L Y . . B E T H .
. . . F E E . B A K E . . . .
T H R U . A S S U R E . S I S
R E A L . C H A N C Y . W O E
U L N A . C O U G H . G O N G
S I B . H E A D E D . L O I N
T O Y . I N L I E U . U N C O
. . P E T S . . C W M . . . .
F O R A . . S C H E M A T A .
L A U G H . D A R E D E V I L
A T S E A . A V E S . S E L L
T H E R M . W E E S . T R E Y
```

130

```
S P R A G . B E R G . M A T E
E R I C A . A V E R . A B U T
A I M E R . P I S A . H A T H
S M Y R N A . C O C K A T O O
. . . B E T . T W E E T E R S
P L C . R O R O . P A M . . .
R A H . E M E R G E . A N K H
O V E R D I D . A R C S I N E
M E Z E . C O O L I E . F E W
. . . T O W . B L O T . F E N
S O R R I E S T . D A M . . .
C R E A K I E R . S C U F F S
A L E C . G R U B . E N U R E
R O V E . H O D S . A G R E E
S P E D . T W E E . N O S E D
```

131

```
C U P O L A S . . G O T A T
A N O R E X I A . H A U G H
T I N I N E S S . R E P L A Y
. . D O T . S H O E . S I M
O P E L . S L U E S . P A N E
T O R E . C O M P E T E . . .
T O O . P A G E . W H E L P S
E L U S I V E . C O R P O R A
R E S U M E . C H O U . C O D
. . B A N D A I D . T A E L
A R M S . G A U D S . E L M Y
P O O . L E W D . D A T . .
S A U C E R . A C C U S I N G
I S S U E . . L E U K E M I A
S T E E R . . P R E T E X T
```

132

```
R A D S . J A B . O R A N G
A B U T . A V E R . M E D E A
G O E R . W I L E . B R A W L
A U T O . S A L T . R E P . .
S T O P . N I H . E A T I N
. . H A S . N I T . D A D O
E N T E R T A I N E D . B I N
G A Y . M A D . K E A . L O G
Y U P . S I D E S T R E E T S
P R I G . N U T . H E P . .
T U F F S . C O D . I D Y L
. Y O U . E N O L . G H E E
W H I R R . R I G A . R O S E
O U N C E . S A G S . A L E C
E G G E R . N O T . M E S H
```

133

```
T R A P S   Y O B   S H U T
I O N I C   S A L E   N O N O
N I N T H   C H E E S E D I P
S L I M E   R O O T L E
  S H A M P O O   L I Z A R D
    I N A L L   R E N E G U E
P A L   S O L V E   G R E B E
A F A R   D I E T S   S O L D
N O T E R   N E W T S   F E Y
D U E L I N G   E U L E R
A L S A C E   D E B O N E D
    T I C K E T   S C A R F
A R G E N T I N E   H O S E R
G O E R   A W E D   E R O S E
M O N S   R I B   D E N S E
```

134

```
C U D S   T H O R   T A B B Y
O P E L   Y E A H   A V I S O
D E L E   R A S E   H E L E N
A N T I S E P T I C I S E
  D A G O   S N I T
    H A D J   G I N G K O
M A M   V I E W S   U L N A
E G O C E N T R I C I T I E S
Z E B U   S Y N O D   B E T
E D E M A S   S O I L
    L A V S   O A K S
  P R E D E T E R M I N E S
W H O O P   R A L E   R O L E
A I T C H   D I M E   D U M A
D E S K S   I D Y L   S T A R
```

135

```
B L A B   D E C K S   S W O P
R O D E   I N L A W   C H O U
A I M S   A D O R E   R E P S
W R I T   L O T T E R I E S
L E X I C O N   T A M
    R U G   C O P Y   F U R
C H I R P   B L U E   P A L E
R U L E   P L I C A   R U N E
A G E D   L E C H   Z O N A L
P O X   G A W K   S E X
    B U T   S E E I N G S
  D I R T Y P O O L   M A L I
N A N A   P O U F S   A V E S
I C K Y   U N S A Y   T E A S
B E Y S   S T E R N   E L M Y
```

136

```
S P I C     T H A T C H
T E N O N   B R A V U R A
I R E N I C   W E A P O N E D
M I X   P U P I L S   W A D
  T O G   P A R T H I A
F O R U M   M E W   S L I P
I N A N E R   R A M S   N H S
N E B   T I C   Y O U   T O P
D A L   A G U E   P E L O T A
  L E A L   N A B   S A X O N
    U S I N G U P   V I M
  N O S   R E L Y O N   C E P
D I A S P O R E   T O M A T O
O P T I O N S   W A T E R
B A S E L Y     T E R N
```

137

```
B Y T E   P A T S   I N P U T
B O O N   A G U E   N A I R A
Q U O D   D I N E   L A N G E
    P H A S E D   A N G E L
  B A R I U M   C A W
B E M O C K   A X S E E D
A B E D   B O S E   S L I P
T O L U   T R I E D   C U R L
S P I C   W O K S   R A G U
  S A T E E N   S M I T E S
    F E Z   S P A T E S
C H A F F   E V E R S O
L E V E E   A I R Y   I N C H
A M E N T   G A U L   R O U E
P E R S E   E L M Y   E M M Y
```

138

```
B A B E     W H O S   B B Q
U G A N D A   O I N K   Y O U
M E T R O S   K E P I   T O O
  D H O T I     A P P E N D
  S L A M S   P O L
    G O U T   E L A N D S
A C H I E V E R   R E T O O L
G O A D   T A X   T U T U
U N C L A D   P R E T E N S E
E S K I M O   S A G O
  N O G   Y O U R S
I M A G E R   I S A A C
N O W   B O L T   S L I V E R
C U R   A S B O   M E D I C I
H E Y   N E W T   S N A G
```

139

```
S C U M   B A R T   I N C H
U L N A   G L U E Y   M O L E
B A R S   O U T E R   M U O N
  N A T   G E O L O G I S T S
  V E T O       S A X
S T E R O L   S O I L   P O T
H I L L Y   I N A N E   L A W
I N L Y   P L A T E   P A K I
V E E   B O E R S   D O N U T
S A D   L U X E   T O T E M S
    P U L     W H E T
A F T E R T A S T E   N A B
B A U D   I L L E R   T R O W
U R G E   C L U N K   L I L Y
T O S S   E Y E D   Y A L E
```

140

```
M A N N   A L G A L   S L O B
O L E O   G A R D A   T I N E
L O W S   U M A M I   A B U T
A N T I S E P T I C   D I S H
R E S E T   S E X   K I D
      R E F     L I A I S E
B S E   T A C K S O N   N A M
Y O N   T R U E I N G   A G M
T O T   I C E A X E S   L O Y
E T E R N E       R I D
  R I G   P U S   Z A X I S
B R I G   H A P P Y E V E N T
O A T H   E N S U E   I N F O
F L I T   E D E M A   T O R E
F E S S   L A T E R   S N A P
```

141

```
S W I M   G A D S   M O O D
L I N U M   A B I T   A R V O
U L T R A   B A S E   M E A L
G L I D E D   C E P   M A T E
  M E N U   I N S P A D E S
C H A R A D E   T O I L
R A T E D   L Y I N G   D O T
A V E R   B E E T S   T O P I
W E D   D E C A L   A R C E D
  A U N T   E N T I T L E
G O L D B E R G   A M B O
A X E D   F O E   G O U R D S
S E A L   I N C H   S N A I L
P Y R E   T I K E   T E T R A
S E N D   S C O W   S E E M
```

142

```
M I S O   O F F S   A T B A Y
I N C H   P O L O   R O U G E
S C U M   P R O F   C O M M A
S U B I T O   P A P A
  R A C I S M   O N I C E
      M E A S U R E M E N T
S M I L E   T A N K   B A D E
H O N O R   R I D   M E S O N
E X E C   N O N O   I D E N T
D A R K L A N T E R N
  S T E A M   S O U R C E
    Z E S T   T S H I R T
L Y C R A   W O N T   O L E O
T O W E R   A G U E   M I C K
D U M P S   B O N N   B A T E
```

143

```
L O S S   E C H T   C O D E
E R N E   K A Y O   L O B A R
A M I D   E T E R N I Z I N G
P O P U P   A N T O N Y
E L E M I   P A S S E   B L T
R U S S E L L   U R E A
    R E A P P E A R I N G
  S P A C E S H U T T L E S
A I R T E R M I N A L
S L O E     C L A B B E R
P O D   H U T C H   S U A V E
  Z A G R E B   T I B E T
T O C O P H E R O L   L O N E
O R A L S   K I W I   D O S S
E T N A   S A L E   S N O T
```

144

```
B L A H   B A S   S C H U S S
R I F E   W R Y   P O O T L E
A M A L G A M S   A D R I A N
T E R M I N A T O R   S L I D
    L A D E N   W E E N S
C Y R I L   A M I D E S
W O O D S Y   S O O N E S T
M U T E   O R A N G   N O I R
  S A N J U A N   E A S I L Y
    T A R M A C   F E L L A
A T R I P   P L A T O
B A I T   P S Y C H O P A T H
O S S I F Y   S H U T A W A Y
R E H E A R   T O M   C A R P
T R I S T E   S U B   T Y P E
```

145

S	L	A	W		S	P	A	W	N		S	T	O	P
O	U	C	H		H	A	N	O	I		P	U	P	A
B	R	I	E		A	N	T	E	C	H	A	P	E	L
S	E	N	T	R	Y	G	O		A	E	D	I	L	E
	D	I	S	H		A	N	G	R	Y				
			T	O	G		Y	E	A		E	F	F	S
C	H	R	O	M	O		M	A	G		S	O	L	I
R	A	I	N	B	O	W		R	U	S	T	L	E	R
U	R	G	E		D	O	T		A	M	I	D	E	S
X	M	A	S		N	O	W		N	A	M			
			B	E	D	I	M		S	A	P	S		
M	I	S	S	U	S		N	A	P	H	T	H	A	S
I	N	T	E	R	S	T	I	C	E		O	I	N	K
S	L	A	G		M	U	N	R	O		R	A	T	E
T	Y	R	O		E	G	G	O	N		S	L	A	P

146

C	U	P	P	A				S	C	R	I	M	S	
I	N	L	A	N	D		A	P	H	O	N	I	A	
G	R	A	P	N	E	L		C	L	E	A	N	L	Y
S	I	N	U	A	T	E		C	A	N	N	O	L	I
	G	A	L	L	A	N	T	R	Y			V	I	N
	R	E	S	I	D	U	A			T	W	A	N	G
			N	E	B		C	O	R	T	E	S		
F	A	W	N	E	R		L	A	W	Y	E	R		
T	I	B	I	A	E		F	I	N					
A	N	E	N	T		M	O	L	O	C	H	S		
M	A	Y			P	A	R	A	N	O	I	A	S	
A	L	A	S	K	A	N		C	L	O	T	T	E	D
L	I	N	N	E	T	S		S	A	L	T	I	R	E
E	S	C	A	P	E	E			W	E	E	N	I	E
S	T	E	P	I	N				D	R	Y	A	D	

147

M	O	K	E		E	M	U			W	R	I	T	
P	R	E	P		S	E	N			H	U	L	A	
G	R	E	E	N		T	N	T		S	I	M	O	N
	L	E	I		O	A	R		A	P	P			
			L	A	N	G	U	I	D					
S	W	U	M		D	I	E	T	S		S	N	A	G
M	E	T	A	Z	O	A		H	O	S	T	I	L	E
O	B	I	T	E	R			T	O	O	N	I	E	
T	E	C	H	N	I	C		O	O	L	O	N	G	S
E	R	A	S		N	A	A	C	P		D	Y	N	E
			E	G	E	S	T	E	D					
	P	E	W		S	H	E		U	F	O			
C	L	I	M	E		U	L	T		O	L	I	V	E
H	O	P	I			R	A	T		O	L	I	O	
A	P	E	R			A	R	E			C	Y	A	N

148

S	W	A	T		C	L	A	D			T	R	A	M
P	I	S	A		L	O	G	I	A		R	I	V	E
O	R	Y	X		A	X	E	R	S		A	F	E	W
D	E	N	I	M	S		D	E	P	O	S	E	R	S
			C	R	E	P	T		H	A	H			
A	R	H	A	T		H	A	C	E	K		S	A	D
B	O	R	N		O	R	R	E	R	Y		C	U	R
A	M	O	K		M	A	O	R	I		P	O	N	Y
F	E	N		F	I	L	M	I	C		L	U	T	E
T	O	Y		A	T	L	A	S		S	A	T	Y	R
			G	U	T		E	N	A	C	T			
S	P	U	R	N	I	N	G		E	X	A	R	C	H
U	L	N	A		N	O	O	N	E		R	O	U	E
S	O	D	S		G	E	T	U	P		D	O	T	E
S	T	O	P		S	O	T	S			S	P	E	D

149

D	E	V	A		S	C	A	U	P		F	A	C	T
A	V	E	R		H	I	P	P	O		A	W	R	Y
V	E	R	T		A	V	A	S	T		R	E	A	P
I	N	T	E	R	M	E	N	T		D	O	D	G	E
S	T	E	R	E		T	A	R	S	I				
			B	I	B	S		G	E	T	S		P	U	G
S	P	R	O	U	T		E	A	R	P	H	O	N	E
C	O	A	L	T	A	R		M	I	R	A	N	D	A
O	C	T	E	T	T	E	S		C	A	N	D	O	R
W	O	E		A	U	N	T		T	I	D	E		
			L	E	E	R	S			S	C	R	A	M
G	R	A	S	S		G	I	N	G	E	R	A	L	E
R	I	G	A		M	A	F	I	A		A	B	I	T
A	F	E	W		A	D	E	P	T			F	L	E	E
F	E	D	S		Y	E	S	E	S		T	E	N	D

150

B	O	A	S			C	A	M	P		W	H	O	
E	R	R	O	R	S		O	D	O	R		A	I	L
R	E	G	L	E	T		N	O	V	E	L	I	S	E
M	A	L	A	C	O	S	T	R	A	C	A	N	S	
			D	E	N	U	M	E	R	A	B	L	Y	
				D	R	A	W	A	B	L	E		A	N	A
I	S	L	E				I	L	E	A		M	E	L
B	O	U	R	G		O	N	E		R	E	I	V	E
E	R	G		I	C	E	D			N	A	I	F	
X	I	S		A	U	D	I	T	O	R	S			
	A	N	T	E	C	E	D	E	N	C	E			
	S	Y	S	T	E	M	A	T	I	C	A	L	L	Y
H	O	U	S	E	S	A	T		S	T	R	I	F	E
A	M	A		S	I	T	E		T	A	E	N	I	A
T	A	N		S	E	A	S			D	E	N	S	

151

S	L	U	G		V	E	R	S	T		G	O	D
E	U	R	O	S		A	R	E	T	E		R	O	W
A	N	G	E	L		R	E	C	O	G	N	I	Z	E
T	E	E	S	U	P		M	A	D		O	P	E	L
			T	R	A	C	I	N	G		W	E	S	T
S	H	M	O		L	O	T	T	E	D			
L	O	O	P		P	R	E	S	S	U	R	I	N	G
A	L	O	O	F				G	E	N	O	A	
B	E	S	T	I	R	R	I	N	G		S	K	I	T
		T	A	E	N	I	A		T	Y	R	E	
I	F	F	Y		C	H	U	T	Z	P	A		
T	O	L	U		K	I	T		E	A	R	I	N	G
C	L	A	M	B	E	R	E	D		R	E	N	I	N
H	I	C		U	T	E	R	I		D	A	C	C	A
Y	A	K		T	Y	S	O	N		S	H	E	W

152

S	L	A	P		H	Y	P	O	S		T	H	U	S
H	E	B	E		A	U	R	A	L		Y	A	R	E
M	A	I	N		S	M	O	K	E		R	A	G	E
O	P	T	E	D		P	E	P	P	E	R	E	D
			T	U	R	N	E	D	T	O		
N	E	A	R	B	E	E	R		D	I	R	E	R
U	L	N	A		S	I	F	T	S		N	A	N	A
M	I	T	T		E	G	R	E	T		A	W	A	Y
B	O	R	E		T	H	A	N	E		M	E	T	E
S	T	A	S	H		C	E	N	S	O	R	E	D
		A	B	A	T	T	O	I	R		
E	S	O	P	H	A	G	I		B	A	C	K	S
F	O	U	R		R	O	O	D	S		T	O	O	L
F	U	Z	E		E	N	N	U	I		A	U	T	O
S	L	O	P		D	E	S	E	X		S	P	O	T

153

S	U	M	A	C	H	S		C	L	A	S	P	S
P	L	A	G	U	I	N	G		L	A	G	O	O	N
I	N	T	E	R	P	O	L		E	X	E	D	R	A
R	A	I	N		T	O	F	F		D	A	N	G
T	E	N	T	H	S		B	U	S	H		
		A	I	D	E	R		A	N	G	S	T
B	L	I	N	D	G	U	T		O	P	I	A	T	E
R	I	C	E		H	E	R	B	S		S	P	A	N
O	C	K	E	R	S		O	U	T	L	I	E	R	S
S	K	Y	P	E		S	T	R	I	A		
		G	O	U	T		A	B	A	S	E	S
D	A	S	H		A	B	I	T		G	A	V	E
A	V	A	U	N	T		N	I	C	T	A	T	E	D
D	E	N	G	U	E		G	R	O	O	M	I	N	G
A	R	G	O	T	S		E	X	P	A	N	S	E

154

P	U	D	S		G	H	A	T		B	U	S	S
O	S	I	E	R		L	O	B	O		I	N	L	Y
T	H	R	E	E		Y	A	R	N		D	I	A	Z
M	E	E	D	S		C	R	A	G		E	N	V	Y
A	R	C	S	I	N	E		D	A	M		T	E	G
N	I	T		T	E	R	S	E		A	P	E	R	Y
	N	O	W		W	O	T			C	O	R	
	G	R	O	G		L	E	V		S	O	R	B
		G	O	D			N	O	G		F	U	R
S	T	E	L	A		M	O	L	A	L		P	A	M
C	O	N		Y	O	U		C	R	O	A	T	I	A
A	W	E	D		C	U	B	A		B	L	E	N	D
T	H	R	O		C	M	O	N		O	L	D	I	E
T	E	A	L		A	U	T	O		S	O	L	E	D
Y	E	L	L		M	U	S	S		T	Y	R	O

155

S	A	S	H		T	H	E	A		A	P	O	R	T
A	U	T	O		A	I	R	S		B	L	A	I	R
D	R	A	M		S	C	U	P		B	A	S	S	O
D	I	R	E	C	T		C	E	M	E	N	T	E	D
O	C	T	R	O	I		T	R	A	Y		
		R	E	G		T	S	U	R	I	S
W	I	T	H	D	R	A	W	S		N	O	N	U
A	C	H	Y		T	O	W		D	O	C	S
S	K	E	P		T	E	A	C	L	O	T	H	S
H	Y	M	E	N	S		P	O	O		
		A	I	M	S		U	S	H	E	R	S
L	A	C	R	I	M	A	L		N	E	U	R	A	L
A	F	O	U	L		L	E	F	T		R	A	G	U
S	E	N	S	E		T	E	A	R		S	T	A	R
T	W	E	E	R		S	P	R	Y		T	O	S	S

156

D	U	R	S	T		E	F	F	S		S	E	E	M
E	R	A	T	O		M	I	L	T		U	L	N	A
E	G	G	A	R		B	L	U	R		B	L	A	T
M	E	A	N	T		R	O	B	E		L	I	T	E
		Z	I	T	I		A	B	U	S	E	R	
S	A	G	A	C	I	T	Y		M	U	N		
P	U	D		O	C	T	E	T		F	A	T	W	A
A	T	A	L	L		L	A	W		F	R	I	A	R
R	O	Y	A	L		E	R	O	D	E		T	U	M
		V	I	N		S	H	I	R	T	I	L	Y
C	R	U	I	S	E		A	D	Z	E		
H	A	N	S		W	A	R	N		O	N	T	A	P
I	N	C	H		A	W	E	D		N	A	O	M	I
P	U	L	E		G	A	T	E		E	N	D	O	N
S	P	E	D		E	Y	E	D		S	T	O	K	E

157

S	U	R	F	■	J	E	S	S	■	O	R	B	E	D
C	L	I	O	■	A	M	O	K	■	P	O	L	A	R
U	N	D	O	■	M	I	D	I	■	S	W	A	G	E
P	A	S	T	■	B	L	A	S	P	H	E	M	E	S
■	■	■	B	A	S	E	■	■	L	O	N	E	R	S
C	A	P	R	I	■	■	S	T	O	P	■	■	■	■
H	I	L	A	R	■	A	W	A	Y	■	K	I	S	T
A	R	A	K	S	■	G	O	P	■	P	I	N	E	Y
D	Y	N	E	■	M	E	R	E	■	I	L	L	E	R
■	■	■	K	I	D	D	■	■	C	L	Y	D	E	■
S	T	R	A	I	N	■	B	A	K	E	■	■	■	■
H	E	A	R	T	T	H	R	O	B	■	R	A	P	T
I	N	S	E	T	■	E	A	S	Y	■	B	R	I	O
M	E	T	A	L	■	F	L	U	E	■	E	M	M	Y
S	T	A	L	E	■	T	E	N	S	■	E	Y	A	S

158

S	L	A	M	■	E	A	C	H	■	S	T	I	F	F
T	O	D	O	■	F	A	R	E	■	L	U	N	A	R
O	U	Z	O	■	F	R	O	W	■	A	D	D	T	O
W	R	E	N	■	L	O	R	N	■	P	O	R	E	S
■	■	S	C	O	N	E	■	A	U	R	I	S	T	■
S	T	A	T	O	R	■	V	I	P	■	■	■	■	■
A	R	M	O	R	E	D	C	A	R	■	S	A	P	S
L	O	O	N	■	S	H	O	R	T	■	P	U	R	E
T	Y	K	E	■	C	O	P	Y	E	D	I	T	O	R
■	H	E	W	■	■	R	U	N	O	F	F	■	■	■
H	E	A	V	E	D	■	M	A	M	B	A	■	■	■
A	R	G	U	E	■	F	O	C	I	■	L	A	M	B
D	R	I	L	L	■	L	O	I	N	■	T	R	E	Y
S	O	L	V	E	■	U	L	N	A	■	A	V	E	R
T	R	E	A	D	■	B	A	I	L	■	P	O	K	E

159

B	L	A	B	■	A	C	H	Y	■	R	A	L	E	■
R	U	B	E	■	F	L	U	E	■	R	E	C	O	N
I	N	L	Y	■	R	A	G	A	■	E	A	T	O	N
O	D	Y	S	S	E	Y	S	■	S	T	R	I	N	E
■	■	■	H	E	P	■	H	E	R	N	I	A	■	■
■	■	B	A	T	I	S	T	E	■	A	G	E	D	■
■	B	I	G	■	G	L	U	E	■	N	O	S	■	■
■	T	E	G	■	D	E	I	S	T	■	G	U	T	■
■	H	A	H	■	R	O	T	C	■	M	E	T	■	■
R	O	U	E	■	U	N	S	A	T	E	D	■	■	■
A	R	G	A	L	I	■	L	O	W	■	■	■	■	■
T	I	E	R	E	D	■	C	O	D	L	I	N	G	S
R	A	S	T	A	■	W	H	O	A	■	C	A	R	E
U	T	T	E	R	■	E	A	S	Y	■	K	N	E	W
N	E	E	D	■	B	R	A	S	■	Y	A	W	N	■

160

M	A	P	S	■	S	A	L	V	E	■	B	R	A	W
A	B	U	T	■	T	W	E	E	R	■	L	A	V	E
T	I	M	E	S	E	R	V	E	R	■	A	G	E	D
S	T	A	N	L	E	Y	■	■	O	T	H	E	R	S
■	■	■	T	U	P	■	M	E	R	E	■	■	■	■
A	R	B	O	R	■	M	U	N	■	G	H	O	S	T
C	H	A	R	■	L	A	B	A	N	■	I	N	K	Y
C	E	D	I	■	A	L	A	M	O	■	P	A	I	R
R	I	G	A	■	B	I	R	O	S	■	P	I	N	E
A	N	E	N	T	■	G	A	R	■	P	O	R	T	S
■	■	■	■	O	I	N	K	■	P	I	C	■	■	■
E	P	O	N	Y	M	■	■	T	A	N	K	F	U	L
F	L	U	E	■	I	M	M	O	R	T	E	L	L	E
F	A	Z	E	■	D	I	A	L	S	■	T	O	N	E
S	N	O	T	■	E	N	D	U	E	■	S	P	A	R

161

S	N	O	B	■	S	U	R	G	E	■	S	L	O	P
C	O	R	E	■	P	R	I	O	N	■	H	A	U	L
U	N	A	S	S	I	G	N	E	D	■	R	I	C	O
M	O	N	T	E	N	E	G	R	O	■	A	C	H	Y
■	■	■	G	R	E	Y	■	■	W	E	N	■	■	■
S	P	E	E	D	■	M	A	P	M	A	K	I	N	G
C	R	A	W	■	P	O	S	I	E	S	■	M	A	Y
H	I	D	■	B	A	L	C	O	N	Y	■	P	I	P
W	O	E	■	A	L	L	O	U	T	■	H	O	L	S
A	R	S	O	N	I	S	T	S	■	G	A	S	S	Y
■	■	■	B	E	N	■	■	F	A	Y	S	■	■	■
C	Y	M	E	■	O	B	S	T	E	T	R	I	C	S
H	O	A	R	■	D	E	L	E	C	T	A	B	L	E
O	U	Z	O	■	E	N	U	R	E	■	C	L	A	W
W	R	E	N	■	S	T	E	M	S	■	K	E	Y	S

162

S	H	O	T	■	A	M	B	O	■	■	C	L	A	D
L	I	V	E	■	G	U	I	R	O	■	H	E	M	E
I	D	E	A	L	I	S	T	I	C	■	R	O	O	F
P	E	R	S	I	S	T	E	N	T	■	I	N	K	Y
■	■	■	W	E	N	T	■	■	G	A	G	S	■	■
S	M	O	L	T	■	■	■	G	A	M	I	N	E	■
A	I	R	S	■	S	Y	P	H	O	N	■	M	A	M
D	A	K	■	S	H	O	O	I	N	G	■	M	A	C
D	U	E	■	E	R	U	P	T	S	■	D	O	N	E
O	L	D	A	G	E	■	■	■	B	U	R	S	E	■
■	■	N	O	W	T	■	■	T	O	A	T	■	■	■
S	H	M	O	■	D	R	I	V	E	L	L	E	R	S
W	E	A	N	■	L	A	C	E	R	T	I	L	I	A
O	A	K	Y	■	Y	I	K	E	S	■	S	L	O	G
P	R	O	M	■	T	Y	R	E	■	M	E	T	E	■

163

A	R	R	A	S				A	M	E	R	C	E
B	A	O	B	A	B			M	I	L	E	R	S
A	D	M	I	X	E	D		A	S	I	T	I	S
S	I	A	L		Y	A	K		R	E	T	I	N	A
I	C	I	E	R		C	O	P	E		I	N	K	Y
N	A	N	N	A		H	A	R	T		S	A	L	E
G	L	E	E	S		S	N	O	T		M	E	E	D
			H	A	H		T	O	M			
S	L	I	D		S	U	R	E		I	C	T	U	S
C	O	N	E		S	N	A	G		N	O	R	S	E
R	O	T	C		A	D	Z	E		G	R	E	E	N
A	P	E	R	C	U		Z	E	D		R	A	D	S
P	I	N	E	A	L			S	I	R	O	C	C	O
I	N	S	E	R	T			P	E	D	L	A	R
E	G	E	S	T	S			B	E	E	R	Y

164

B	R	A	T		S	L	A	W		J	O	L	T	S
L	I	N	E		C	O	D	E		O	B	E	A	H
U	L	N	A		H	A	Z	E		L	E	A	S	E
B	L	O	S	S	O	M	E	D		L	I	N	K	S
			T	E	A	L		S	K	I	S	
G	L	A	D	R	A	G	S		I	T	A	L	I	C
N	I	T		D	R	A	T		D	Y	N	A	M	O
A	B	I	T		R	O	W		T	U	B	A
R	E	V	I	E	W		M	A	I	D		N	U	T
S	L	E	A	V	E		A	G	N	U	S	D	E	I
			M	I	N	D		H	A	A	R	
F	A	R	A	D		E	S	C	A	L	L	O	P	S
A	F	O	R	E		C	O	O	S		A	M	O	K
G	E	T	I	N		A	U	N	T		D	A	C	E
S	W	E	A	T		F	R	E	E		S	T	O	P

165

S	W	A	P		A	W	A	I	T		S	A	P	S
L	A	V	E		Z	A	I	R	E		C	L	E	W
A	X	E	D		T	Y	R	O	L		U	L	N	A
P	Y	R	I	T	E		S	N	U	B	B	I	N	G
			C	A	C	K		I	G	U	A	N	A	S
S	A	M	U	R	A	I		C	U	R	
A	M	A	R	A	N	T	H		Y	O	L	K	S
C	O	L	E		H	I	T		V	A	I	L
S	K	I	D	S		C	O	N	C	E	R	T	I
			H	I	D		B	O	A	R	D	E	D
T	R	I	B	U	N	E		Y	I	P	S	
R	I	B	A	L	D	R	Y		S	E	I	S	M	S
A	G	E	D		U	M	A	M	I		G	L	U	E
L	O	A	D		C	A	R	O	L		H	U	L	L
A	R	M	Y		E	L	E	G	Y		T	E	L	L

166

S	E	L	F		T	A	M	S		B	E	R	G
W	A	U	L		W	R	I	T		E	Y	E	D
A	C	C	I	P	I	T	E	R		J	A	V	A
T	H	Y	R	O	N	I	N	E		M	E	S	S	Y
			T	O	T	S		P	R	O	W	
S	T	A	Y	P	U	T		O	B	E	A	H	S
T	U	N		B	I	B		W	E	L	L	I	E
A	M	O	K		C	O	Z		S	I	L	L
M	O	D	I	S	H		G	U	V		N	A	M
P	R	E	S	T	O		C	A	L	D	E	R	A
			S	I	B	S		C	L	O	Y	
O	C	C	A	M		E	T	H	I	C	I	S	T	S
F	L	A	B		P	O	I	S	O	N	O	A	K
F	I	L	L		T	O	N	E		G	O	R	E
Y	O	K	E		S	K	I	S		S	N	A	P

167

T	H	E	N		F	L	A	P	S		H	I	S	T
H	O	M	O		L	A	M	I	A		I	N	L	Y
U	M	B	O		U	M	B	E	L		T	H	O	R
M	I	E	N		S	P	O	R	T	S	P	A	G	E
B	E	D	E	W				L	A	B	
			H	A	W	S		E	A	R	I	N	G
S	P	R	A	Y	C	A	N		A	B	A	T	O	R
K	E	E	N		T	Y	I	N	G		D	E	L	E
I	N	C	A	S	E		C	U	R	S	E	D	L	Y
S	N	I	P	E	D		K	N	E	E	
			P	A	W			X	E	B	E	C
F	R	I	E	N	D	L	E	S	S		N	O	A	H
R	O	E	S		R	O	Y	A	L		A	U	T	O
A	U	N	T		A	B	A	C	A		C	L	O	P
G	E	T	S		M	E	S	S	Y		T	E	N	S

168

S	U	B	S		S	K	U	L	K		A	W	A	Y
K	N	I	T		E	N	D	U	E		S	H	M	O
I	C	K	Y		L	E	D	G	Y		S	O	A	K
N	O	I	R		F	E	E		M	U	R	R	E
S	I	N	E	W		R	E	F	E	R	E	E
	L	I	N	E	A	R		D	I	G	E	S	T	S
		E	N	L	I	V	E	N		D	O	T	E
G	A	B		A	G	A	M	A		N	I	X
O	I	L	S		T	H	R	A	L	L	S	
P	R	O	P	H	E	T		S	E	A	T	E	D
	T	O	L	E	D	O	S		W	A	V	E	S
T	O	P	U	P		W	E	B		T	E	C	H
H	A	I	R		P	L	A	Y	A		I	N	K	Y
R	I	N	G		O	O	Z	E	S		S	E	L	L
U	R	G	E		O	X	I	D	E		T	R	E	Y

ANSWERS

ANSWERS

169

```
S N A P . B A P . G A T E
T A C H . L U C Y . W R A P
A U T O . P A Y E R . Y O K E
F R I N G E D . T A W N I E R
F U N E R A L H O M E . N O G
. . O C E A N I D . T U N
. T W O E D G E D . B I T E
. P R A M . . . D E N S
T R O D . A D H E R I N G
H I M . G R E A S E R
W E B . E R A S T I A N I S M
A D O R N E D . E N C O M I A
C I N E . A S H E S . M A X I
K E E P . R E A M . A G E D
S U S S . S A D . D O S S
```

170

```
M A T T E . . D Y N A S T S
A B H O R . D E C E N N I A
C I R R I . D E P L E T I N G
S T U N G . A N T E D A T E S
. . . E M M Y . P E G .
. K A R E N . T R O T H
S H A D O W S . N O O N
A A R O N . . P I T T A
D I O R . C L O S E S T
. L O N G S . H E L M S
. M A T . C A V E .
T H R E N O D E S . M I L L S
R O U N D W O R M . I C E U P
A E S T H E T E . S K A T E
P R E S I D E . T Y P E D
```

171

```
R E S T . R A B B I . B A C H
E A C H . A G A I N . A C H Y
B R I E . V E R N E . R U E D
. H E R D E D . R O T T E R
G O N E O N . A N T I H E R O
A L C O V E . S E L L . S I X
B E E F E D . P A Y S . T O Y
. . . D I P . . .
W O T . P O O R . A R A R A T
H U H . L U N E . T E R E D O
I T E R A T E S . W A R N E D
S T R A N D . M O R E E N
T R E F . A P T E R . S W O P
L A S T . T O O T S . T A M E
E Y A S . E M M E T . S L A G
```

172

```
H A S . F A D . . B A B E
Y I P . L O W . B Y W A Y
P R O C U R E . D O N A T E
E S T H E T E . F O R A Y E D
. . A N A B O L I S M .
S T A R T S . P A N C E T T A
A R M Y . H I G H . R I B
N O B . A T H I R S T . Y E A
D U E . L O A D . T O R C
S T R O B I L I . G D A N S K
. . B E L E A G U E R .
S T R I D E R . R I P O F F S
O R A T O R . I N U T I L E
D O G E S . M E T . S E X
S T A R . M A Y . H E Y
```

173

```
S L A W . B U Z Z . S H U L
P O U R . C U R I E . C O N E
L U G E . A R G O N . H U F F
A I M S . S P E N D . W R I T
T S E T S E . A W A I T S
. I N L Y . O R I Y A .
D A T E S . C O N A R T I S T
I N E R T . C U T . P E N N I
P A R S O N A G E . A T T I C
. L A M E R . T R E F .
A R M L E T . W H A R F S
B O Y O . I D A H O . R A L E
U M B O . O R M E R . C L I P
T E A T . N O B L E . H I N T
S O D S . S P O D . S A G S
```

174

```
M A C K S . F E E . S C U R F
A U R A L . L A X . H O R A L
S T A M I N A T E . I N G L E
H O M E M A K E R . K N E E D
. . . T E N T H S .
. J A B . . Y A N K E E
N O N U . S Y N G E . A I R Y
I N K Y . Q U E E N . W O R E
P A L E . U M B R A . A W E D
S H E R P A . . B A D
. . S T A R C H .
S T A G Y . C O L O R B A R S
P U B I C . O M O P H A G I A
A P I S H . R E G . E L E M I
D I T T O . N O S . A I D E D
```

175

```
S H I R R S . . . . . W I L D
P I N E A L . . A R T P A P E R
E N G A G E . . B I O A S S A Y
A D O R E D . . S L O W P O K E
K I T . . . D W E L L . . F A R
. . . . Z I O N . . . M A G S
. . P L A N E T . E D U C E
. E Y I N G . . . V O L T S
. G R E Y S . S T E R E O
W O O F . . P U N Y
H I M . . D R I P S . . B U R
A D A P T I O N . O C T O P I
R E N O U N C E . N O I S E S
F A I R N E S S . G A M I N E
S L A T . . . . . S T E E D S
```

176

```
L A O S . S N A P . S C O L D
A B I T . T A N H . H A N O I
M O L E . A U T O . U N I O N
B A L M . B R A S . T U C K S
D R A M . S U R P L I C E
A D M E N . C H U N K
. . P R O M P T E D
. . S T A L I N I S T
. . R A C E C A R D
. L O G I C . D A R E S
. S E L E N I D E . M E N U
T H E Y D . T R U G . C A R L
H O R D E . I C K Y . A M O K
E L V E S . F L A P . R U B E
A M E N T . F E S T . S P E D
```

177

```
G N A W . T A R S . V A S T
Y A R E . O R A C H . I C K Y
R I V E . R E T R O . C H I P
E L O N G A T I O N . H Y P E
. . . R H E O L O G Y
. R O B E . S L U E . B A G
R E D E E M S . B R O M A T E
O C E A N I A . A E R O S O L
A T O M I S T . R E G A I N S
D I N . S L U T . I N L Y
. . C H A R I S M A
S H M O . B A T H I N G C A P
P O O H . E T H O S . R A G A
U M B O . L E E R S . A F E W
R O S E . D R E Y . F E D S
```

178

```
M A T . . B A B U . F O P
A B U T . M A V E N . F L U E
P I P E . O R E A D . O A S T
S T I M . I N S U R G E N T S
. . . A F L U T T E R
D I A Z O . M A S S E U S E
E L D E R . . S A T A N G
S L O P E . . T I L D E
K E B A B S . A L E U T
. R E M O T E S T . P I M P S
. . D E N T U R E S
S P A C E P R O B E . E A S Y
T O F U . D O L E S . R U L E
A G E D . A B O R T . S N U G
R O W . D E N S . . T E G
```

179

```
B R A T . . S A D . B Y R D
R A T E R . Q U A . R O U E
A N T R E . U N S H A K E N
G U A R S . P I T H I N E S S
. P R O P H E S I E D
. . R O U G H E R . P L U G
S T R I N G . S T R U M A
L O E S S . . H E R B Y
A S L E E P . C A M E O S
W H Y S . A S S H O L E
. . H I T P A R A D E S
I N S P I R E R S . M I L L S
N A T A T O R Y . I C E U P
K N O W . F E E . C A M E O
Y A W N . F O R . L I S T
```

180

```
J A P E . P L E B . S N I T
E L A N D . L O V E . N O N O
S A T A Y . A G E D . O A K Y
T R I C K S T E R S . W H Y S
. M O T I L E . T O G S
. . N U N . E R E C T L Y
. P H A G E S . D E N A R I I
B A A L . . . . P A L P
A N A L Y S T . A C C E P T
R E R O U T E . C A R
. C M O N . O P E R A S
D A D A . M A P L E S U G A R
R I O T . A B L Y . T R A V E
U R G E . C L O T . S A T I N
B Y E S . H Y P E . L E N D
```

181

S	U	P	S			M	I	S	S			S	P	E	D
P	R	O	P	S		I	N	C	H			P	O	M	E
A	G	R	E	E		S	L	U	R			R	U	I	N
R	E	N	E	W		T	Y	P	I	C	A	L	L	Y	
		D	E	W	Y			M	A	T	T	E			
A	S	P	I	R	E		S	A	P	S					
W	H	E	E		B	A	W	D		T	O	F	F	S	
R	O	E	S		B	R	A	Z	E		P	A	R	E	
Y	E	N	T	A		M	I	E	N		P	R	O	W	
		G	W	Y	N		V	R	O	O	M	S			
	S	L	I	E	R		B	Y	E	S					
A	M	E	N	D	A	B	L	E		B	I	F	F	S	
M	E	E	D		P	O	U	T		U	T	E	R	I	
B	A	R	E		U	N	D	O		S	E	T	I	N	
O	R	Y	X		P	E	O	N		S	A	G	E		

182

S	L	A	P		A	B	L	Y		F	E	T	C	H
P	I	S	H		R	O	U	E		O	V	O	L	O
I	N	K	Y		T	A	X	A		R	E	L	I	T
T	A	E	L		C	R	E	S	C	E	N	D	O	S
S	C	R	A	W	L			T	O	A	T			
		H	A	S	T		B	R	U	N	C	H		
S	U	B	S	Y	S	T	E	M		M	A	O	R	I
K	N	I	T		S	U	N	U	P		T	O	O	K
I	D	L	E	D		D	E	C	A	D	E	N	C	E
M	O	L	A	R	S		T	H	R	U				
		M	O	U	E			C	E	L	L	E	D	
D	I	S	P	O	S	A	B	L	E		Y	A	R	E
U	N	T	I	L		R	O	I	L		S	N	O	B
S	L	O	P	E		T	Y	K	E		O	A	S	T
T	Y	P	E	D		H	O	E	D		L	I	E	S

183

S	K	I	V	E				S	T	I	F	F	S
A	N	N	E	X			M	O	R	C	E	A	U
C	O	L	I	C			M	O	N	I	K	E	R	S
S	T	Y	L	E		C	O	D	I	F	Y		
		P	R	O	D	U	C	E		R	E	G	
A	C	E	T	O	N	E	S		C	H	I	N	O
L	U	X		P	U	L	P		T	E	D	D	Y
S	U	B	T	L	E	R		O	T	A	L	G	I	A
U	M	B	R	A		B	O	N	E		L	E	V
S	N	E	A	K		A	R	E	A	C	O	D	E
S	A	D		E	A	T	I	N	T	O			
		H	E	L	I	O	S		U	N	A	R	M
H	Y	P	E	R	I	O	N		R	O	M	E	O
A	E	O	N	I	A	N		T	U	B	A	S	
H	A	W	S	E	S			S	N	O	R	T	

184

I	R	I	D		E	D	G	E		R	A	C	Y
W	A	N	E	D		T	A	L	A		E	U	R	O
I	N	T	R	O		A	B	U	T		A	R	I	D
S	K	I	M	P			B	O	S	S	D	O	M	S
		A	S	P	E	N		H	E	R	E		
A	L	S	O		E	A	R	S		E	R	A	S
G	E	O	R	G	I	C	S		E	R	S		
O	U	T	C	A	S	T		S	A	P	H	E	N	A
		H	M	M		D	E	T	A	I	L	E	R
D	R	E	E		P	U	R	E		P	L	E	B
R	E	S	T		A	L	A	R	M				
S	Y	S	T	E	M	I	C		A	G	I	S	T
P	E	E	R		E	S	E	S		U	N	L	A	Y
A	R	E	A		T	A	T	E		T	A	L	U	K
T	S	K	S		A	N	S	A		W	Y	L	E

185

I	R	A	D		O	H	M			S	A	G	O
D	E	M	E		R	E	I		R	U	I	N	E	R
O	D	I	C		A	B	S	T	E	R	G	I	N	G
L	U	N	A	R		E	D	E	M	A		L	E	Y
	B	E	F	O	G		R	A	S	E	S		
		S	C	U	T	E	S		M	A	K	A	R
O	R	B		L	O	W		T	I	M	E	L	Y
C	A	R	A	B	A	O		L	I	C	E	N	S	E
A	N	A	L	O	G		C	O	L		S	O	S
S	T	E	E	L		C	O	O	E	E	S		
		C	I	G	A	R		R	O	U	G	H	
A	B	A		V	E	I	N	Y		N	I	H	I	L
F	R	I	C	A	N	D	E	A	U		N	O	P	E
A	I	D	E	R	S		A	N	D		T	U	P	S
R	O	S	E		E	G	O		S	L	O	T	

186

H	A	R	A	M		A	B	L	Y		D	I	S	S
A	L	I	B	I		L	A	I	C		I	N	C	H
S	E	V	A	S	T	O	P	O	L		S	H	O	E
P	R	E	S	S	U	P		N	E	P	H	E	W	S
S	T	R	E	A	M	E	D		P	O	O	R		
		L	U	C	E		T	O	N	I	C	S		
B	L	A	H		L	I	N	K		F	E	T	A	L
R	A	L	E		T	A	T	E	R		S	O	F	A
E	N	T	R	Y		S	I	V	A		T	R	E	Y
D	E	I	C	E	D		N	I	F	F				
		M	U	L	E		E	N	T	O	M	B	E	D
S	H	E	L	L	A	C		R	E	L	I	E	V	O
P	A	T	E		R	E	P	U	D	I	A	T	E	D
R	H	E	A		T	R	A	D		A	M	O	N	G
Y	A	R	N		H	E	L	D		R	I	N	S	E

187

B	U	S	K			S	P	A	R			C	O	M	P
A	L	T	A	R		E	A	C	H			H	A	A	R
S	T	E	R	E		A	N	T	I	P	A	S	T	O	
I	R	I	S	H		R	E	E	N	A	C	T	E	D	
C	A	N	T	A	B			D	O	S	H				
			N	U	M	B		S	T	A	L	A	G		
A	R	P	E	G	G	I	O	S				C	E	D	E
M	O	O	N			T	O	W				H	A	Z	E
B	O	N	D			T	R	A	Y	B	A	K	E	S	
O	D	E	O	N	S			S	T	A	R				
			C	O	O	N				K	I	S	S	E	R
M	I	C	R	O	C	O	S	M			N	I	T	R	E
U	N	L	I	K	A	B	L	E			K	N	E	A	D
S	K	I	N			G	L	U	E			S	E	N	S	E
H	Y	P	E			E	Y	E	D			W	O	E	S

188

A	R	G	O	T						M	A	N	S	E
W	A	R	P	A	T	H		I	N	I	T	I	A	L
E	R	I	T	R	E	A		M	A	G	E	N	T	A
D	E	M	I	S	E	D		P	U	R	L	O	I	N
				M	I	N		D	E	T	A	I	N	E	D
S	K	U	A			H	A	L	I	T	E			
W	E	N		M	E	A	L		C	O	R	P	S	E
A	R	D	O	U	R	S		M	A	R	S	A	L	A
G	F	O	R	C	E		J	U	L	Y		P	I	C
			D	I	M	S	U	M			H	A	T	H
F	A	M	I	L	I	E	S		V	E	E			
E	M	A	N	A	T	E		P	E	N	A	N	C	E
E	N	C	A	G	E	D		O	R	A	T	O	R	Y
L	I	O	N	E	S	S		M	Y	C	E	N	A	E
S	A	N	D	S						T	R	E	N	D

189

S	H	A	M			M	A	T	S				D	A	S	H
C	O	X	A			A	B	U	T			C	E	N	T	O
R	U	I	N			L	I	T	E			A	F	O	U	L
A	D	L	I	B	I	T	U	M			N	I	M	B	Y
P	I	L	A	U				G	L	A	C	I	S		
E	N	A	C	T		P	R	I	A	P	I	C		
D	I	E	S		B	L	A	N	K	E	T			
			K	L	U	D	G	E	S					
		H	O	A	R	I	E	R			D	E	C	K
	C	O	R	S	A	I	R		M	E	L	O	N	
	S	H	T	E	T	L			A	F	I	R	E	
R	A	I	T	A		I	S	T	H	M	U	S	E	S
A	D	M	E	N		S	H	O	E		N	I	L	S
C	H	E	S	S		T	U	F	F		D	O	L	E
Y	U	R	T			S	T	U	T		S	N	I	T

190

R	E	E	L	S					S	P	A	S	M	S
A	Q	U	A	T	I	C		S	P	I	R	A	E	A
S	U	L	T	A	N	A		L	E	A	V	I	N	G
P	I	E	T	I	S	T		E	N	F	O	L	D	S
	P	R	E	D	I	C	T	E	D					
				S	H	I	T	S	C	A	R	E	D	
M	A	G	N	E	T	I	C		A	G	A	M	A	
A	B	R	E	A	S	T		P	H	L	E	G	M	Y
I	L	I	A	C			W	E	E	K	D	A	Y	S
L	Y	M	P	H	G	L	A	N	D					
				H	E	X	A	G	R	A	M	S		
F	L	A	T	T	O	P		N	E	E	D	I	E	R
L	I	M	I	E	S	T		C	R	E	M	A	T	E
O	D	O	N	A	T	A		E	S	K	I	M	O	S
P	O	K	E	R	S					S	T	I	N	T

191

C	O	S	E	C			S	P	I	C			P	R	O	D
O	R	I	Y	A			T	A	N	H			L	E	V	O
G	A	M	E	S			U	R	G	E			A	F	E	W
S	N	I	D	E			B	O	E	R			C	U	R	E
		G	A	R	S		B	L	A	T	H	E	R	E	R
	S	N	O	T	T	I	E	R		A	B	B	A	S
		S	P	U	R	N	S		F	R	O	S	T	
			D	U	G			P	U	D				
		R	E	J	I	G		B	A	N	A	N	A	
C	A	N	O	E			B	O	L	D	N	E	S	S
A	N	T	I	S	E	R	U	M			D	O	P	E
S	A	W	S			R	U	N	T		F	L	I	R	T
T	W	I	T			U	N	D	O		A	I	R	E	R
L	A	N	E			P	E	E	P		S	T	E	N	O
E	Y	E	D			T	I	N	S		T	H	R	E	W

192

A	D	H	O	C					S	C	A	R	P
B	R	E	V	E				L	O	A	T	H	E
L	O	R	E	N			G	U	N	S	H	I	P
A	P	A	R	T		S	U	N	S	H	I	N	Y
T	I	L	D	E		W	O	R	D		B	R	O	S
E	N	D	O	R	P	H	I	N		J	O	S	S
			F	U	E	L		R	I	O	T		
		C	O	P	T		B	O	N	K			
	V	E	L	A		W	E	A	R			
	T	O	L	D		P	A	L	M	I	T	A	T	E
S	A	X	E		P	E	R	T		K	A	S	H	A
T	I	P	S	T	E	R	S			I	N	S	E	T
A	P	O	T	H	E	M				S	N	O	R	E
T	E	P	E	E	S					H	I	R	E	R
S	I	S	S	Y						A	N	T	S	Y

193

C	A	N	S	T			I	F	F	Y		L	O	O	N
A	M	A	T	I			T	I	R	O		A	R	V	O
L	I	V	E	N			C	L	E	W		M	I	E	N
K	N	A	P	S			H	E	E	L		B	E	R	G
S	O	H	O			B	I	R	D			B	E	N	T
		O	N	I	O	N			O	M	E	N	T	U	M
			D	U	G			M	A	S	C	A	R	A	
B	O	B	B	E	R				D	O	Y	L	E	Y	
I	R	E	L	A	N	D			W	E	T				
G	A	L	I	L	E	E			R	U	S	T	Y		
		T	O	N	S		C	H	I	P		R	I	P	S
C	O	N	K		P	I	O	N			S	U	P	R	A
U	R	G	E		A	M	O	K			A	S	P	I	C
B	I	E	R		D	A	H	L			S	T	E	E	R
S	O	D	S		S	L	A	Y			H	Y	D	R	A

194

F	R	Y	E	R			W	R	I	G	G	L	E	R
L	I	E	L	O	W		H	I	M	A	L	A	Y	A
I	S	A	I	A	H		A	P	P	R	O	V	E	D
C	H	R	O	N	I	C	L	E	R		W	E	D	S
K	I	S	T		T	H	E	S	E					
			D	E	I	S	T	S			C	A	R	B
A	F	F	L	I	C	T			S	P	E	W	E	R
G	A	L	O	S	H				I	O	D	A	T	E
E	V	E	R	S	O		M	O	S	E	Y	E	D	
D	E	W	Y		C	O	L	O	N	Y				
				O	B	E	L	I			T	A	R	E
L	A	B	S		L	I	V	E	S	T	R	E	A	M
A	B	R	O	G	A	T	E			T	R	A	G	I	C
P	I	A	M	A	T	E	R		S	A	L	I	N	E
S	T	E	E	P	E	R	S			M	A	S	S	E

195

D	A	U	B	S					S	T	A	D	I	A
U	N	L	A	C	E			S	T	A	V	I	N	G
E	N	T	R	A	N	T			K	A	R	A	C	H	I
T	U	R	T	L	E	R			O	R	E	S	T	E	S
	M	A	H	A	R	A	J	A			C	A	R	T	
				V	I	A	L			C	U	T	E		
	D	E	F	A	N	G			H	A	L	O	N		
	D	I	V	O	T	S			H	O	B	A	R	T	
	O	S	A	G	E		M	E	S	S	R	S			
	M	E	N	S		H	U	R	T						
S	I	N	G			O	M	E	L	E	T	T	E		
I	N	G	E	S	T	S			T	E	R	R	O	R	S
D	E	A	L	O	U	T			O	R	G	A	N	O	N
L	E	G	I	O	N	S				S	O	L	I	D	I
E	R	E	C	T	S						T	A	C	E	T

196

C	H	U	F	F			S	I	A	N		A	W	R	Y
L	A	S	E	R			U	N	D	O		C	O	H	O
I	N	U	S	E			P	L	O	W		C	L	E	W
M	O	R	S	E			P	Y	R	A	M	I	D	A	L
B	I	P	E	D	A	L			E	Y	E	D			
				M	I	N			S	T	E	N	C	H	
K	E	L	P		B	E	A	D			A	N	E	L	E
N	A	I	L		O	R	B	E	D			T	A	I	L
O	C	C	U	R		S	O	F	A			S	P	O	D
T	H	E	M	E	D		B	A	Y						
			M	A	U	L			U	S	I	N	G	U	P
W	A	T	E	R	F	O	W	L			C	O	R	N	U
A	B	U	T		F	I	A	T			T	R	A	C	K
R	I	T	E		U	R	G	E			U	M	I	A	K
S	T	U	D		P	E	E	R			S	A	L	P	A

197

M	A	S	H			C	R	A	M			S	T	A	R
A	U	T	O	S			O	O	Z	Y			C	U	B	A
C	R	A	S	H			R	O	O	F			I	N	L	Y
H	I	K	E	R			A	T	T	O	R	N	E	Y	S
		C	E	D	I			H	O	O	T					
				F	Y	K	E			T	W	I	R	P	S
P	L	A	N	T	A	I	N			S	L	E	E	P	
L	O	G	O			K	R	A	F	T		L	E	A	R
E	G	E	S	T			C	A	U	S	A	L	L	Y	
B	E	D	E	W	S			T	Y	P	E				
			B	I	T	S				E	A	C	H		
I	M	M	A	N	E	N	C	Y			D	U	R	E	R
N	O	O	N			R	O	L	E			E	R	O	D	E
C	U	R	D			N	O	I	L			D	U	N	G	S
H	E	N	S			S	T	O	P			M	E	E	T

198

F	R	A	G			M	I	M	E			A	M	B	O
L	I	F	E	S	A	V	I	N	G			F	O	R	A
O	C	E	A	N	L	I	N	E	R			F	L	A	K
C	O	W	R	O	T	E			R	E	W	I	L	D	S
				B	A	D			G	E	E	D			
S	P	O	D						C	I	N	N	A	B	A	R
C	A	R	E			T	E	A	S	E			V	I	C	E
U	N	D	O			I	N	N	E	R			I	N	C	H
T	I	E	D			D	A	I	S	Y			T	A	R	A
A	C	R	O	N	Y	M	S						S	L	A	B
				R	A	T	E			P	A	M			
S	T	R	I	G	I	L			A	L	I	T	T	L	E
T	H	I	S			P	I	C	N	I	C	A	R	E	A
U	R	G	E			S	N	U	G	G	E	R	I	E	S
B	O	A	R			G	R	A	N			S	P	R	Y

S	N	O	B		C	E	A	S	E		A	F	E	W
W	O	V	E		H	A	U	L	M		N	O	N	O
A	G	E	D		A	C	T	U	P		A	R	V	O
M	O	R	T		P	H	O	T	O		L	A	Y	S
	M	I	N					W	H	Y				
M	I	A	M	I		D	I	S	E	A	S	E	S	
O	N	S	E	T		O	V	E	R	S	E	L	L	S
J	E	T			P	L	I	E	S		D	I	P	
O	P	E	N	F	A	C	E	D		B	R	E	D	E
	T	R	E	E	L	E	S	S		A	I	R	E	D
	W	E	T					D	O	B				
S	H	A	M		R	U	B	L	E		T	E	A	T
T	O	D	O		I	N	L	A	Y		A	R	M	Y
O	U	Z	O		E	D	U	C	E		C	R	O	P
W	R	E	N		R	O	B	E	D		T	Y	K	E

B	A	T	O	N		D	U	F	F	S		W	A	G
A	M	I	N	O		I	N	U	I	T		H	A	H
R	O	P	E	D		S	I	N	G	A	P	O	R	E
S	K	I	N		W	A	T	S		S	O	L	O	N
		I	V	O	R	Y		W	E	R	E	N	T	
S	T	A	G	I	E	R		R	E	S	T			
H	I	G	H	S		A	W	E	D		W	O	M	B
A	R	E	T	E		Y	E	A		M	I	A	U	L
M	O	D	S		K	E	N	S		I	N	K	L	E
		T	I	E	D		C	H	E	E	S	E	D	
A	L	B	A	N	Y		P	E	O	N	S			
B	A	R	N	S		S	E	N	D		T	U	G	S
U	N	A	D	O	R	N	E	D		H	A	N	O	I
Z	A	G		L	E	A	V	E		A	I	D	E	D
Z	I	G		E	G	G	E	D		S	N	O	R	E